This book is dedicated to William Bagley and the Reiki Guides
who were the inspiration for its artistry
My endless gratitude

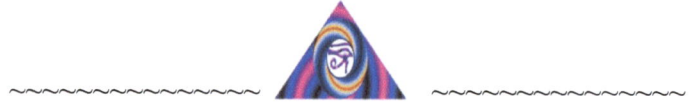

These sacred symbols reflect the Divine spiritual healing essences of those that were once commonly used during the Atlantian, Lemurian Era to transmit the Divine Aspects of The Source of all Creation, as part of the daily teachings and spiritual practices within the temple systems that existed then. The essence of these images and the transformative power they possess lies within the vibrations of their sacred geometrical arrangement and the sentient intention of Divine Enlightenment that Reiki radiates through them.

These prints are blessed and attuned to the life force of Tanran Reiki, and the Universal Source. When used as tools of meditation and visualization their energy becomes alive. They possess the power to activate one's divine intentions for healing and enlightenment and to positively restructure one's life to align with ones divine blueprint and purpose as a spiritual being. Many have found the symbols enable them to transcend various limitations in consciousness effortlessly just by setting the intention and without having to direct them. Reiki Artistry is sentient and has the ability to purify the energy within the environment they are displayed in. All one need do is to be open to receiving the miraculous and let go of what no longer serves them.

Prints are made without titles imbedded in them but can be purchase with labels when specifically requested. All prints are available as a limited edition on canvas, acrylic, or metal print that complement the 3 dimensionalities of the artistry. To place an order and for customized sizing please visit our website below.

Framed glass, glossy prints, calendars, cards and other various healing artistry items are also available in various sizes and can be ordered at www.debra-mchelle.fineartamerica.com.

Thank you for your interest and support of this artistry may you find this artistry to be a source of healing, Self-realization and enjoyment.

Artistry by D'MChelle
Information on Symbolism by William Bagley & D'MChelle

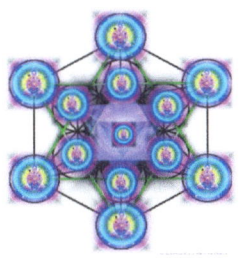

TANRAN REIKI HEALING ARTISTRY COLLECTION

This Series of Artistry derived from the Tanran Reiki symbology which is an expansion of Michao Usui's lineage. The symbols originated by William Bagley of Ashland Oregon, founder of the Tanran system. They have been found to be a visual personification of Divine Sentient Sacred Geometrical Imagery. Each piece possesses the ability to transfer the healing power and Ascended consciousness within Universal Life Force that each symbol depicts whenever one attunes to its energy through open meditation whether one's intention is set to do so consciously or unconsciously. These images started to reveal themselves in 4th dimensional form during healing sessions where I was either incorporating Reiki in with my Vibrational Anatomy massage sessions with clients or during my personal Qi Kung meditative movement practice after having received my Tanran Reiki Masters level attunement in May 2008. The imagery continues to build upon itself as new forms, designs, and arrangements in and around the physical and subtle bodies emerge with the innerstanding of the connectedness and the dynamics of the healing purposes for their various expressions and formations. The sentient healing life force of these symbols became evident as they became a moving meditation within themselves arranging themselves in various combinations based on the healing intentions held for myself, for others, for the planet, and towards the healing of the Soul of the universe as a whole. Though their illustrations may be depicted differently, the element of life force, their purposes, and combined energies and the Divine Unconditional Source of love that they come from are the same as those that were once commonly used during the Atlantean, Lemurian Era. These Divine Aspects of The Source of All Creation were a part of the daily teachings and spiritual practices within the temple systems that existed then here on planet earth.

Each print has a life force energy of its own and is attuned with the life force of Tanran Reiki, and the Universal Source that they symbolically depict. When used as tools of meditation and visualization their energy is able to transmit it healing properties into whatever areas of your life that it is needed. One only need recognize the need with a desire to transcend whatever limitations are holding them back from their divine inheritance of living a healthy, happy, and fulfilled life and be willing to make the changes that fulfill one's desires. They have within their design the sentient-ability to positively restructure one's life with one's divine blueprint and to awaken one's conscious awareness as a spiritual being and activate their divine intentions for healing and enlightenment. Many have found these symbols enabled them to transcend various limitations in consciousness just by setting the intention and remaining open to the transformations that take place without having to direct them per say including myself. It also radiates this same sentient-ability to create a peaceful, healing energy within the environment it is displayed in. There is nothing one need do but to be open to one's own internal truth, and let the miraculous take care of the rest.

D'MCHELLE

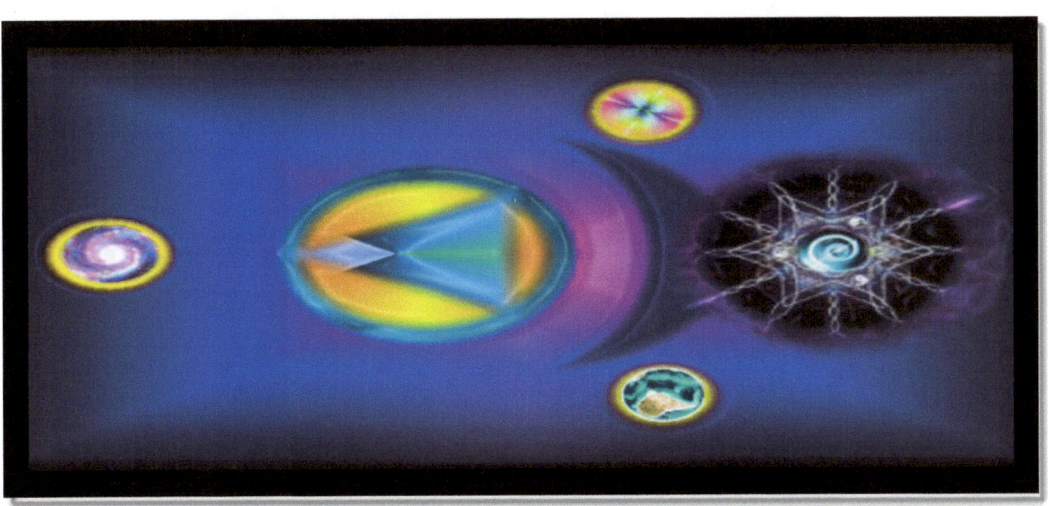

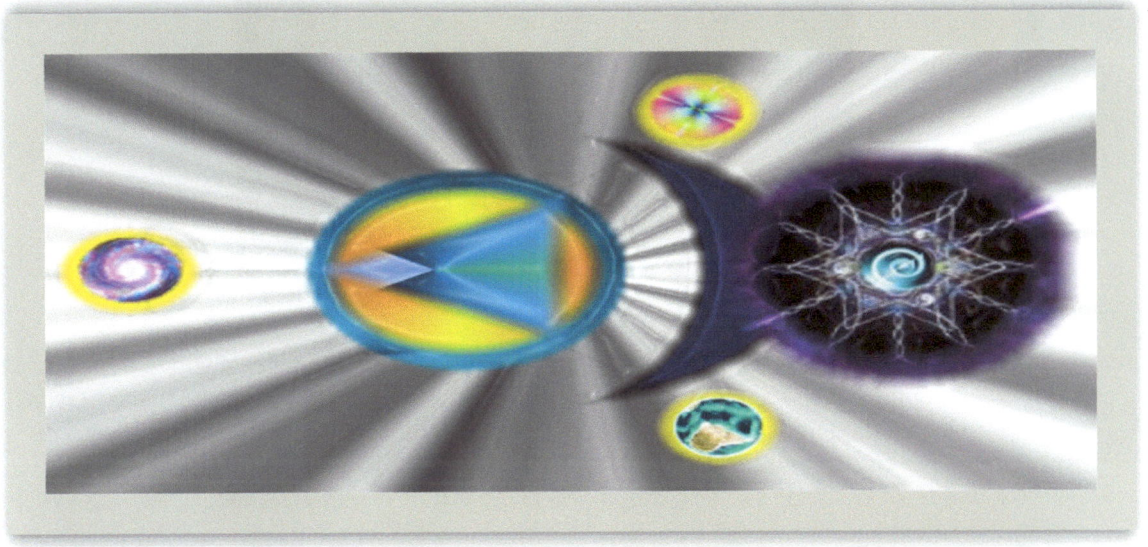

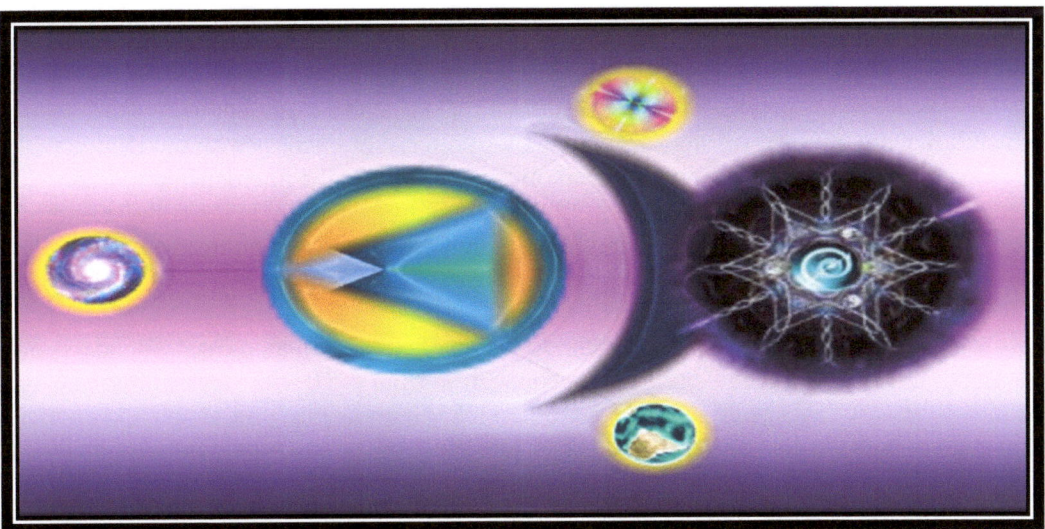

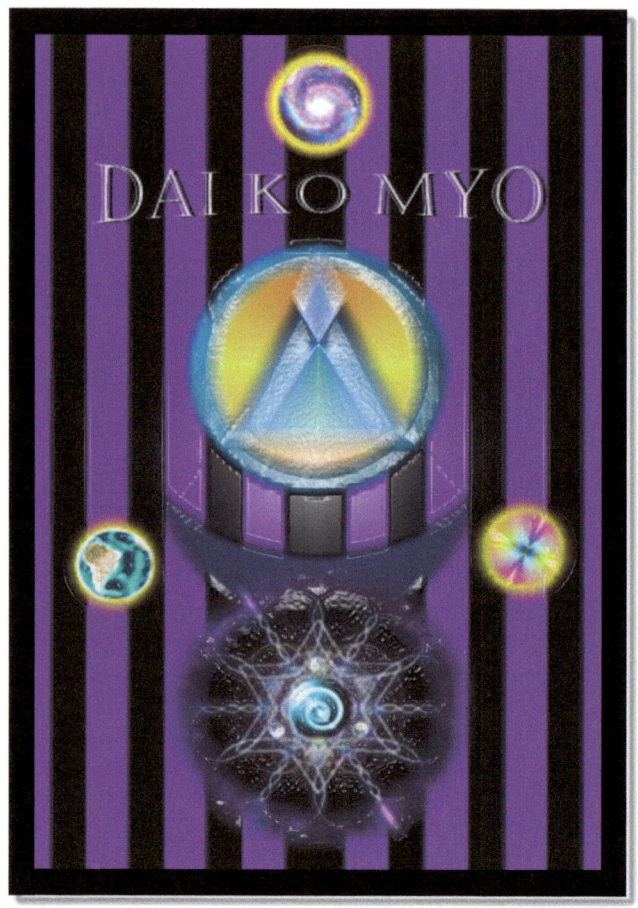

DAI KO MYO is the Master Symbol within all Reiki lineages. It connects you to your Higher Self revealing the Unity and Higher wisdom within life and devotion to spiritual and personal matters, dynamic thought, and energy. As the Master Symbol it reflects the inter-connectedness between cosmic and earthly elements that provide the life force energies that our spirit/soul/bodies are made of. Daikomyo brings the gift of Divine Intelligence and the inward flow of wisdom and knowledge from the Akashic records within the ethers that enable you to see the truth within life concerning illusory ideals, materialistic pursuits, self-limiting concepts, and delusion. It represents that which allows you to experience continuous awareness of your personal and spiritual truth and the wisdom of conscious detachment from personal emotions.

It helps provide you with Unconditional love for self, and all sentient beings through humanitarianism, service, spiritual values, and a true sense of oneness with the Divine within everything. As a master symbol, Daikomyo also reflects the interdependence and interconnectedness that all life shares --from the cosmic to the earthly to the cellular— through the divine intelligence that channels multi-dimensionally throughout all life and within every living entity.

It correlates to the Crown Chakra where the Divine and the human meet. When out of balance, you may experience feelings of disconnection from the Divine, lack of purpose, or an inability to see the Light within yourself or others. When in balance you're able to experience your Oneness with the Divine, your connection and sense of purpose with your Divine plan and to live this out in your daily life.

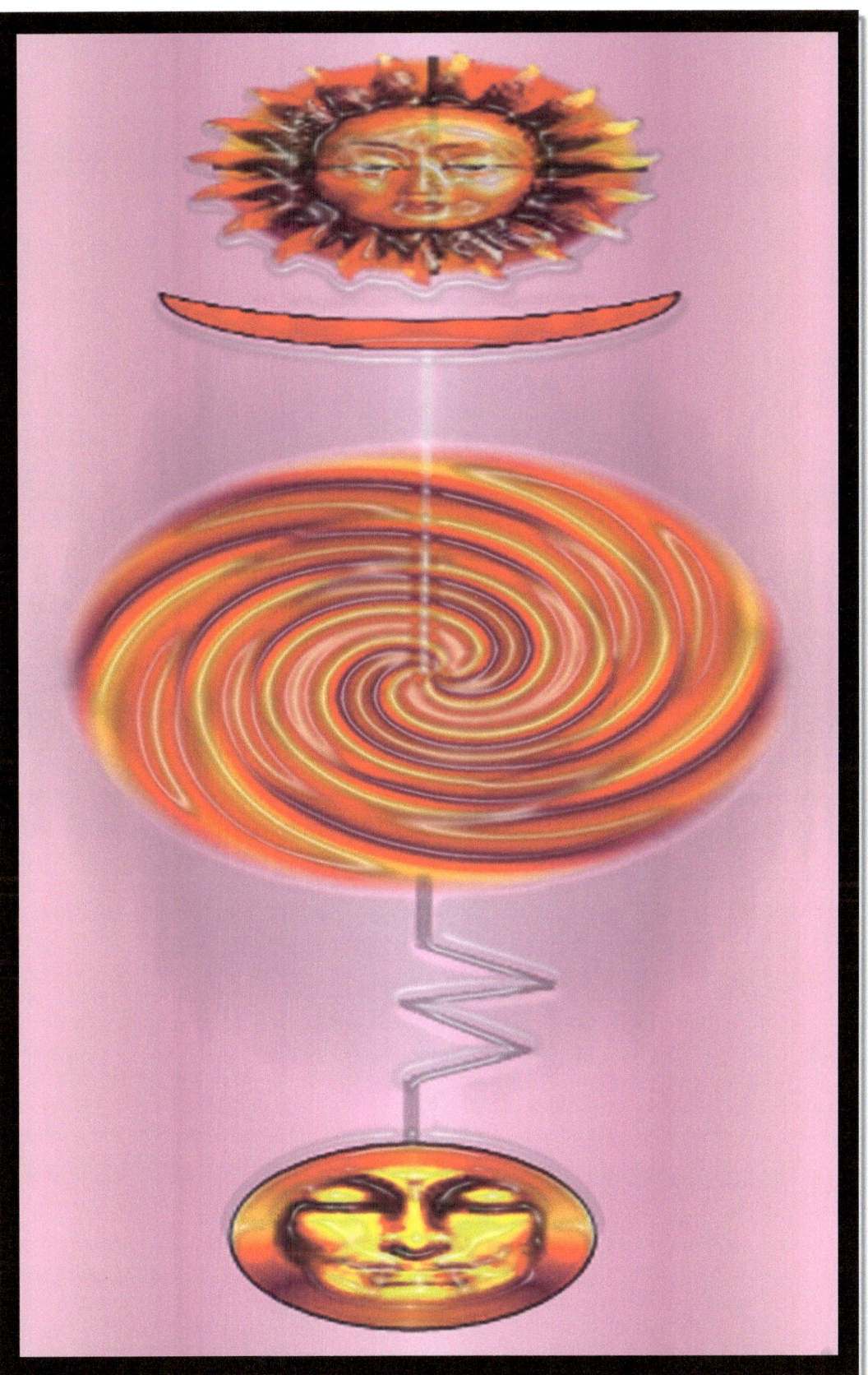

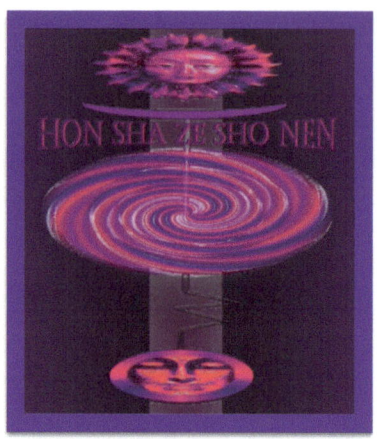

HON SHA ZE SHO NEN provides an inner lens that can help you see past the illusion of one's imperfection in order to relate to all of life with no fear or attachment to what seems to be presenting itself. This powerful healing symbol of many Reiki lineages aligns one to the divinity within themselves in order to recognize the divinity in others and within life itself. It also is used to perform remote or long-distance healing and for sending love, healing intentions and prayers to those whom are open to receive these divine objectives. Honshazeshonen helps to further activate the right brain activity through the 1st eye opening and activating one's conscious awareness of the hidden meaning and personal message below the surface of what's being presented. Its activation ignites the ability to intuit and innerstand what is happening in one's current life so that they're better able to visualize their desired future life through the eyes and mind of their Higher Self with an awareness of the bigger purpose for one's existence and the spiritual power they possess to manifest their visions and dreams as well as identifying the subtle markers that indicate the path.

Hon Sha Ze Sho Nen works with Zee Gah Nah toward the purification of negative tendencies and in the elimination of selfish attitudes, denial, refusal to take responsibility for one's actions and confusion. It does this, both personally and collectively, by revealing in one's awareness the truths behind ones experiences that have previously been hidden within ones subconscious as one has begins to question ones experience and exposures to life and to seek answers to the truths behind these personal and collective quandaries and dichotomies.

This symbol correlates to the 1st Eye Chakra which is the center of I-magi-nation, psychic vision, higher intuitive information, inner wisdom, creativity, and devotion to spiritual knowledge, the energies of the spirit, magnetic forces, and light. This is why, throughout history, the eyes have been referred to as *"The Windows to the Soul"* which can be seen photographically. Next time you look at a photo of a person whom you consider a light worker look in the center of the pupil and one will see that not only do they radiate love but their eyes are radiating white/light.

The anatomy related to this chakra is the Cerebellum, pituitary and pineal glands, liver, gallbladder, nose, ears, left eye, and central nervous system. Some conditions addressed by this symbol are learning disorders, spinal misalignments, hearing, eye problems and tinnitus, fear of being true to one's own needs and desires, understanding the oneness we all share and opening to finding ways to see and appreciate diversity, also to love and to come to value those who've taken on the assignment of teaching them their hardest lessons of spiritual realism and personal evolution.

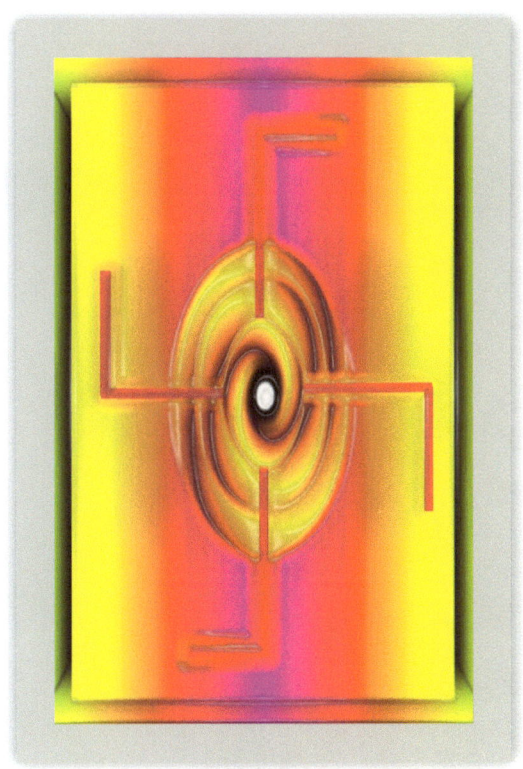
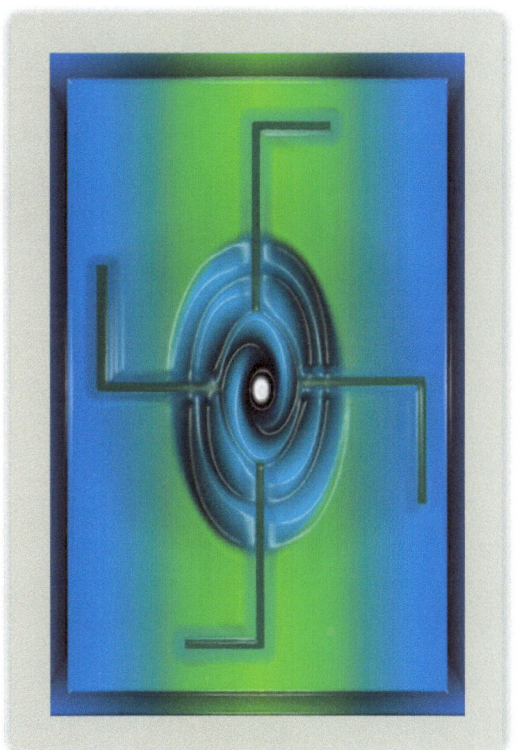
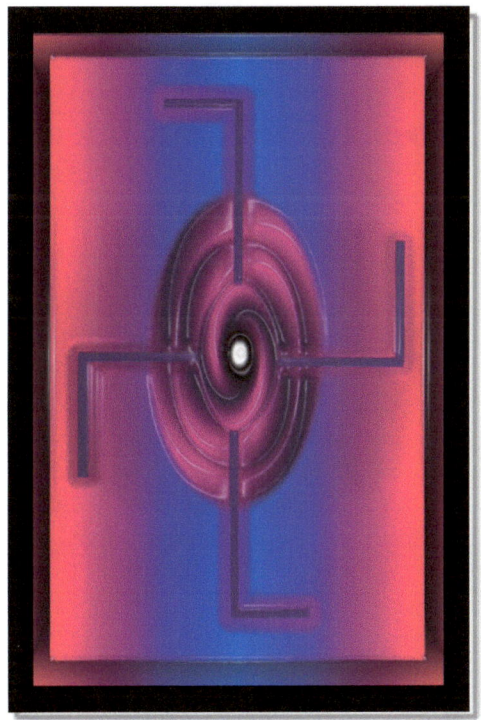
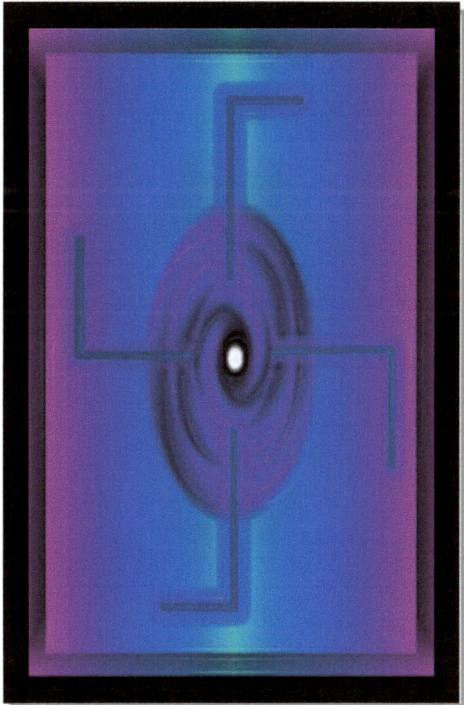

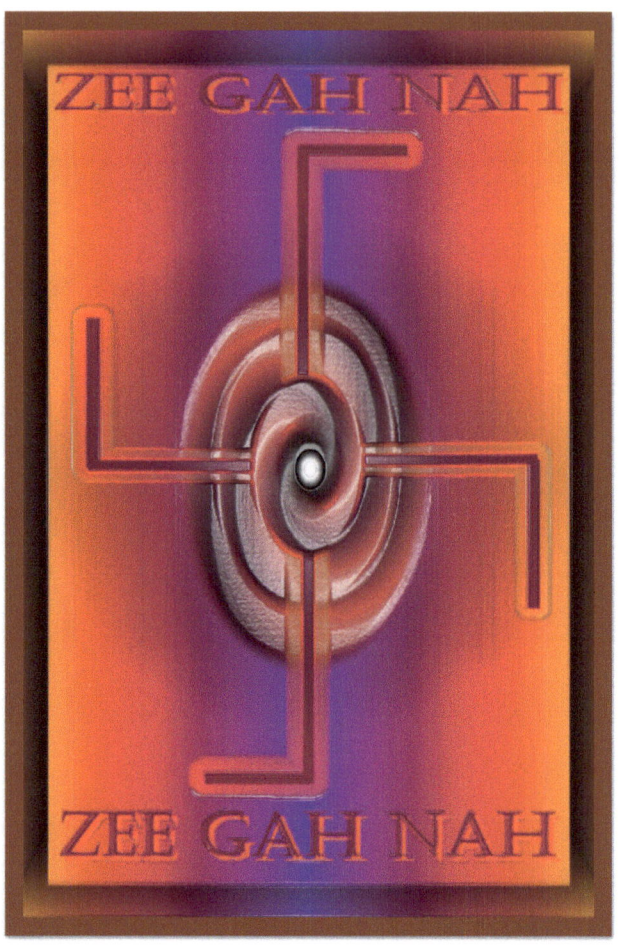

ZEE GAH NAH resides within the Throat Chakra which is the Center of All forms of expression & communication of creativity whether in thought, verbal communication, or movement. This symbol helps empower you to consciously and/or subconsciously manifest one's thoughts and creative intentions within one's life.

All aspects of personality are regulated energetically within the throat chakra and can be purified by Zee Gah Nah through intention and awareness. Zee Gah Nah is designed to transmute ones egoic tendency to suppress anger, sorrows, and fears of exposure or making mistakes into constructive externalizations with the energy and ability to innerstand and communicate one's thoughts and feelings in a positive prolific manner and to let go of their fears, judgments, and need to be in control of the process of Self evolution. From struggling with addictions, unproductive habits, judgments, faith, decisions, and criticisms, to choosing to embrace and incorporate healthy alternatives to the aspects of one's as well as others negative behaviors. We have within us the ability to share the truth of our soul, honor our beliefs, and live one's passions uninhibited which is the embodiment of our divine blueprint.

The anatomy related to this chakra are the vocal cords, throat, mouth and jaw, respiratory system, lungs, large intestine, alimentary canal, thyroid, neck area, teeth, gums, esophagus. Conditions that are addressed range from sore throats, stuttering and glandular problems to writers block, miscommunications, and lack of truthfulness and/or acting on opportunities for creative expression and inspiration.

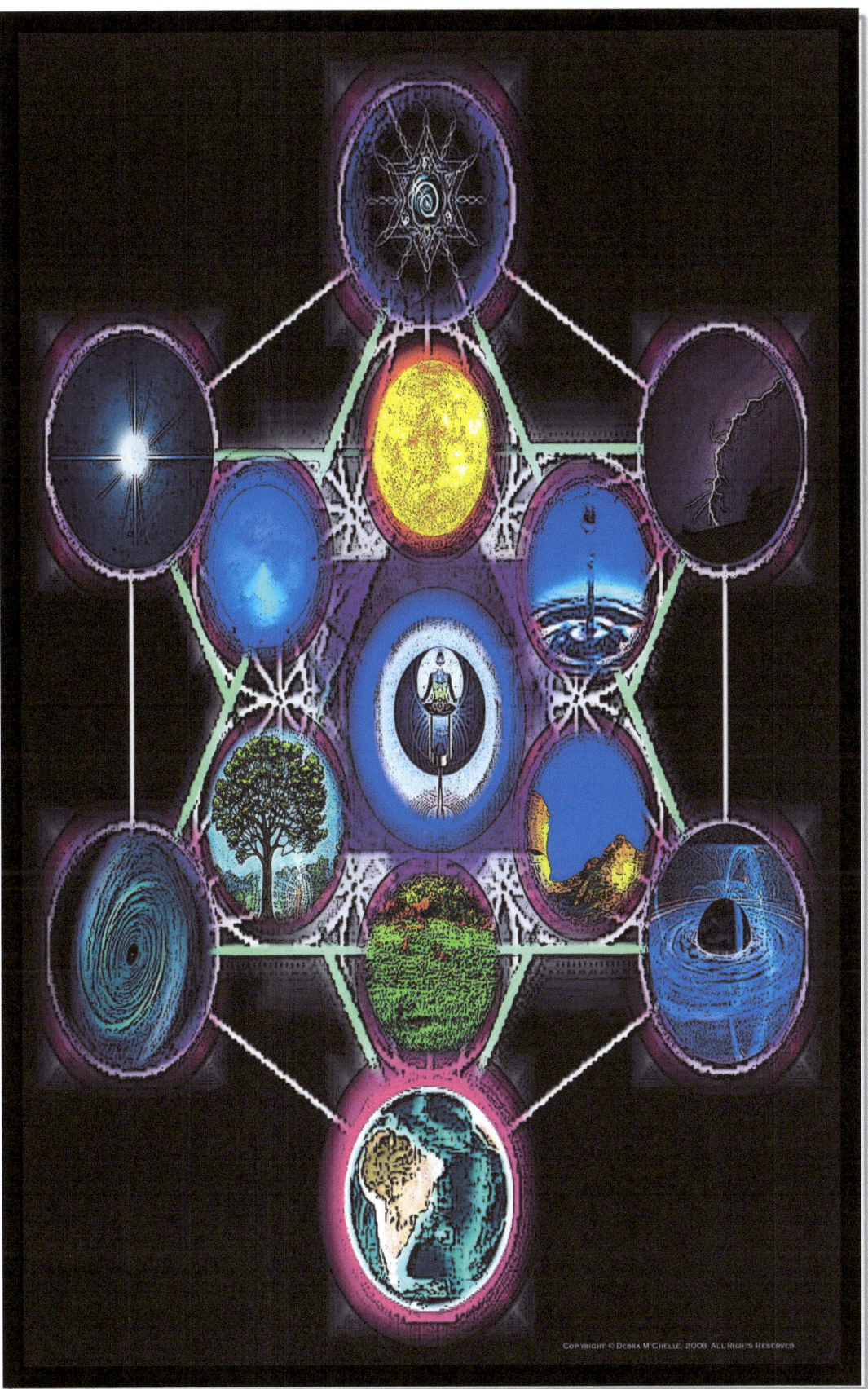

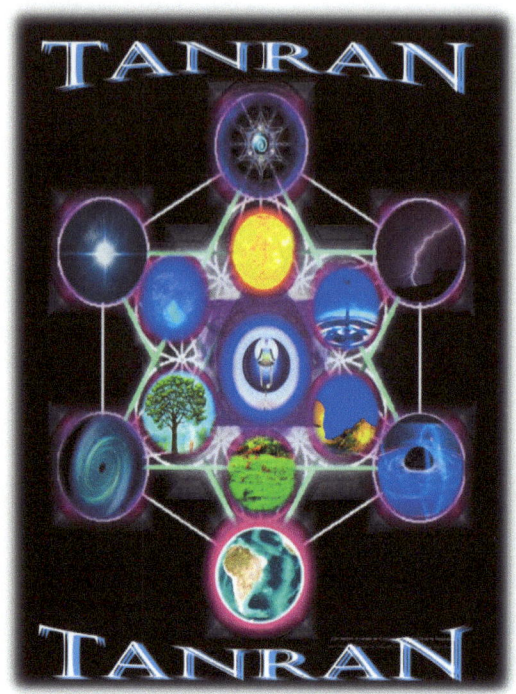

TANRAN is gift to the Reiki experience. It is a vehicle for inter-dimensional travel that affects spirit and body simultaneously allowing one to freely access various dimensions of ascended thought during meditation. As above, so below, its circles represent the elements of earthly and universal life forces and the infinite cycles of life and consciousness contained within its Merkaba structure. The outer Merkaba reflects the sentient universal life forces of magnetism, electricity, ether, light, matter, and intelligence. The inner Merkaba reflect the sentient life force of the elements of solar heat, air, water, mineral kingdom, earth, and plant life with the shared element of sound and Divine Intelligence at its center. These elements are what keep our physical and subtle body forms alive and functioning while embodied here on Earth.

Although the Tanran symbol corresponds to the Heart Chakra, it connects directly with Daikomyo the center of our spiritual connectedness with Divinity and is the nucleus of spiritual life. This helps one to align with the wisdom, love and desire to resolve differences of all types and in all relationships as an expression of the presence of harmony and unconditional love within all life force elements that we are a part of. By this Tanran helps one to access, innerstand, and express the unconditional love, peace, and creativity that reside within one's Higher Self and ground these qualities into one's life experiences.

The physical anatomy related to this chakra are the Heart, pericardium, lungs, thymus, breast, chest area, triple warmer, cardiovascular system, blood, cellular structure, arms, and involuntary muscles. Psycho-spiritual conditions addressed range from breathing problems, upper back, shoulder, and arm problems to sorrow, depression, and the fulfillment of true happiness. Spiritual conditions addressed are the mental/emotional challenges of living up to the demands of those we work for and those we love within the restraints of a socioeconomical restraints being imposed upon most of humanity by corporate entities & institutions who are in control of the way in which we structure our lives socially, technologically, and personally.

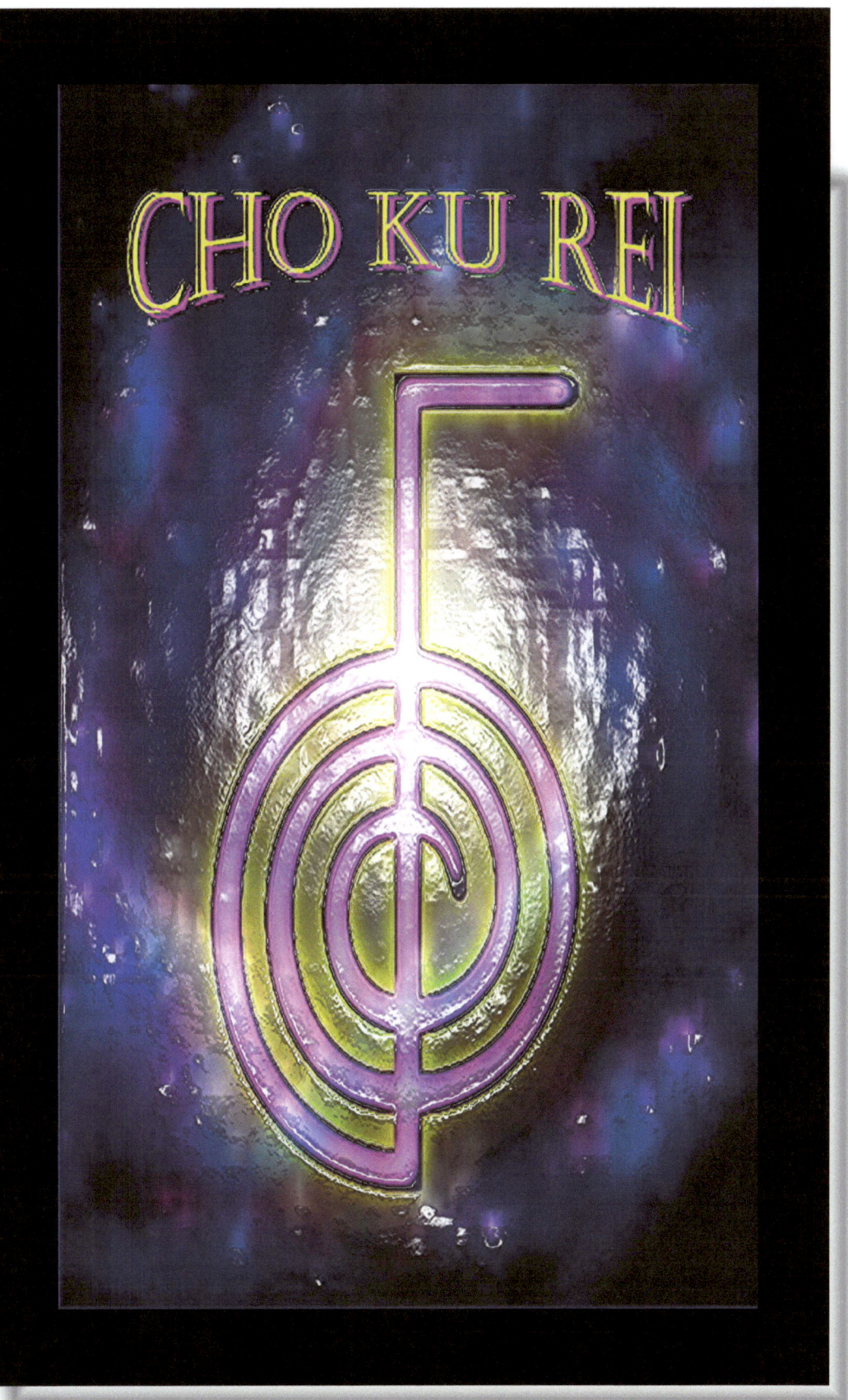

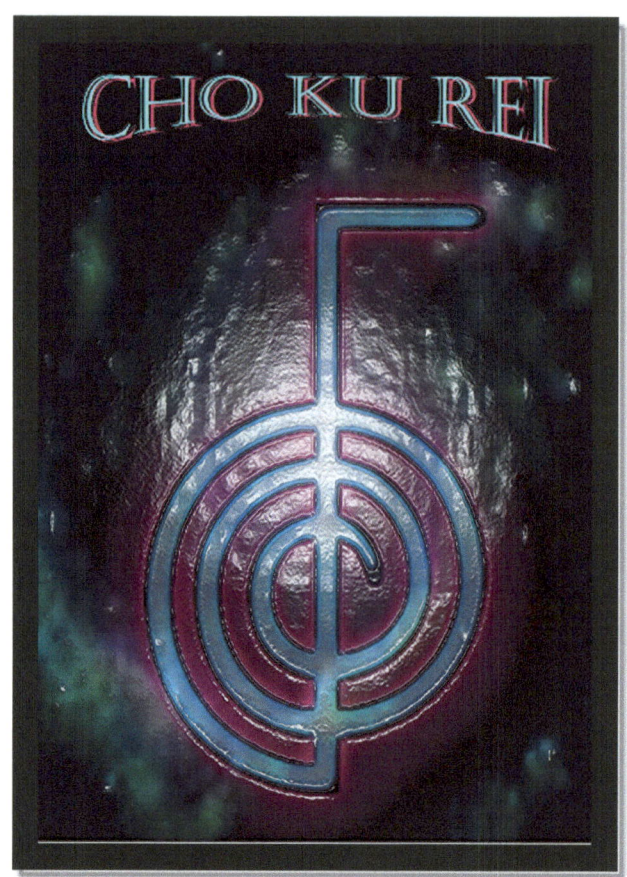

CHO KU REI helps to heal inner child issues by realigning one's sense of personal power to reflect that of one's Divine imprint versus their emotional imprint established during one's formative years. Its energy activates one's personal power to live and operate according to one's true sense of self versus what others have defined them to be in order to control and manipulate their behavior. It also assists in the healing of negative internal and interpersonal relationship views that are held. It inspires the insights that allow one to learn the lessons meant to cause one to gain awareness of what one's true personality is and the courage to set appropriate personal boundaries so that they can remain in alignment with their truth while still being able to actively engage in their relationship with Divine Source, with others and with all of life.

Cho Ku Rei corresponds to the Solar Plexus Chakra which is the center of personal power, ambition, intellect, astral force, self-respect, willpower, self-control, and physical energy. Meditation on Cho Ku Rei can open ones innerstanding promoting a truer sense of self and personal power, a healthy ego and the ability to respond appropriately to conflict in ways that are practical and productive.

The anatomy related to this chakra is the stomach, colon, liver, gallbladder, pancreas, adrenals, immune system, sympathetic nervous system, mid-back, and muscular system. Challenges such as diabetes, arthritis, liver problems, eating disorders, indigestion, to low self-esteem, personal pride and faith in oneself are all issues that can be addressed with meditation on Cho Ku Rei and attuning to one's spirits intention.

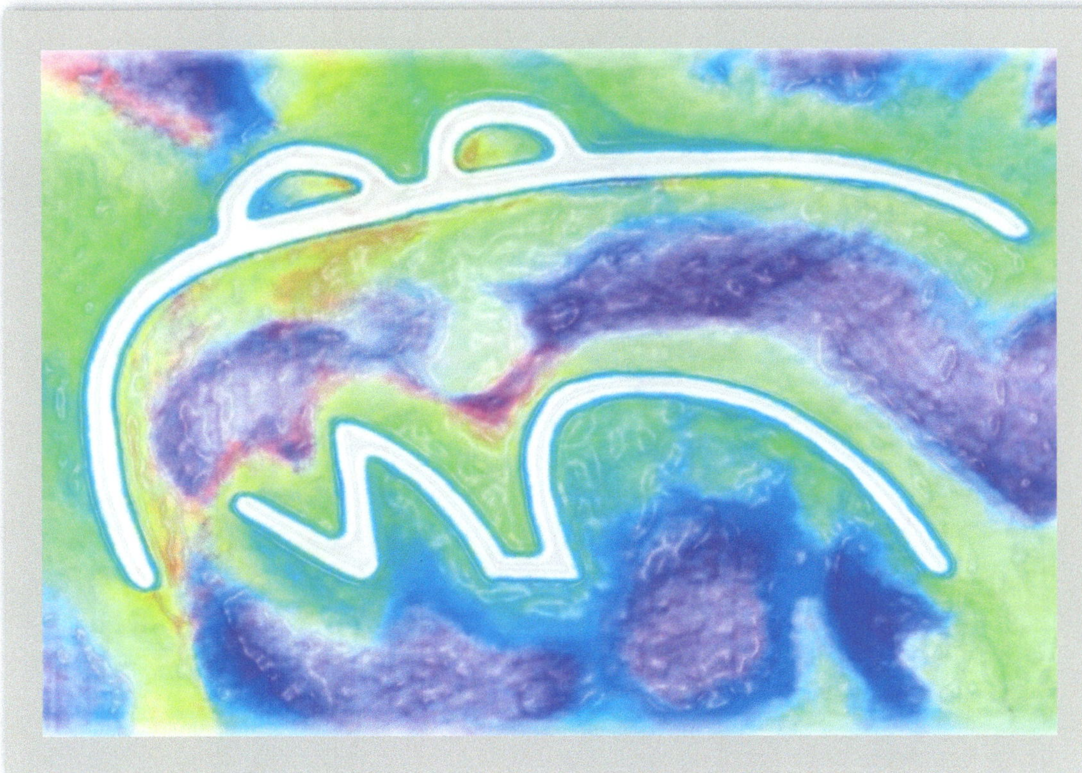

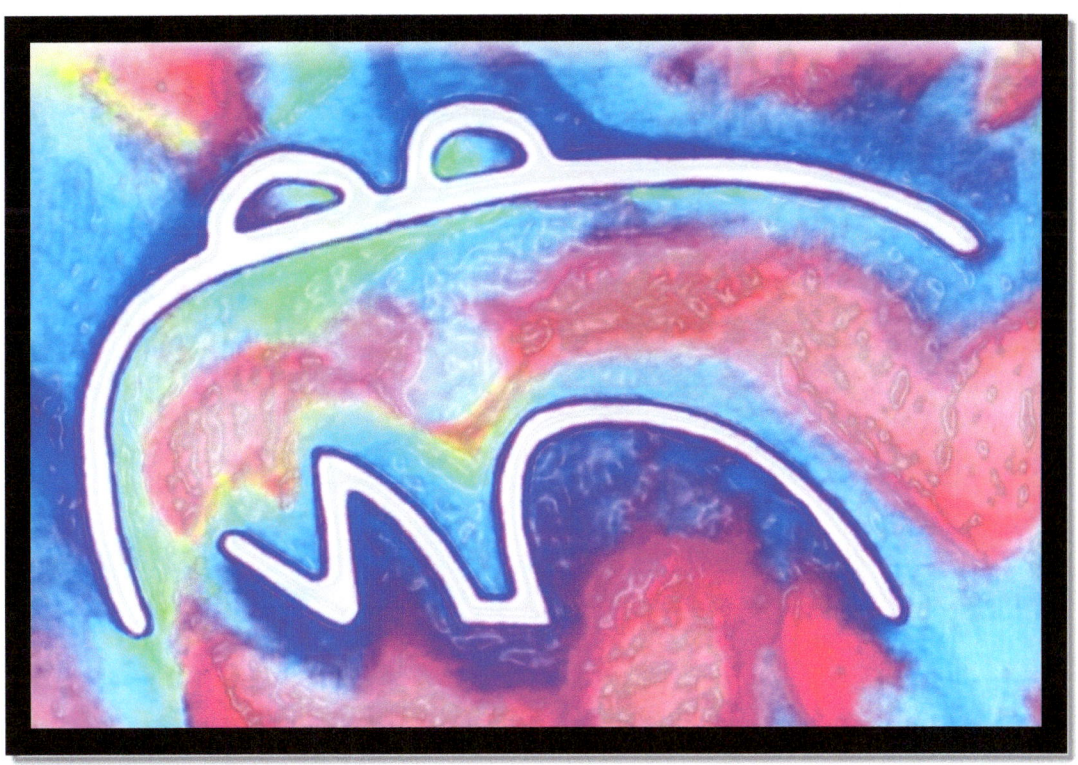

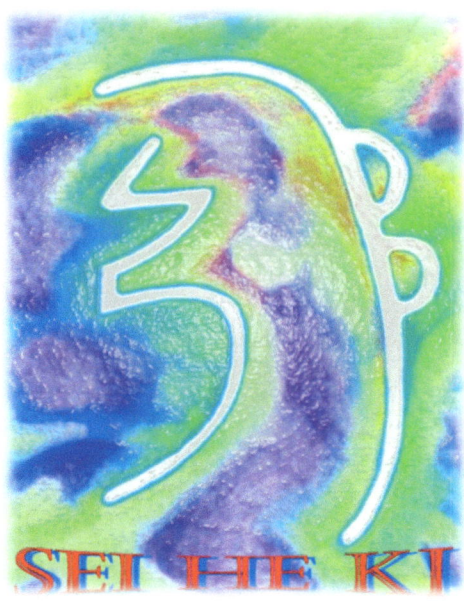

SEI HE KI works to heal the emotional traumas of one's past, present, and future perspectives so that one is able to move on from relationship dysfunctions and abuses perceived or sustained from the past with the innerstanding of the higher purpose and self lessons one was meant to learn in order to handle relationship issues that come with compassionate detachment and honesty and to identify and create healthy relating in the future. The healing energy that Sei He Ki represents also includes the healing of past life traumatic issues that have been passed down or repressed in one's ancestral and memory through present life experiences that trigger these such memories. At times one may experience or witness something that will trigger the traumatic experiences that one's ancestors had experienced which brings these past traumas to mind. Sei He Ki inspires an innerstanding of the situation that can be used as a means of facing ones fears around repeating those past experiences helping one to transcend and heal one's ancestral memory that relates to it. It also is used for the healing of physical and psychosomatic trauma related to the reproductive system by inspiring insights as to holistic options of treatment and healing.

This symbol correlates with the navel chakra, the center of feelings, emotions and their expression, sexuality, desires, creativity, intuition and empathy. Clairsentience is the psychic sense of the 2nd Chakra. power, sexual issues, blame, control, passion, ethics, money, greed, honor in relationship issues, fidelity, feelings of repression or wrongness in sexual matters, reproduction issues and birthing new ideas are all areas of life that associate to this chakra. When out of balance, one may experience co-dependent situations, and the inability to freely bond with others and sometimes even with oneself. When more in tune or in balance one will have a sense of belonging, greater tolerance with others and a more balanced and harmonious relationship with oneself, others, and one's spiritual connection allowing them to experience more open and fluid interactions.

The anatomy related to this chakra are the prostate, genitals, womb, bladder, digestive system, Gonads, (reproductive hormones) spleen, kidneys, hips, Glutes, Iliopsoas, and all musculature attached within and around the pelvic girdle. On a subtle body level, humility and selflessness can be experienced, while honoring one's own needs.

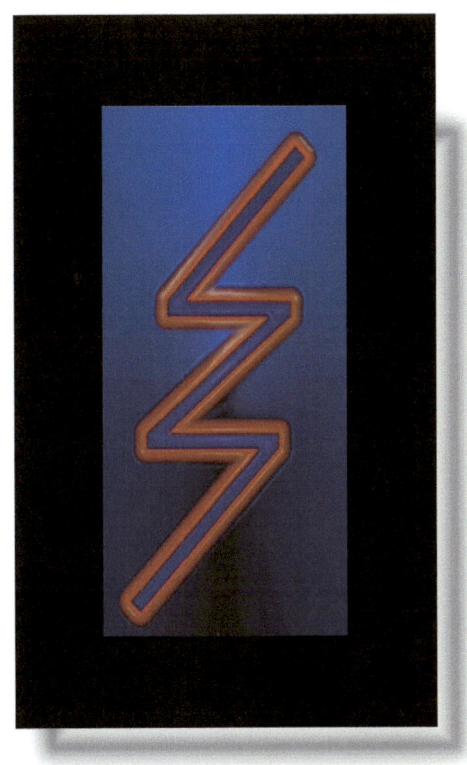
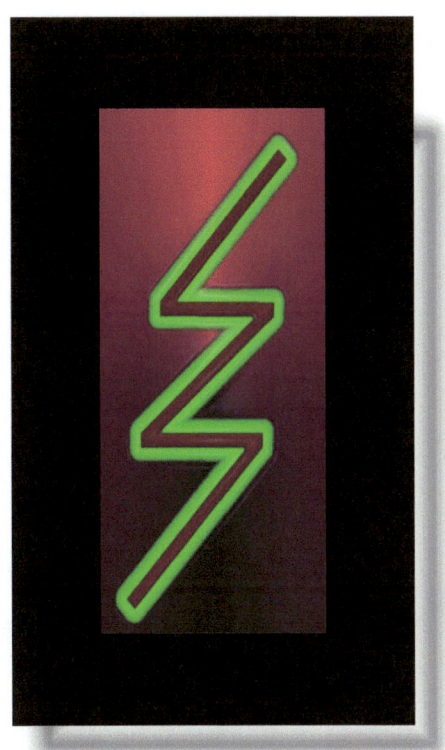
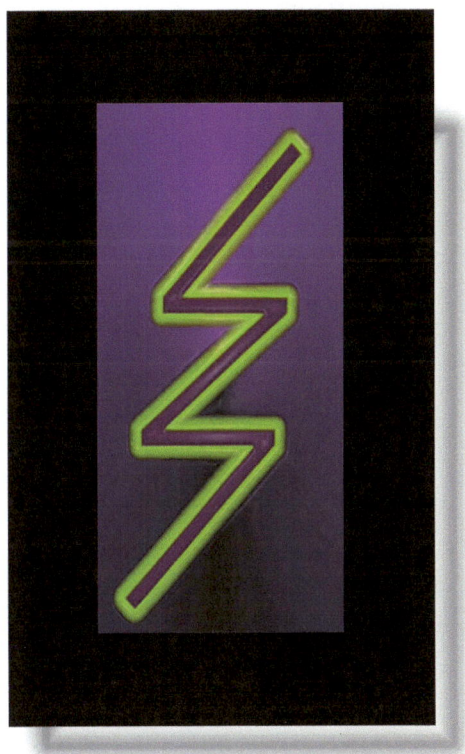
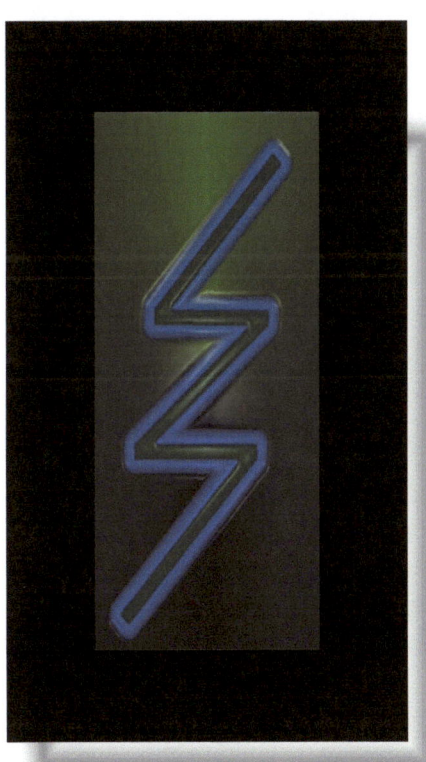

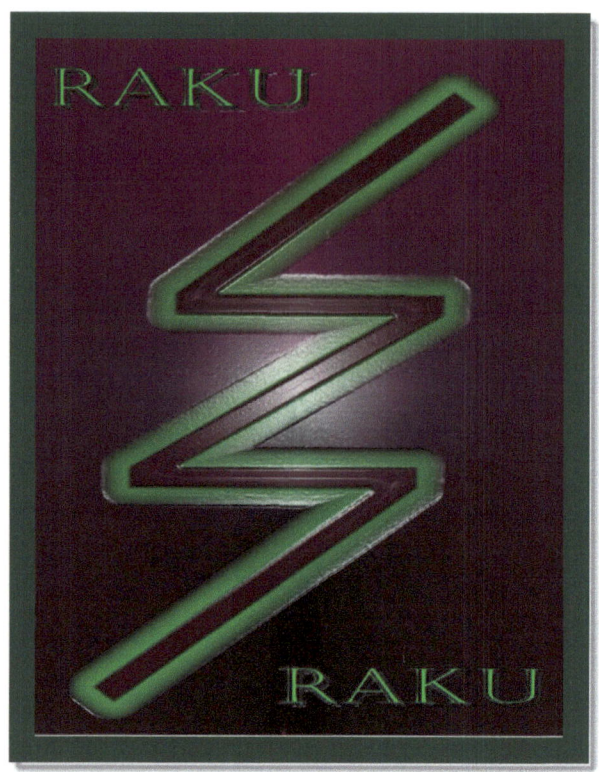

RAKU correlates to the Root Chakra located in the lowest pelvic region which is the seat of our survival instincts and programming. This also relates to tribal and past life issues, family, marriage, parenting, correct behavior, society, and our ability to provide basic needs for living. When this chakra is distorted or out of balance, there may be much fear, timidity, paranoia, and in general fears of the unknown, and an inability to connect to the flow of what's being presented in life. When this chakra is in balance, there will be a feeling of safety, security, stability, desire to maintain or acquire physical health and/or sense of well being, willingness to connect to life, and embrace life's experiences and what it has to offer.

Raku helps to harness and ground our primal life force and survival instinct empowering one to transcend fear based survival instincts in order to create means of survival that empower oneself and others to thrive in ways that promote life, loving support systems, and freedom for all life forms harmoniously. It's designed to nourish one's sense of belonging, their connection to family, community and their oneness with life. Raku can also be used to stimulate one's evolution creating positive changes so that they can make room for new experiences. It also regulates the process so that one can transcend outdated ways of living that no longer serve their best interest or phase of life.

The anatomy related to this chakra are the legs, bones, spinal column, blood, and immune system, kidneys, colon, urinary Bladder, and supra adrenal gland. Conditions addressed the sense of belonging, community, family and the Divine right to thrive on one's gifts and talents versus just survive.

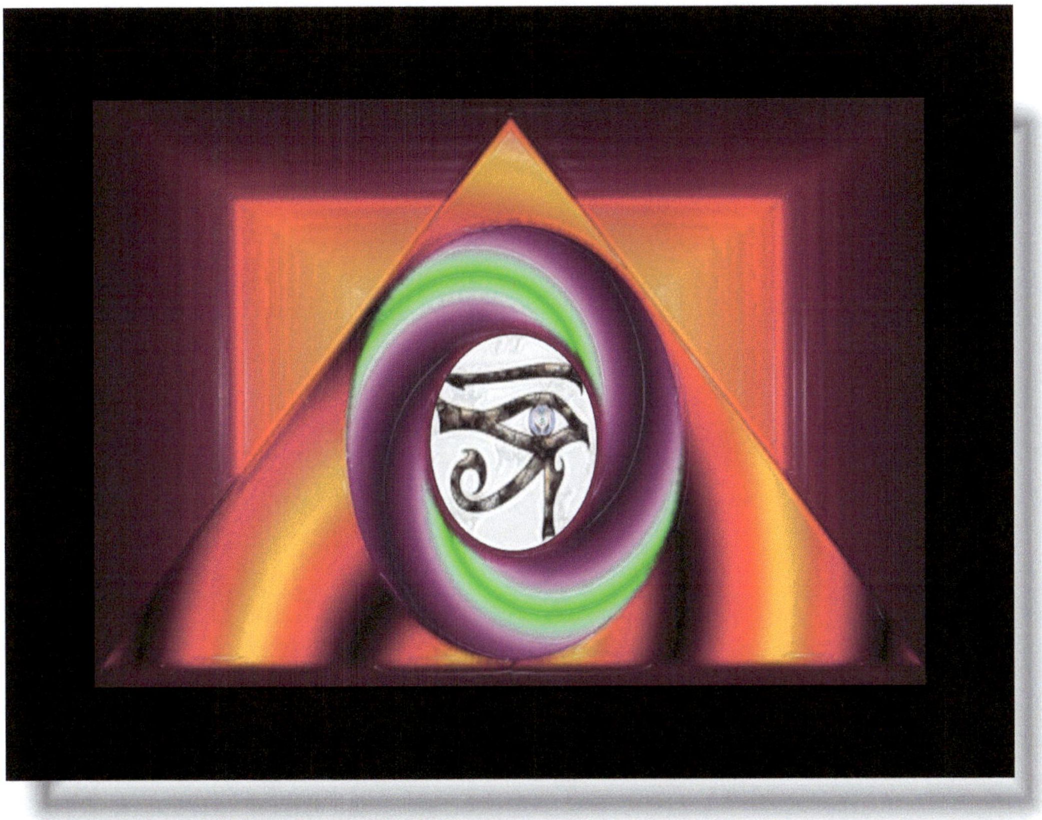

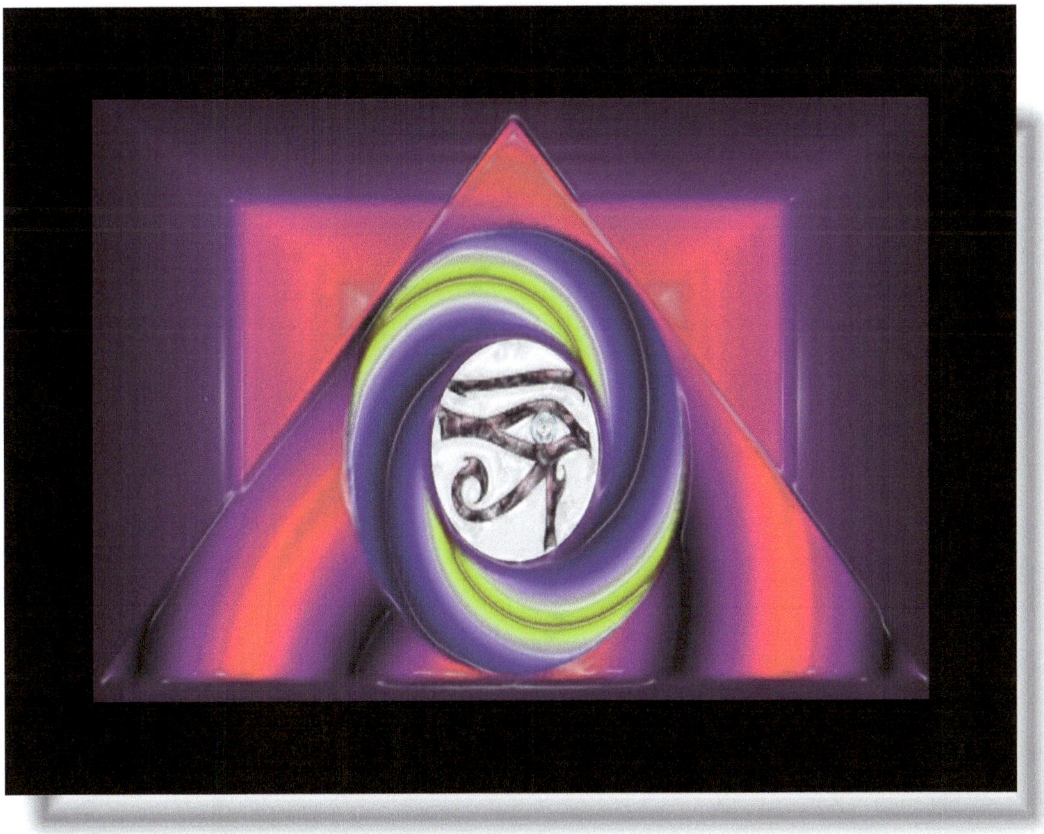

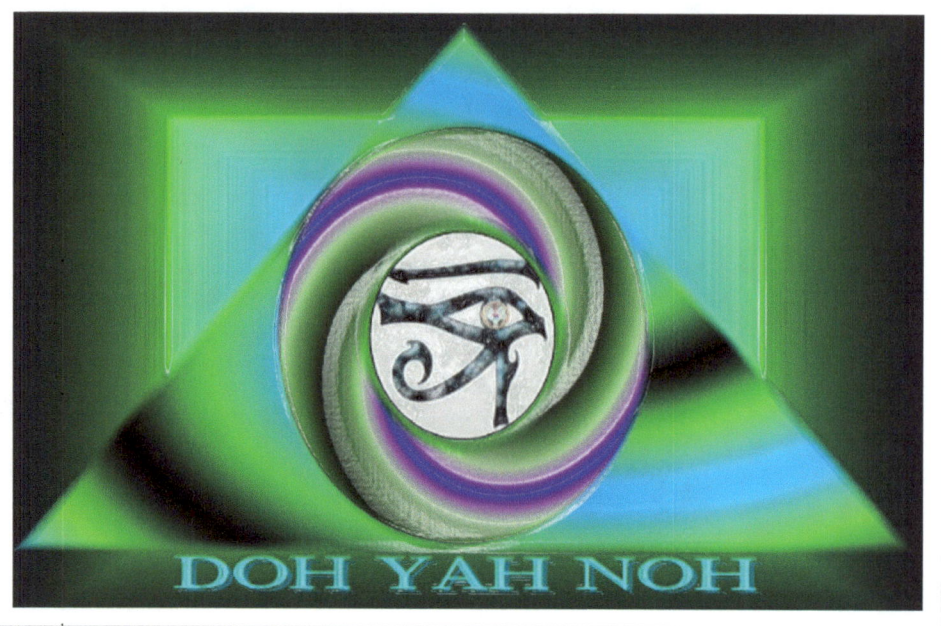

DOH YAH NOH is known as the sentinel and resides within the 8th chakra; also known as, "The Seat of the Soul". The 8th Chakra is an emerging portal into transpersonal awareness and the Universal experience of the Soul and is the temple of human cleansing and the releasing of patterns that are outdated and lifetimes old. By accessing this chakra, one can identify and release old traumas, fears, and behavioral patterns that are causing them pain or limitation in some way. As their awareness expands it enables them to see through illusions and shed old fears that have blocked them from Oneness with the Universal and collective Heart. This in turn leads to an increased innerstanding of the Universal Mind, and greater access to transpersonal aspects of the Self that operates within the chakras. As one's innerstanding grows, they begin to sense not only how all things in life are as they are, but perhaps why especially as it pertains to their knowledge and acceptance of self. It opens the gate of awareness to the divine purpose behind ones past experiences, the divine intelligence within themselves that orchestrated the aftermath of their choices that were designed as teaching tools for greater awareness of the spirit/soul within oneself, within others, and the Oneness of the spirit/soul universally.

Doh Yah Noh, (I found during meditations and Reiki sessions) surrounds the aura protecting one from other's negative thoughts, projections and unwanted influences. It works deeply to protect vulnerable areas within one's spiritual, mental, and emotional bodies as one heals. It can also represents the hermetic seal that surround the outer layers of The Earths magnetic/auric field that is designed to transmute and dissolve the influence of negative thought forms or the manifestation of thought forms that no longer serves our highest good or the highest good of the planet by creating a portal for those beings who have chosen to share spiritual innerstanding of the higher wisdom lessons necessary to re-establish harmony, love and respect for all life forms and their divine rights and purpose as creation to exist without being subjected to dominance by one outside one's own divine intelligence.

The anatomy related to this chakra are the Cerebral Cortex, Pineal Gland, Central Nervous System, subtle body layers, surplus energy, exhaustion problems and sensitivity to the others within one's environment.

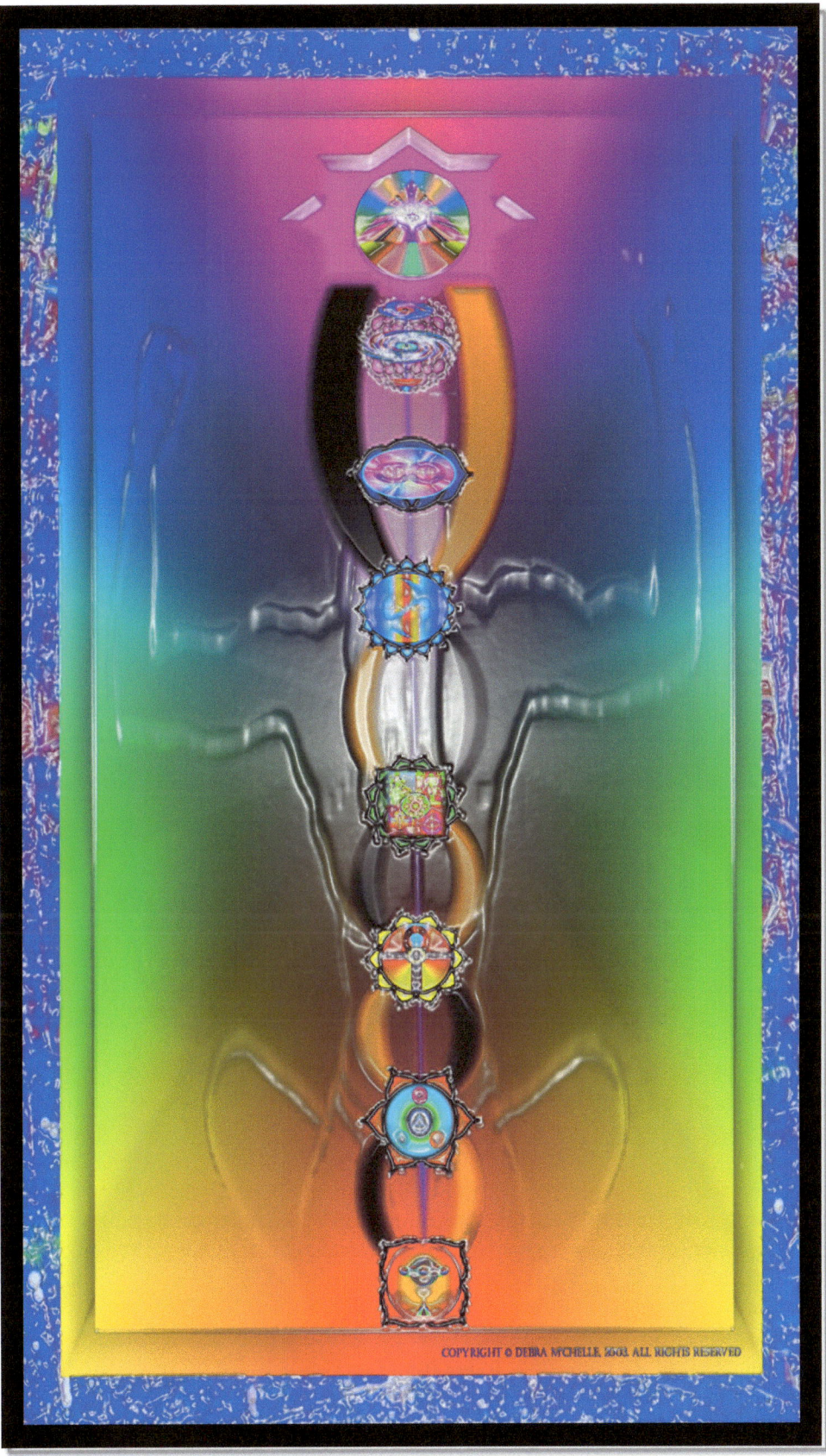

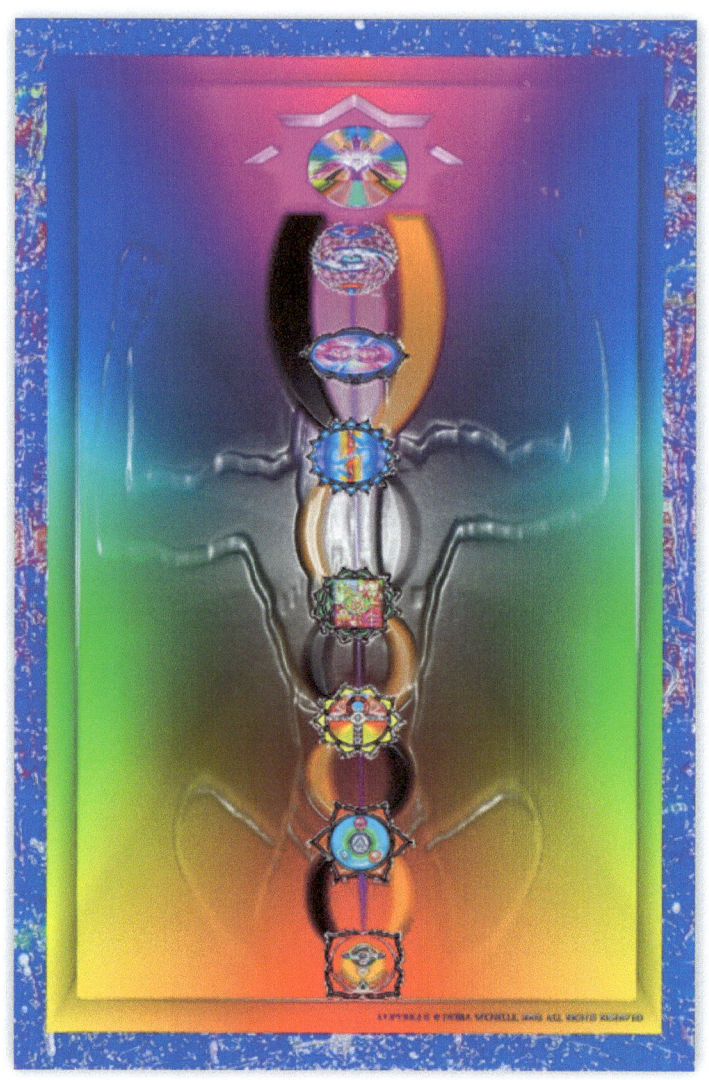

TANRAN LONG LIFE EMPOWERMENT SERIES

This series of imagery derives from the sacred symbols once commonly used during the Atlantean, Lemurian Era to transmit the sentient aspects of The Universe as part of the daily teachings and spiritual practices within the temple systems that existed then. The essence of these images and the transformative power they possess lies within the vibrations of their sacred geometrical arrangements as part of the original long life empowerment that lies dormant within of our DNA structure at this time. As in the previous symbol set, all these symbols while performing their special individual functions work together to perform various tasks in very much the same way as our organ system works to keep the entire body alive and functioning properly as a single organism according to its original design. This symbol set reflects the aspects of original life on Earth that reflect the way in which the animal life forms lived in harmony off of the element of living life force versus living off of the life force of each other.

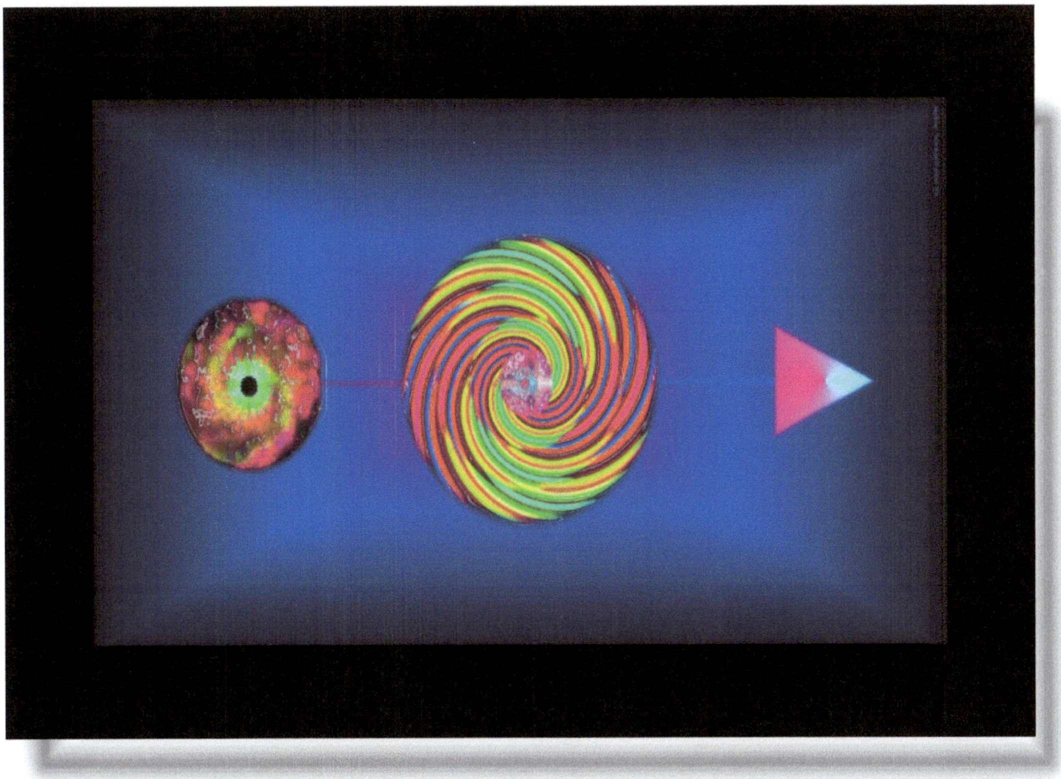

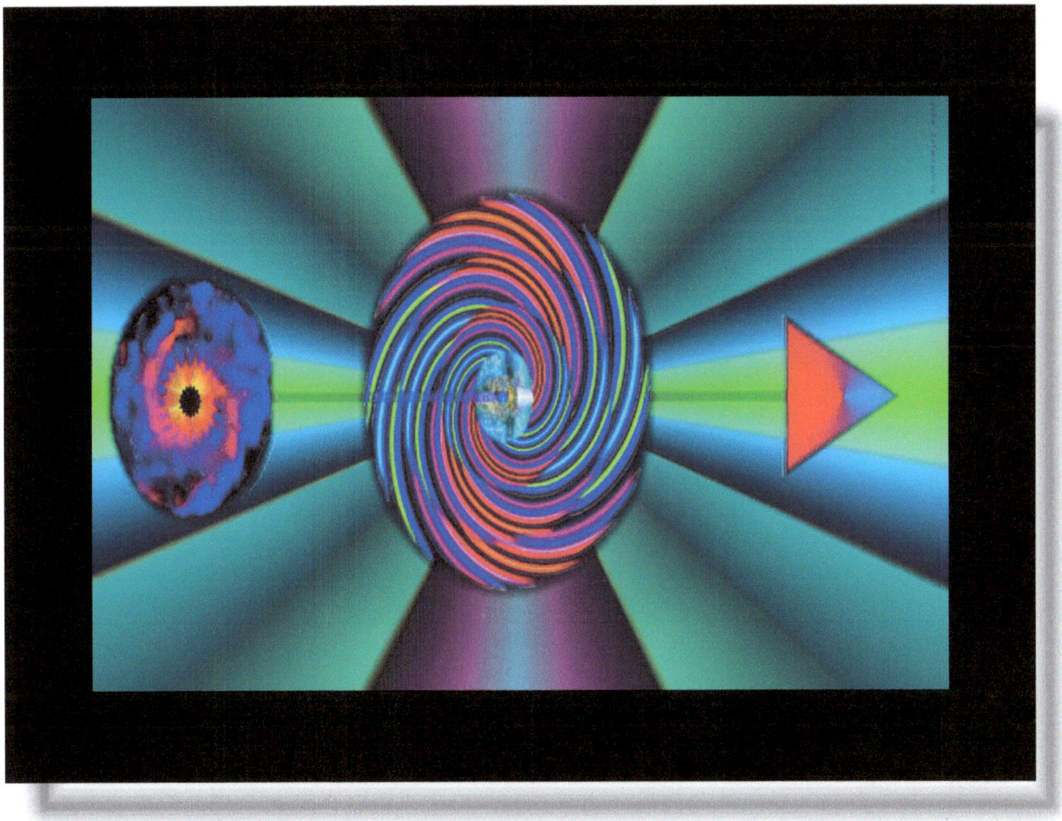

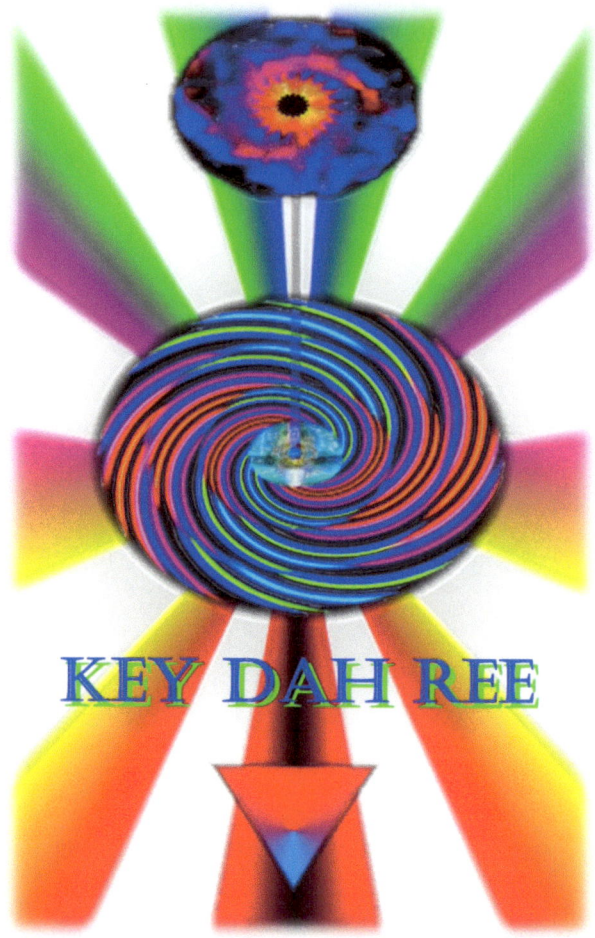

KEY DAH REE

KEY DAH REE assists in the activation of the I Am presence within us, and provides the personal innerstanding of the ways in which we create our life experiences. It works to evolve one into their full potential and to provide them with the wisdom to command their visions of life into existence. It acts like a stargate that helps to open one to their cosmic connections and galactic roots of origin making it easier to innerstand how one Self realizes as a co-creator within this vast, endless, infinite Universe. Meditation on this symbol acts as a portal where one can attune to one's cosmic roots and access one's cosmic story or blueprint in order to glean insights to one's power to transcend limitations in the material world.

It correlates to the Crown Chakra the center of Divine awareness, where the Divine and the human meet and come together down into the heart. It reveals the Unity and Higher wisdom of life and is the center of spirituality, enlightenment, devotion to spiritual and personal matters, dynamic thought, and energy. When out of balance, there will be feelings of disconnection from the Divine, lack of purpose, and inability to see the Light within oneself. When in balance the ability to experience and interact with the Divine. To have "higher mind" knowingness, and a connection and sense of purpose with the Divine plan.

The anatomy related to this chakra Cerebral Cortex, Pineal Gland, Central Nervous System, Right eye, skin and muscle systems, depression, sensitivity to the environment, energy/exhaustion problems.

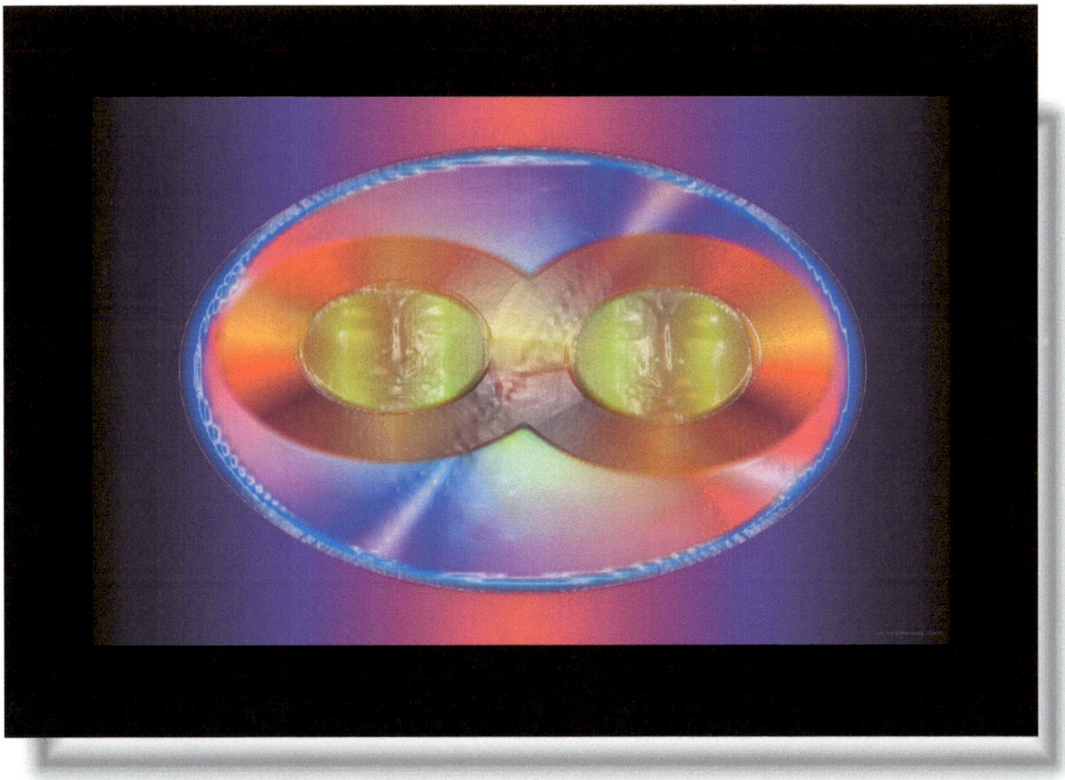

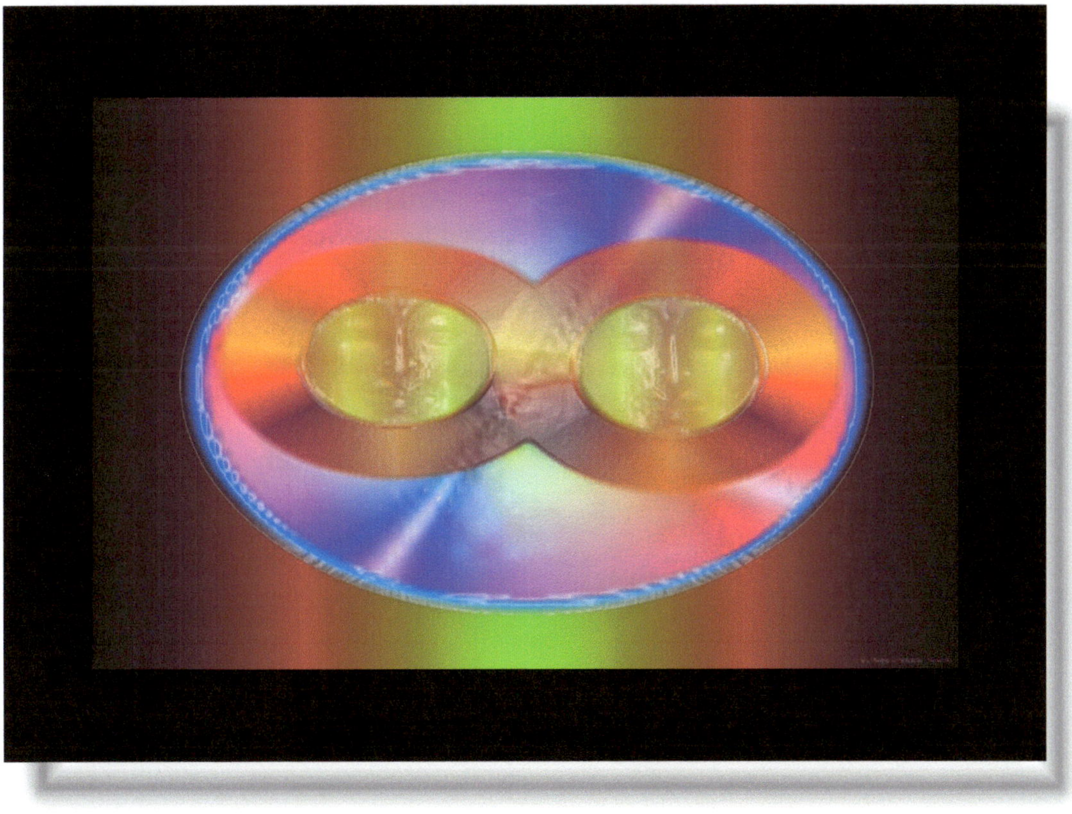

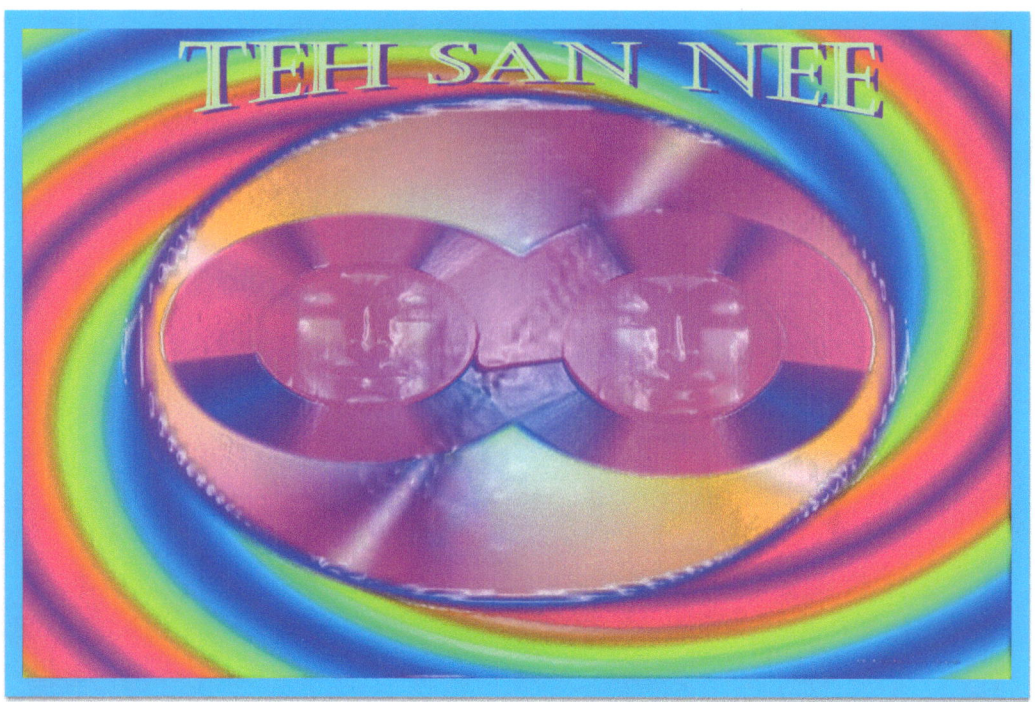

TEH SAN NEE reflects the Divine blueprint of the feminine and masculine principles within all creation and is the activation center where one can access the truth of their Original design as an immortal being. As one breathes in sync with the cycle of infinity within the symbol one will find that they are guided by its wisdom to the knowledge of their divine blueprint as an immortal being which lies within their DNA. The circle sealing this symbol represents the Hermetic force that surrounds spiritual truth and our spiritual body. Teh San Nee helps one to embrace and make sense of the knowledge concerning their galactic connection, the various star groups that are embodied on earth, and their intentions and purposes of evolving the inhabitants on earth such as the Indigo, Crystal, and Rainbow children & adults of today as well as the Reptilians, Pleiadeans, and Nephilim in previous time periods.

This symbol correlates to the 1st Eye Chakra which is the center of psychic vision, higher intuitive information, inner wisdom, creativity, imagination, and devotion to spiritual knowledge, the energies of the spirit, magnetic forces, and light. Teh San Nee can assist with transcending beyond the consciousness of death by healing all fears related to the experience with the death of the body. Teh San Nee helps us to actualize our immortal existence and ascended consciousness. As one evolves into their light "ka" body one will find themselves embracing the concepts of cellular regeneration, breatharians, telepathic communication, teleportation, space travel and seeing these things as a natural aspect of our divine design. One is able then to envision humanity at a level of evolution where we have replaced cellular degeneration and dependency on manmade materials to sustain us and return to natural energy based remedies for healing ourselves, the planet and beyond.

The anatomy related to this chakra Cerebellum, pituitary and pineal glands, liver, gallbladder, nose, ears, left eye, central nervous system, learning problems, spinal problems, hearing problems, tinnitus, eye problems.

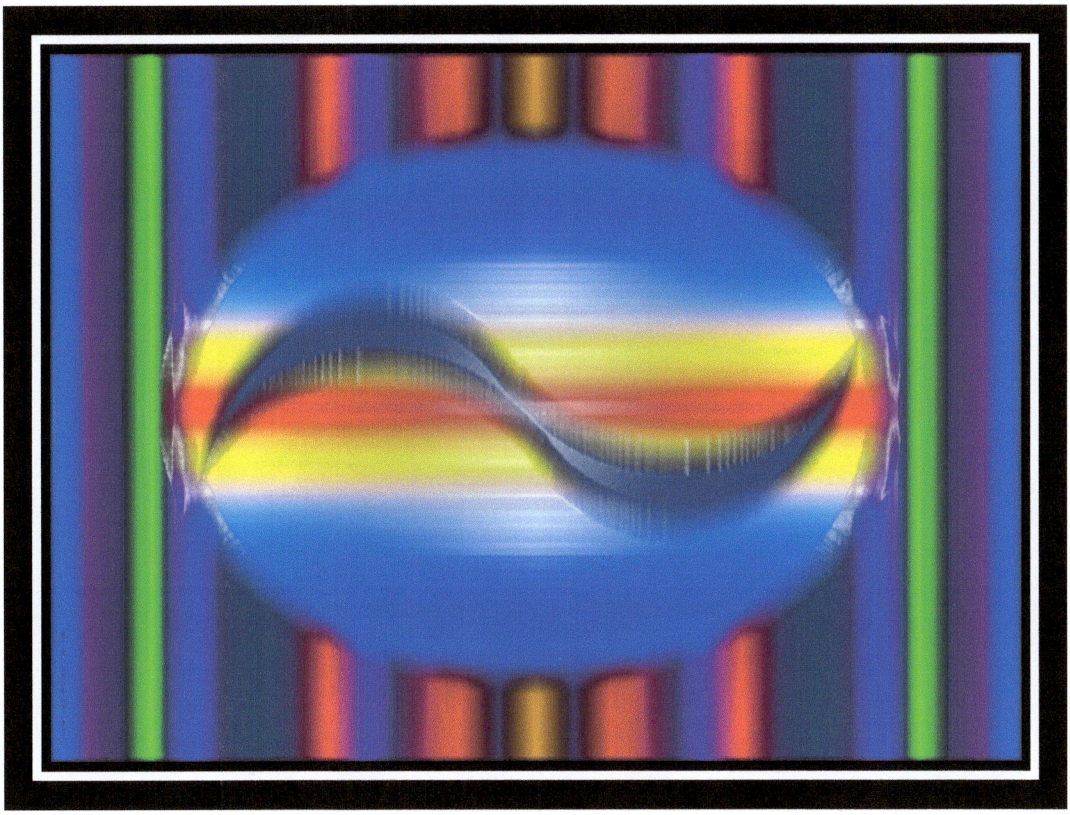

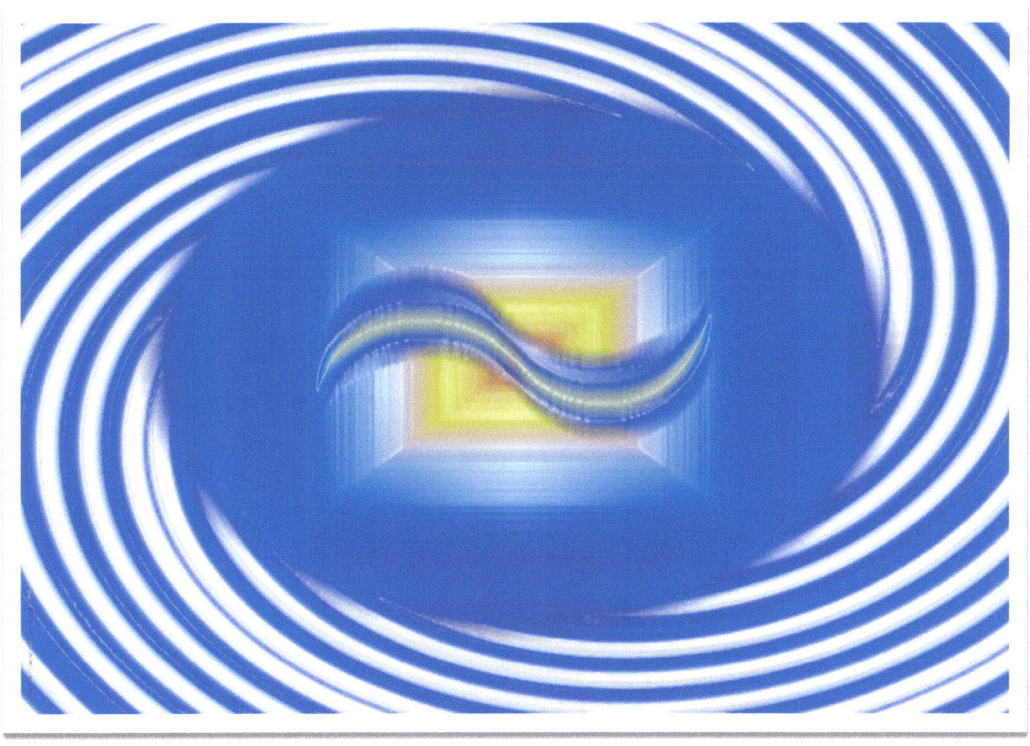

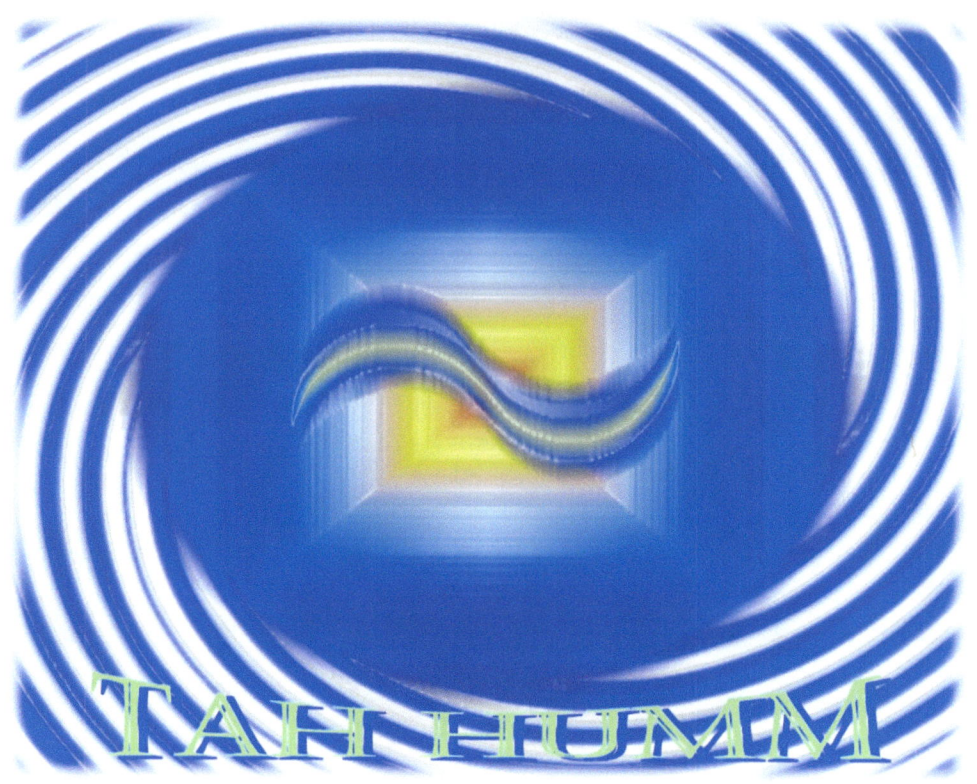

TAH HUMM'S vibrational power resides within the throat chakra. It has the ability to alter one's physical reality through the purification of their thoughts, by focusing them in on only that which produces internal peace, divine health, joy in work, soul fulfillment and divine life. When one speaks from their Spirit each word spoken transmutes all negative thought, words, and expressions into life giving, light radiating forces. The sine wave represents the inhalation of divine thought and the exhalation of divine intention. Therefore, each breath fuels one's words and one's deeds. This form of breathing meditation will help alter one's speech naturally with ease in accessing and speaking words of truth and kindness that resides within one's heart and spirit unhindered. The oval circle is a hermetic seal that surrounds, protects and purifies one's intentions and vocal cords so that their voice can carry the healing power of sound enabling them to hold only those thoughts that one wants to make real in their life.

Tah Humm operates through the Throat Chakra where it is able to influence all our forms of expression, communication, and creativity whether in thought, spoken or written words, song, movement or other. From telling our truth, following our dreams, knowing and being true to our passions, sharing knowledge, wisdom, and kindness, to struggling with addictions, habits, judgments, faith, decisions, criticism, or being true to our word they are all personality aspects of self that are regulated within the throat chakra and affected by this symbol when activated.

As a powerful tool of spiritual healing and ascension, vocal toning has been used in many of the Asiatic African, and East Indian spiritual traditions. Vocal toning allows us to direct the healing energy of TahHumm through breath work and corresponding vibration, into any area one chooses by intention, visualization or physical contact.

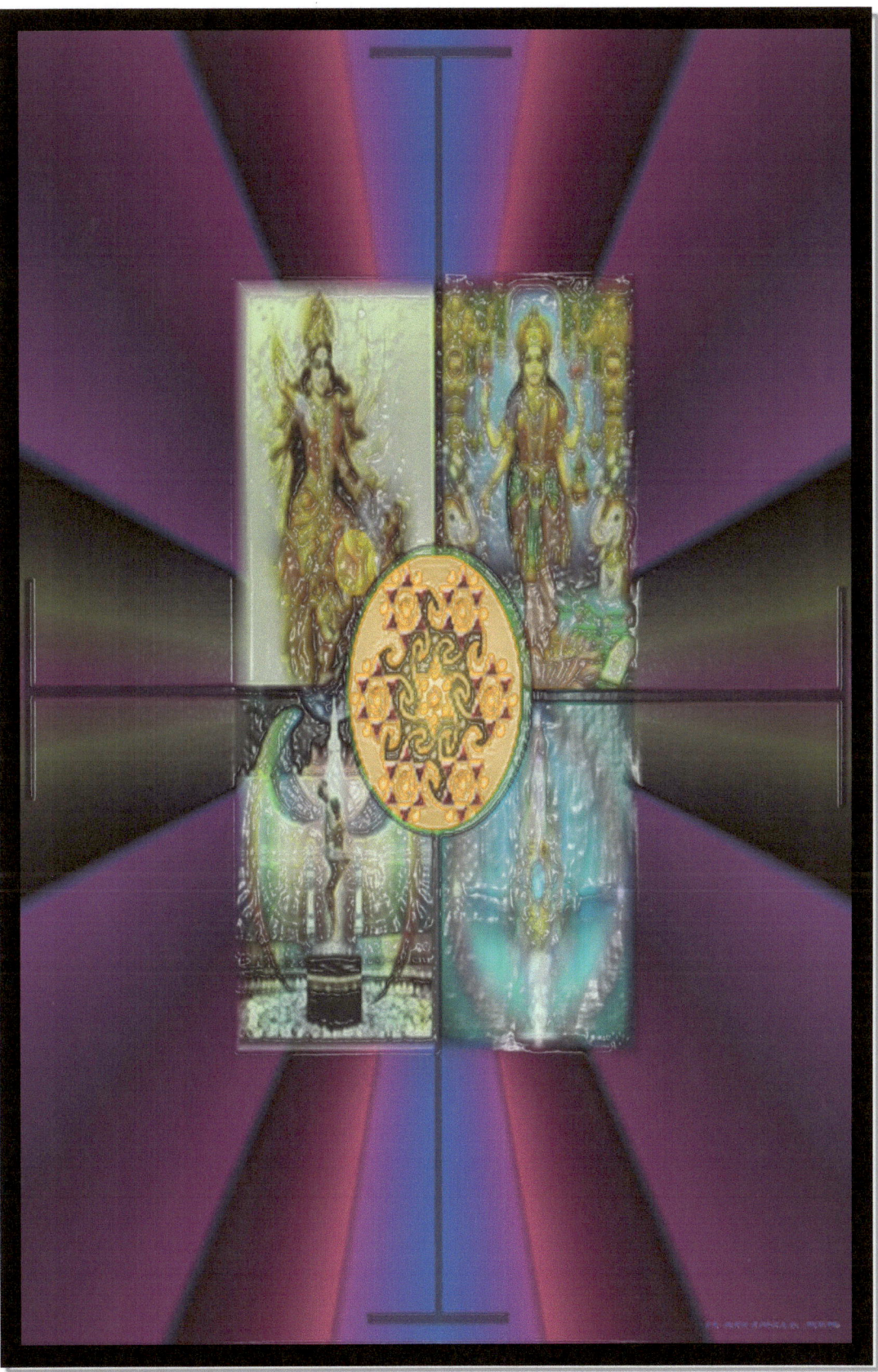

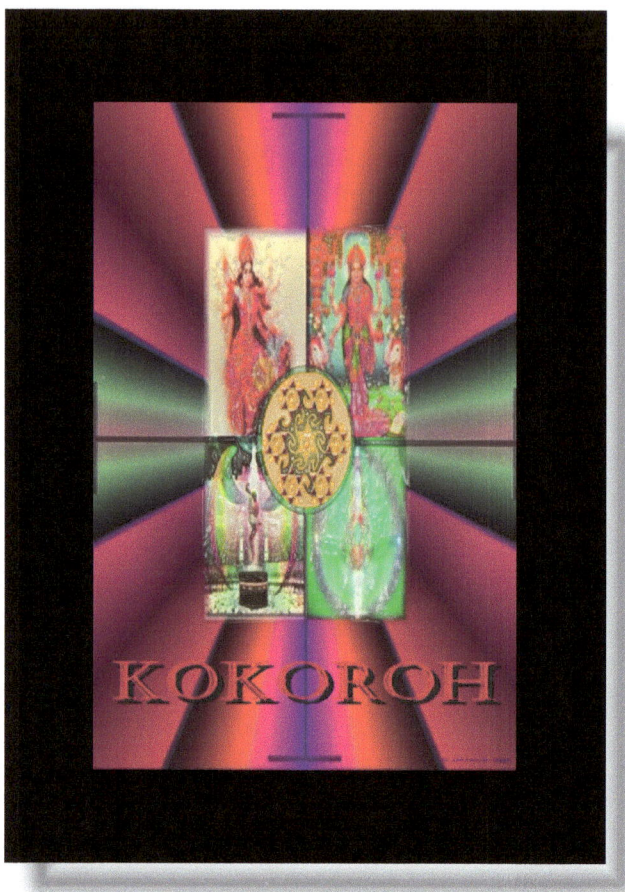

This symbol lies within the Heart Chakra, the center of Divine love, compassion, altruism and acceptance of reality as it is. This is the center of our spiritual connectedness with your divine Self where you are able to express love without condition with healing intentions and align yourself with the truths that allow you to resolve differences of all types and in all relationships for yourself.

KOKOROH represents individual embodiment of divine love which filters into one's level of health, wealth and love experiences through knowledge, acceptance, and embodiment of one's divine Self. It also re-polarizes the spine creating a clear channel for Divine energy to flow into every aspect of one's life and to give them greater access to higher wisdoms that will help them transcend blockages to their ascension into their Divine Truth. It helps to restore one's conscious awareness and commitment to actively loving all sentient beings. It regulates all the chakras and reorganizes the atomic structures within the body to that of the higher vibrations Life Force from of the universe. It helps reacquaint us to the security we're meant to have in our Divinity by helping us break free of the illusion that one can find any form of lasting security within the world.

The anatomy related to this chakra are: heart, pericardium, lungs, thymus, large intestines, triple warmer, cardiovascular system, blood, cellular structure, involuntary muscles, arms, breathing problems, chest area, breasts, asthma and associated allergies, pneumonia, bronchitis, upper back, shoulder, and arm problems.

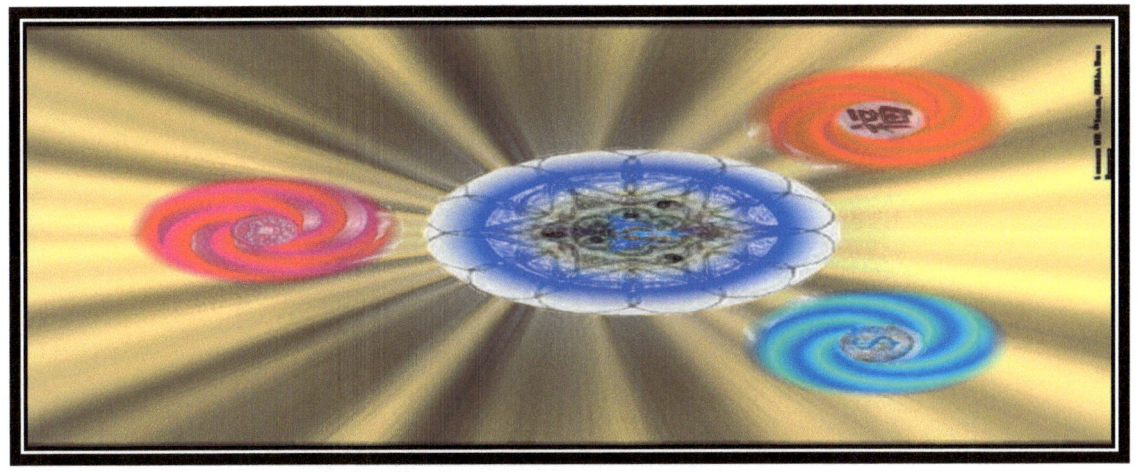

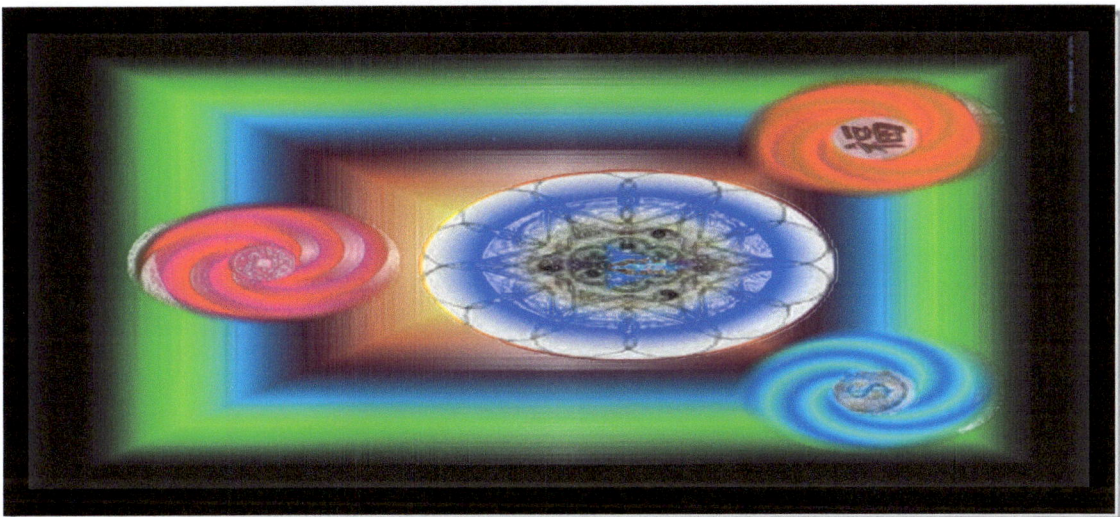

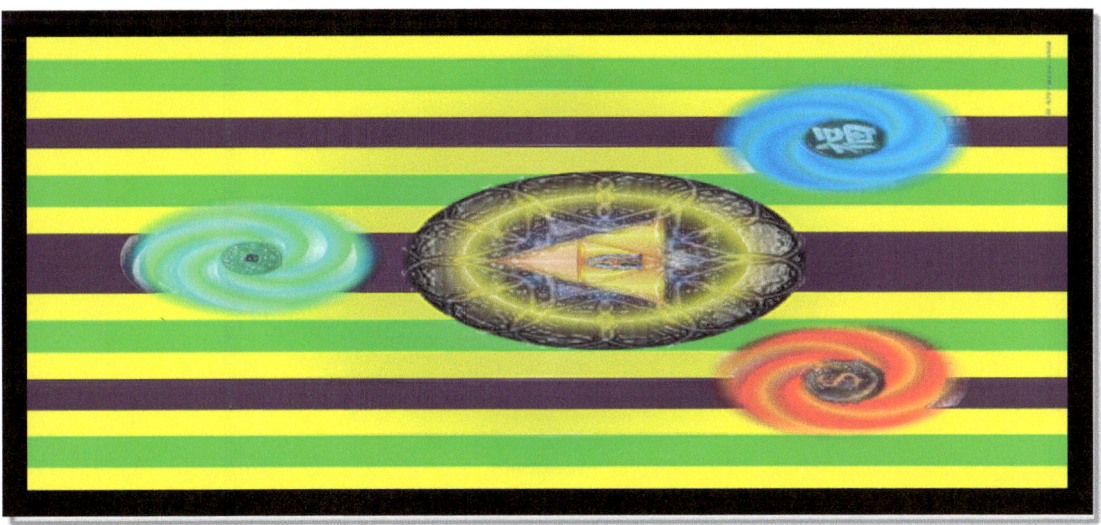

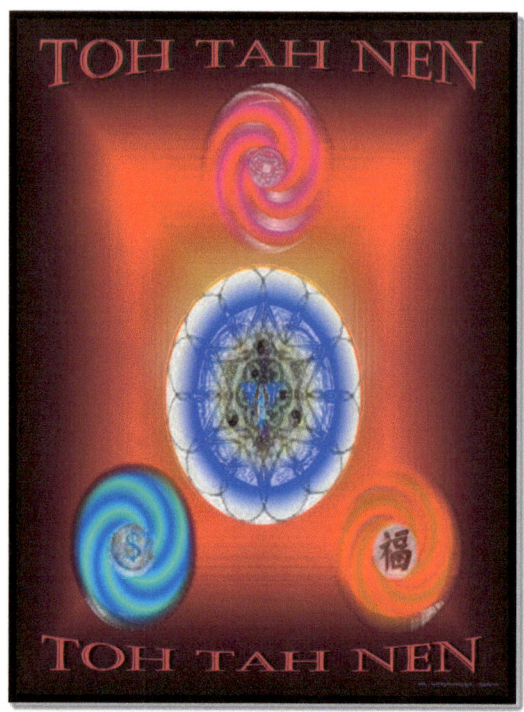

TOH TAH NEN is empowered to purify one's relationship to wealth and abundance removing the masculine tendencies to use brute force or the feminine tendencies to use manipulation in order to achieve wealth. It also helps to release oneself from the false illusions of lack and the need to compete or gain wealth by disempowering another that we have been programmed to believe and allowed to rule one's decisions about money and its relationship to how they live life. Toh Tah Nen aligns us with the insights into our spirit, soul, and heart as to what life and career style will allow one to do what they love and love the work they do based on what's important to them. It can teach us to put Spirit within us first, and to be responsible in regards to our daily duties using the insights, knowledge, and resources available to us to generate abundance and to live self-sustained in ways beyond the current materialistic monetary construct. It is responsible for inspiring humanity to create economic exchanges based on respect and fairness in exchange. These are a part of the new paradigm shift from patriarchal rulership to that of cooperative empowerment and self-sustainability options that lie outside of the constructs of currency alone. Some of these options that are being considered, embraced and implemented are concepts of exchange such as barter, trade, virtual (bitcoin) currency, community voucher exchange systems and more.

Toh Tah Nen operates within the Solar Plexus Chakra which is the center of personal power, ambition, intellect, astral force, self-respect, willpower, confidence, self-control, and physical energy. Issues with fear, guilt, responsibility, caring for others, trust, career, intimidation, personal honor, feelings of victimization, self-concern, self- respect, one's own confidence and courage all affects the health and functioning of this chakra.

The anatomy related to this chakra - the stomach, colon, liver, gallbladder, pancreas, adrenal, immune system, sympathetic nervous system, mid-back, and muscular system. Physical challenges such as diabetes, arthritis, liver problems, eating disorders, indigestion, and any dis-ease related to the associated organs can derive from Solar plexus imbalances.

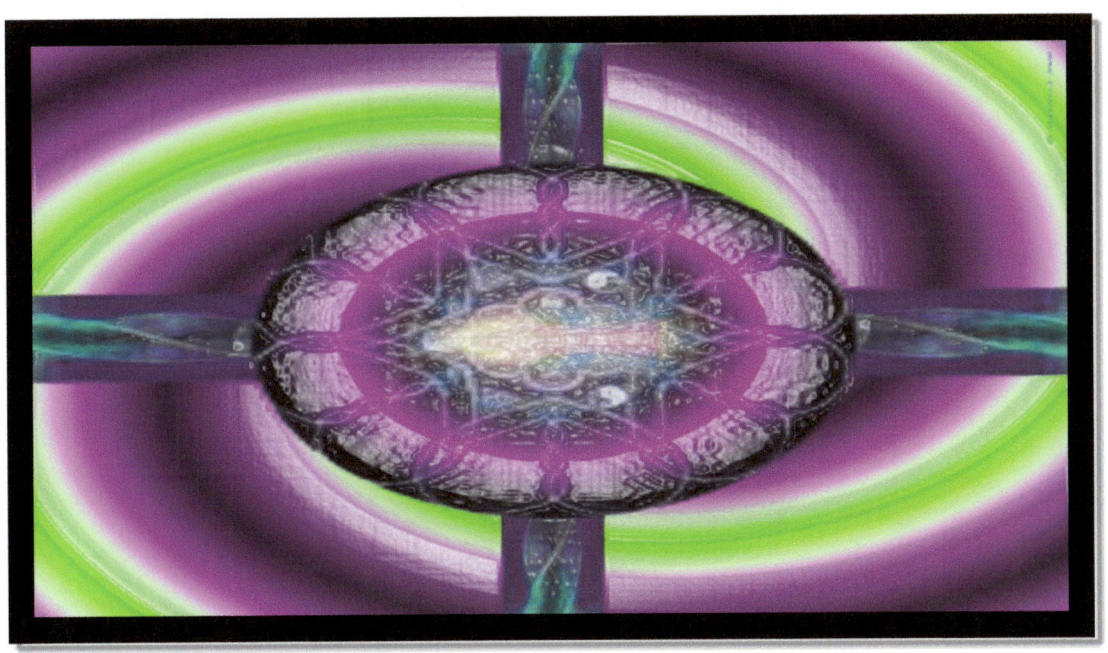

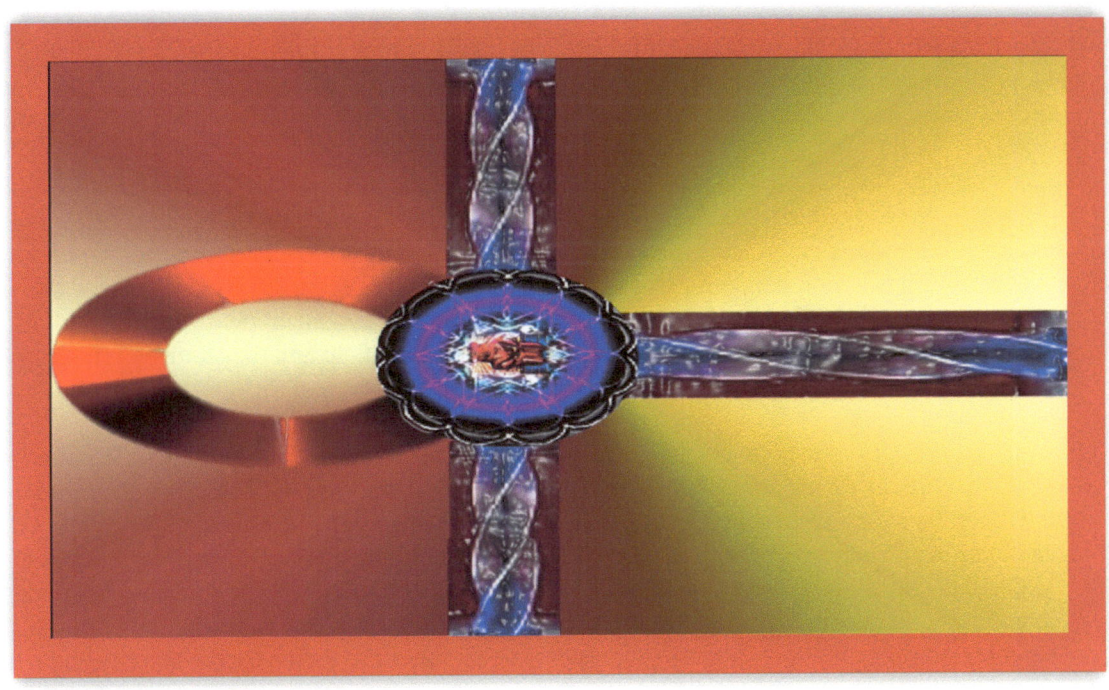

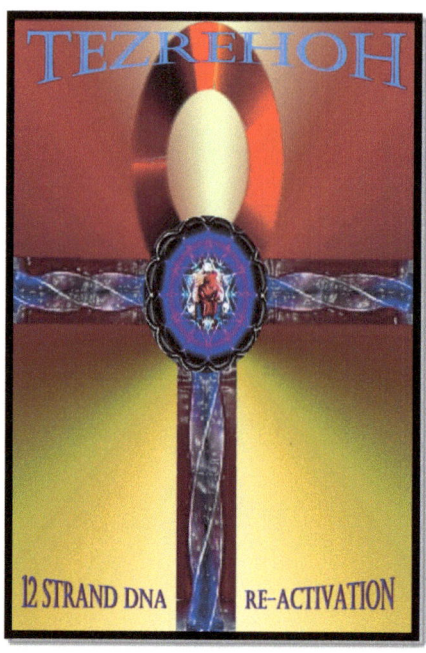

TEZREHOH reactivates the quantum vibrations or, "The God Particles" within our DNA rebuilding and regenerating the DNA strands that have been lying dormant within our cellular design. It activates the light/genetic interface between our cellular structure and that of the quantum universe within the 12 + DNA structure. The genetic wisdom that this symbol represents will cause in oneself a shift from fear based programming and instincts to that of endless regenerative, adaptive, healthy and fulfilling ways of visioning and fulfilling our divine purposes, one's desires and one's dreams for the healing evolution of oneself, one's society and of the planet into homeostasis.

Tezrehoh often works in conjunction with Keydahree and Tehsannee to trigger and open up the info within our DNA that relates to our cosmic blueprint. Keydahree ignites the activation of dormant information concerning our cosmic roots of origin once activated uploads the unlocked info up through the chakras to the1st eye creating a visualization of itself within our conscious minds (Recent Scientific discovery of the God Particle and the elemental makeup that we share with star and planetary matters are examples of this awakening).

This symbol resides in the Navel Chakra yet directly corresponds to the Solar Plexus Chakra as it directly pertains to one accessing dormant aspects of their personal, ancestral, and spiritual sense of self and empowerment. When out of balance, there may be an inability to freely bond, sometimes even with the self. When aligned with Tezrehoh we open up to ways to eliminating the death and aging programs, and remove the encoding of fear, slavery and victimization. It potentiates into greater effectiveness within the immune system, and enhances our ability to regenerate, and eventually evolves our systems to be able to live directly on universal light energy as our source of life force energy.

The anatomy related to this chakra are the ovaries, testicles, prostate, genitals, womb, bladder, digestive system, Gonads, (reproductive hormones) spleen, kidneys, hips, Gluts, Iliopsoas, and all musculature attached within and around the pelvic girdle.

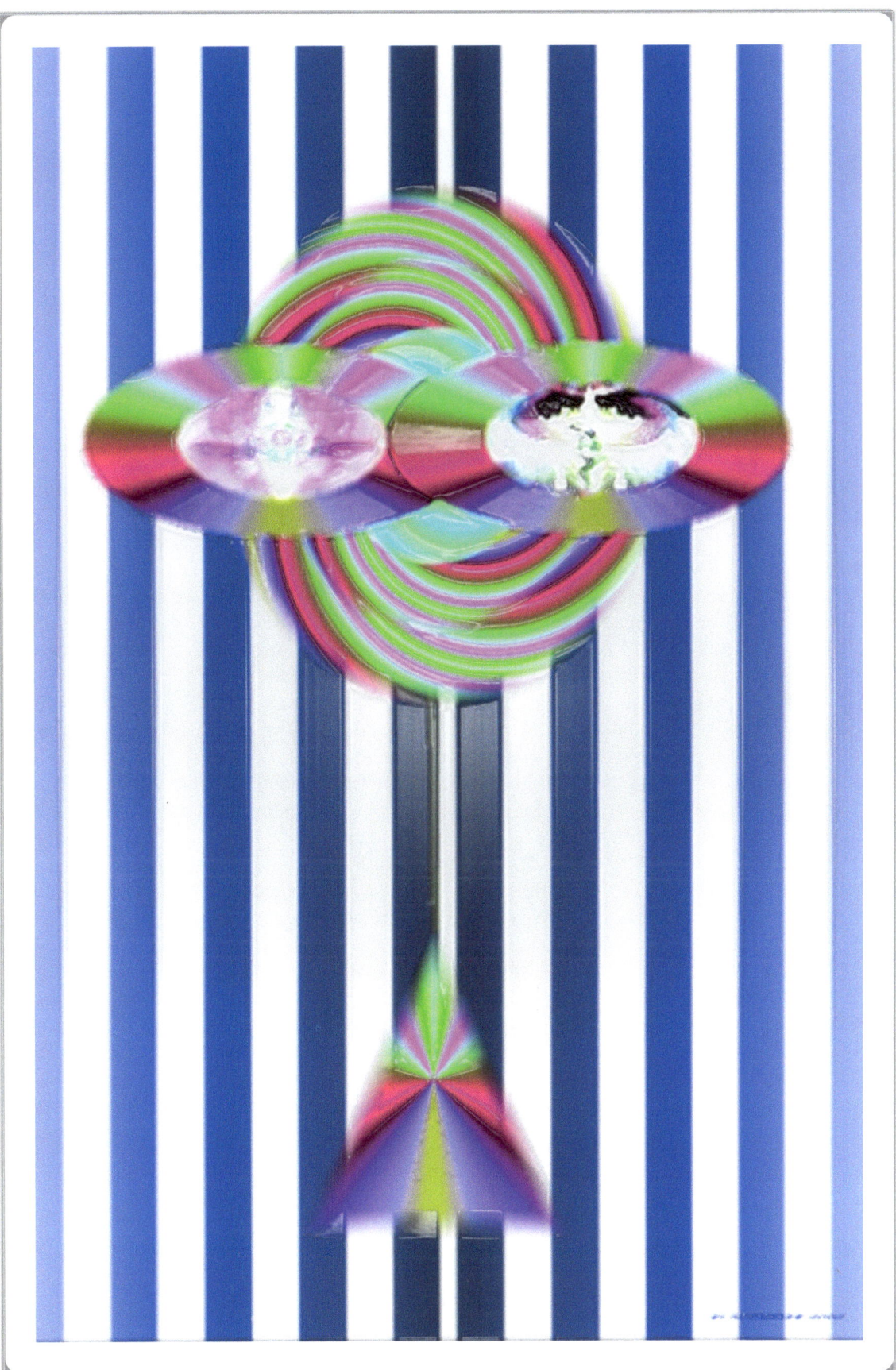

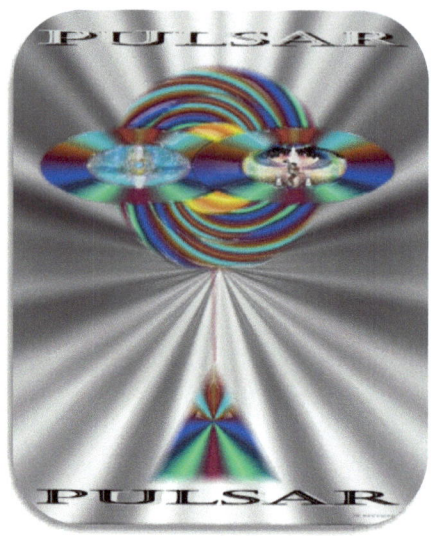

PULSAR helps to keep our desire for freedom and natural tendency for wishful thinking pure, guiltless and unadulterated from societal programming. It can help to purify our desire to live, love, and be free from fear-based cravings and attachments to worldly outside influences and manipulations. It can also establish within our innerstanding that desire is a part of our divine design and is a natural part of enlightenment. And that our freedom to have and be what we dream is a part of our Divine inheritance. And like the free flowing nature of the cosmic and earthly elements our dreams and desires become governed by this free flowing expression harmoniously and intuitively balanced.

Pulsar overlays within the Root Chakra and represents the steady even progressive movement from one point to the next creating a solid foundation and focal point for the manifestation of what we desire. It also represents the Divine Trinity within oneself operating as one unit. Through various life experiences we discover our likes and dislikes and become more self aware of our true values and purpose. Pulsar works to clarify our priorities and the value we place on the things we desire. The ascending line represents the way in which our desires move and evolve into the spiral of fulfillment as they go from general concept of what we want to more specific idea visions of the steps and requirements necessary for manifestation.

The infinity symbol within Pulsar represents the breath of life itself. The inhalation of embracing what we chose in our present experiences, and relationships, the holding of breath that allows us to experience these things fully in order to process, gain insight and determine what is of use and of value to us, to the exhalation of letting parts of our lives go that no longer serve us so that we can give thanks and integrate the lessons learned and again embrace life in the current moment with the promise of greater more fulfilling experiences. Thus, is the cycle of life itself, pulsar empowers us to continue without fear, shame, or outdates concepts of our Divinity.

The anatomy related to this chakra are the legs, bones, spinal column, blood, and immune system, kidneys, colon, urinary Bladder, and supra adrenal gland.

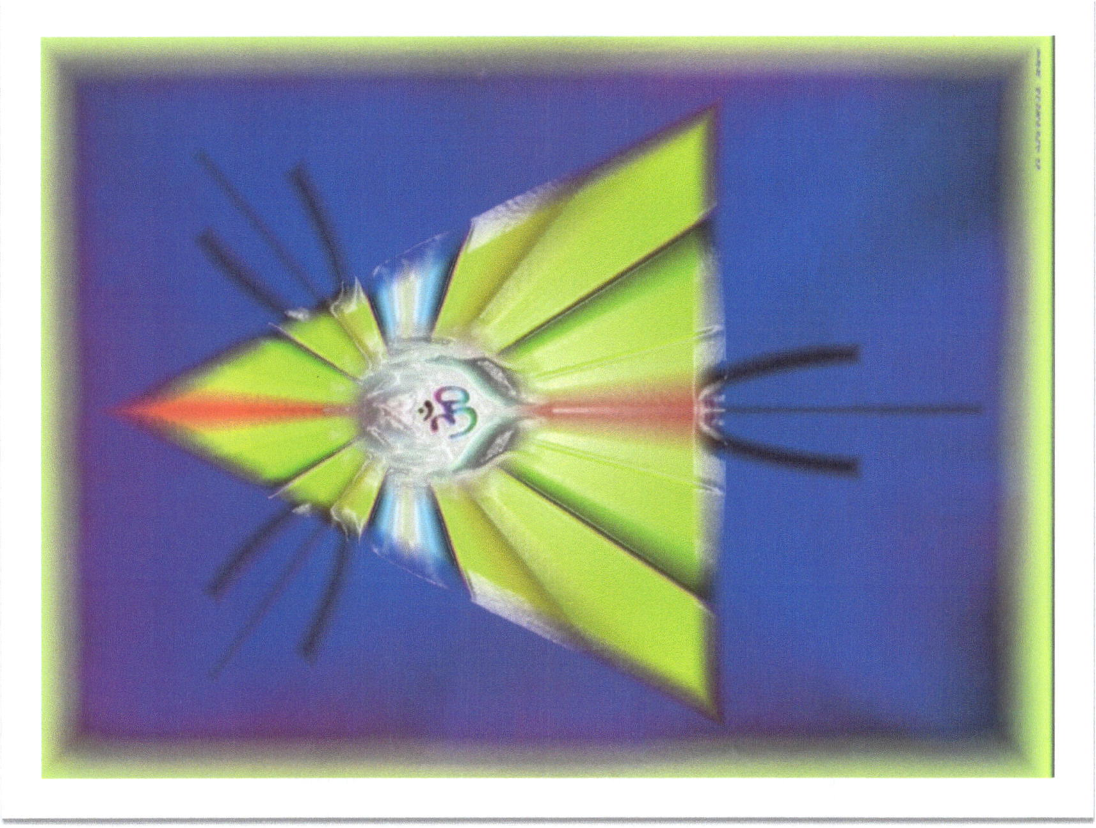

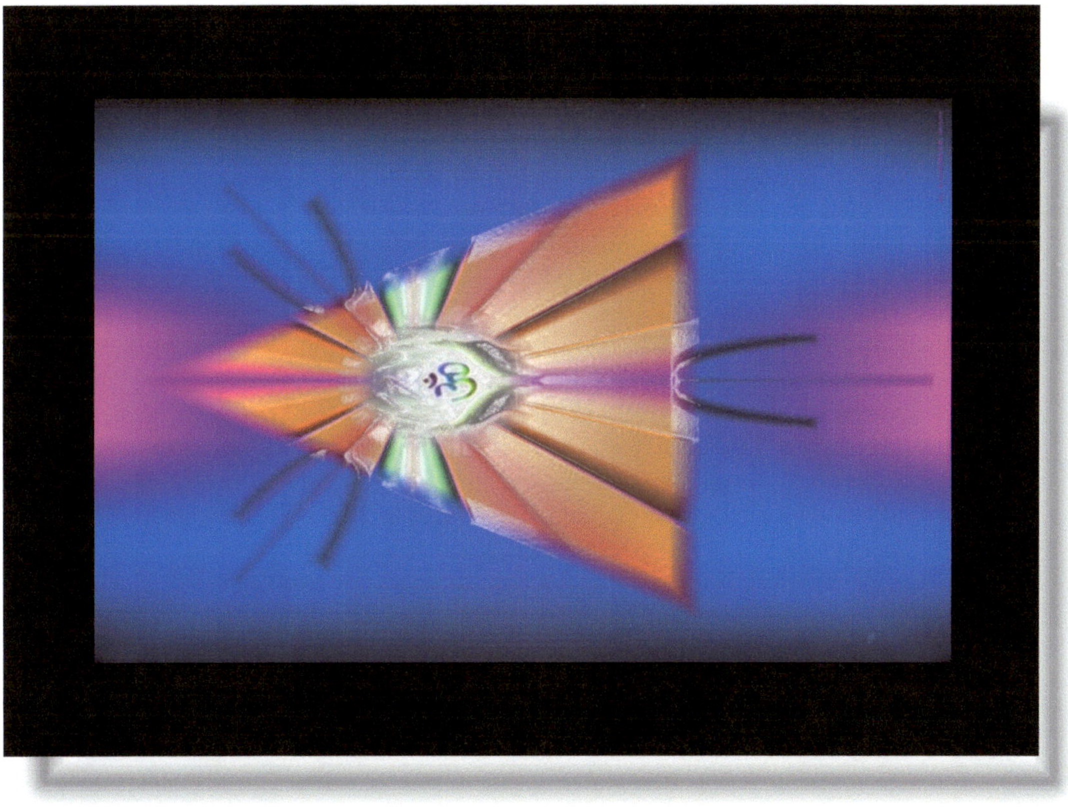

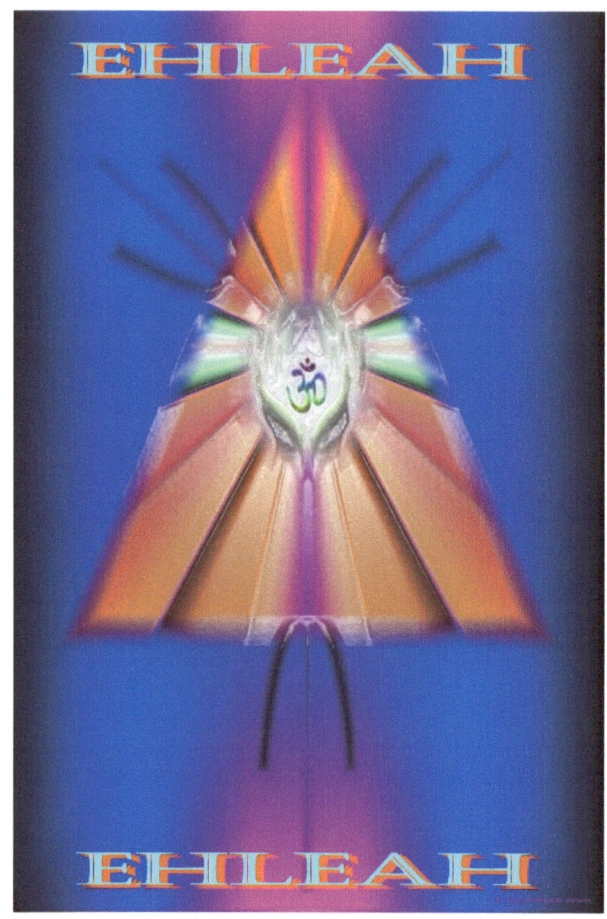

EHLEAH resides in the 8th Chakra along with Dohyahnoh. It is a soul retrieval symbol that assists in reconnecting and healing fragments of one's soul that have been abandoned or cast off due to trauma related to significant events in one's life. Ehleah also assists us by gently processing and re-integration previously repressed or lost soul aspects that have been retrieved and ages them up to date so that their importance to our wholeness and divine purpose can be experienced with ease and grace.

As previously mentioned, The 8th Chakra is an emerging portal into transpersonal awareness and the Universal experience of the Soul and is the temple of human cleansing and the releasing of patterns that are outdated and lifetimes old. By accessing this chakra, you can identify and release old traumas, fears, and behavioral patterns that are causing pain or limitation in some way. As one's awareness expands Ehleah enables them to shed old fears and one will come closer to Oneness with the Universal Heart. This in turn leads to an increased innerstanding of the Universal Mind, and access to transpersonal aspects of the chakras. As one's innerstanding grows, they begin to sense not only how all things in life are as they are, but perhaps why especially as it pertains to their knowledge and acceptance of self.

The anatomy related to this chakra Cerebral Cortex, Pineal Gland, Central Nervous System, subtle body layers, surplus energy/exhaustion problems and sensitivity to the environment.

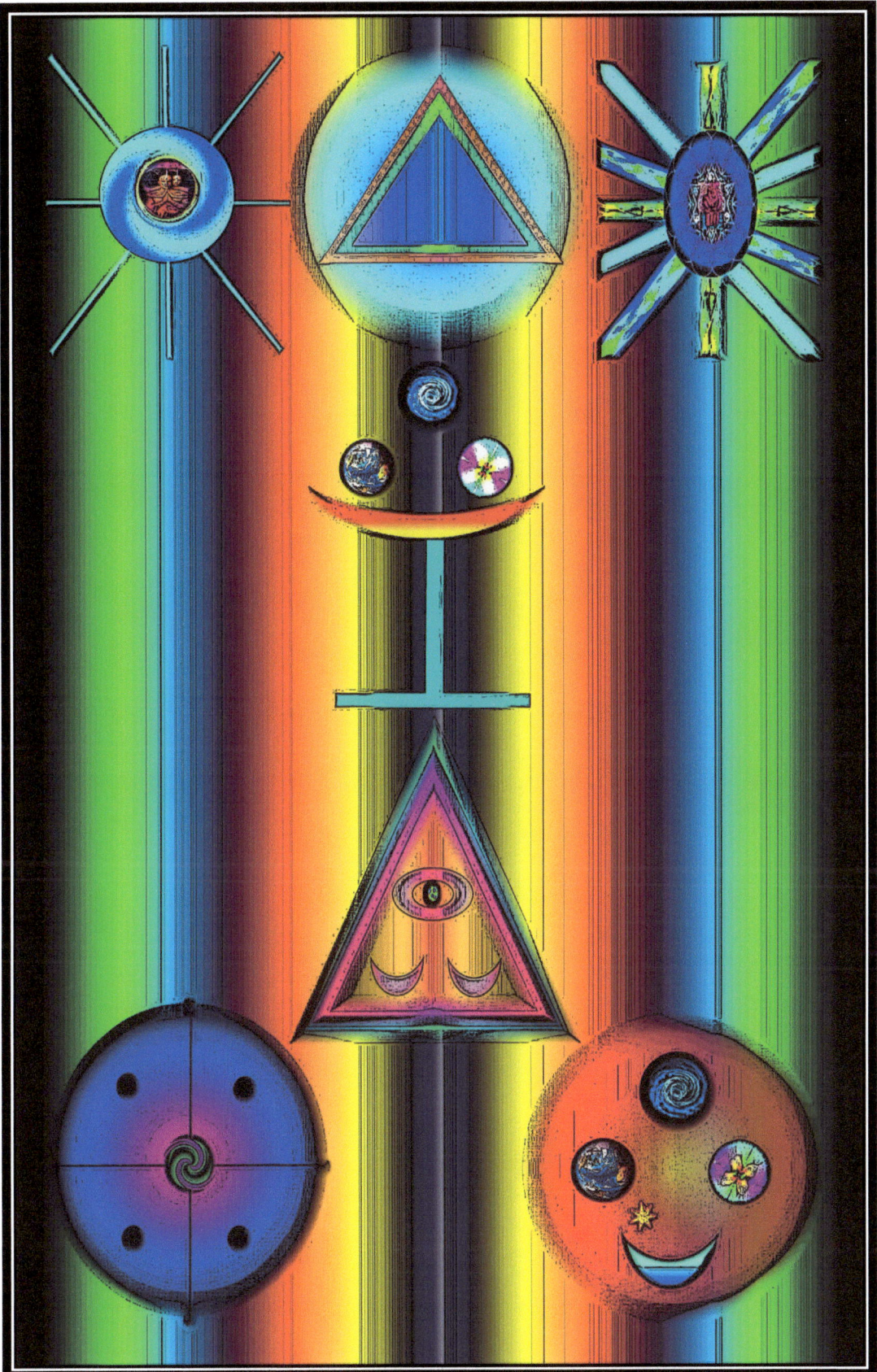

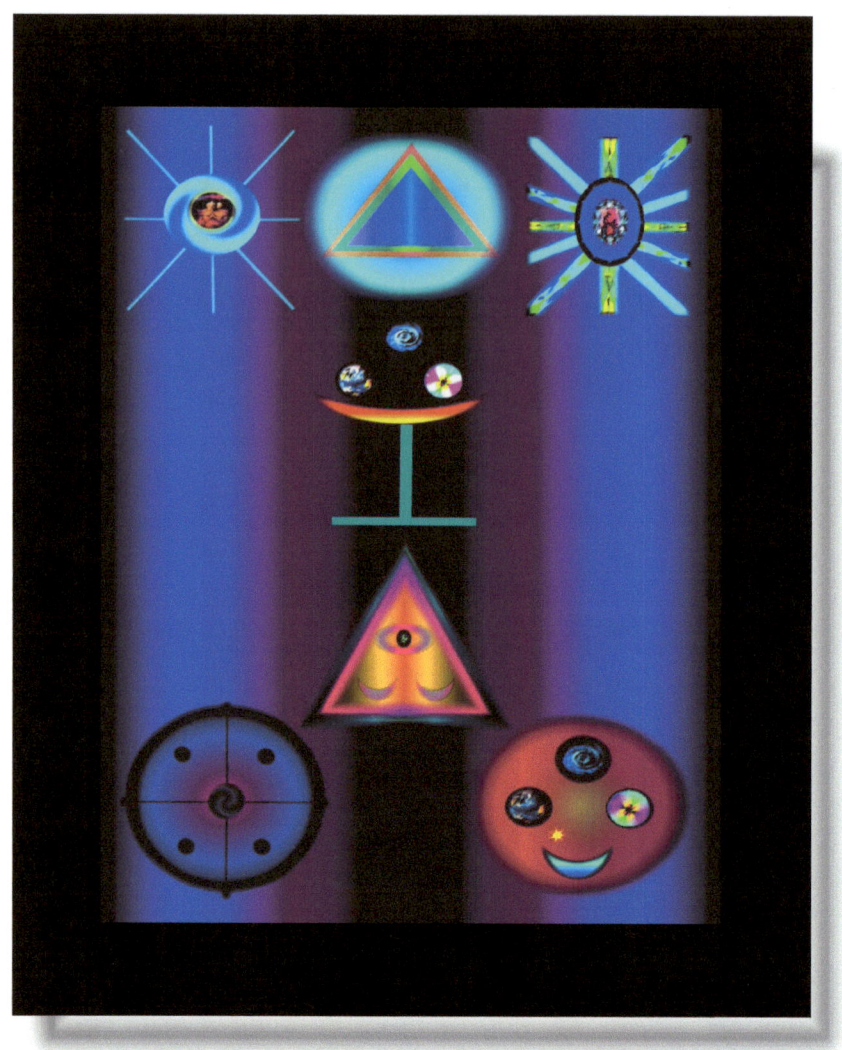

TANRAN REIKI PURE ETERNAL LIFE SERIES

The Tanran Pure Eternal Life Set opens the gateway to innerstanding the Eternal Soul that your current embodiment is a partial co-creative extension of. The Eternal Soul is the collective soul experience of all of one's various embodiments (past, present, future), on earth, in parallel universes, and multidimensional personifications. Some of these you have yet to experience as divine infinite expressions of one's self and of those who are a part of one's Soul group. The symbols within the Pure Eternal Life set express Divine Truth that underly the messages within the teachings of Enlightenment throughout ancient and modern-day spirituality and religion. Each symbol activates aspects of your Eternal essence and guides your mind towards the elevated awareness and innerstanding of who you are and what your experiences as an Eternal Soul expression and who one is as a part of the Source of all life and creation. As the Spirit of The Divine Intelligence embodied in this set activates within oneself, its essence will radiate through their heart, soul and bodily expression, the truth and beauty of love and life unconditional.

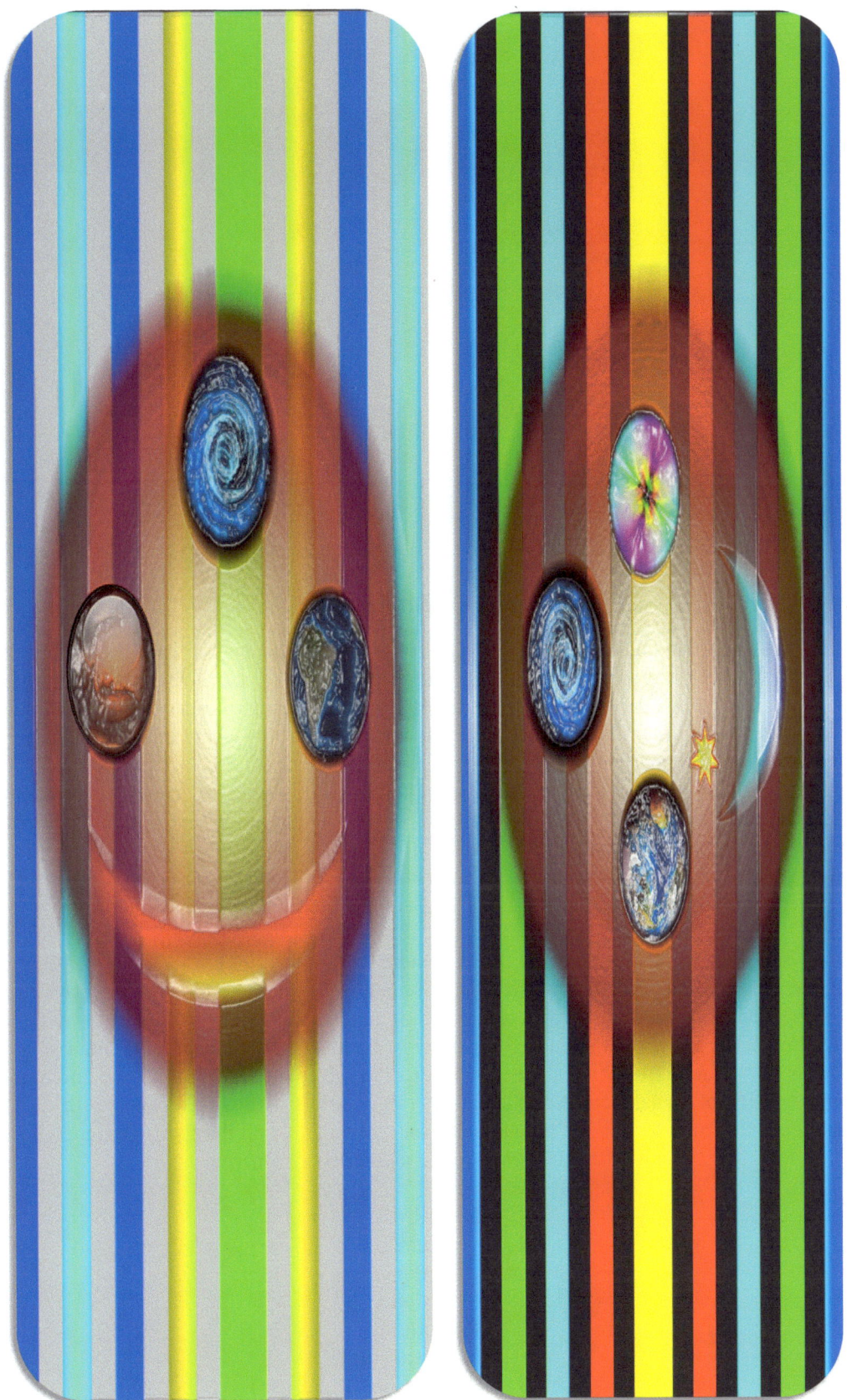

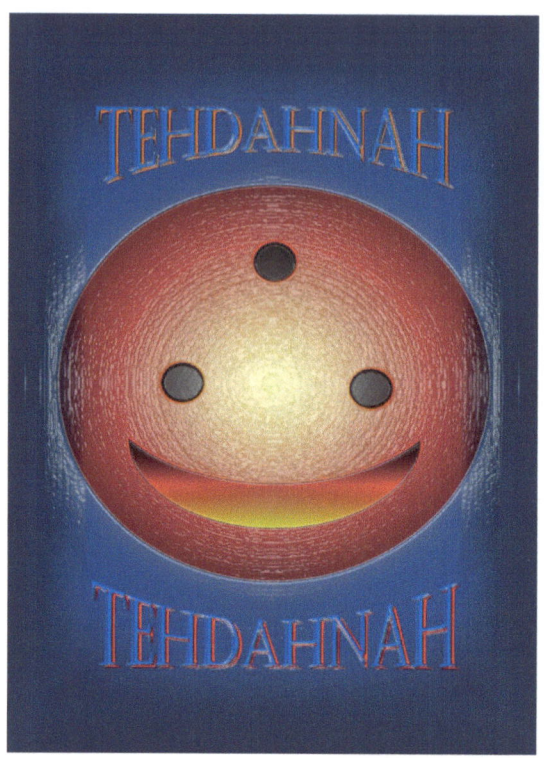

TEHDAHNAH Non-dualistic Bliss; "1ˢᵗ Eye Smiley": Teh Dah Nah reflects the happiness of the person whose 1ˢᵗ eye is wide open. One who is able to see the cosmology or the underlying behaviors regulating all events that are in harmony with the natural order of the cosmic laws and the natural order of earth life. It depicts the state of being where one is able to see everything unfolding perfectly and rest in the perfection of its enfoldment allowing oneself to experience the joy of being in synch with the rhythms of life. When in this state of awareness, the influence of Tehdahnah inspires the trust in God to always guide one to the fulfillment of their divine purpose and envisioned dreams. It helps one identify when they are out of sync with these same rhythms and provides the insights to what one must do to regain synchronicity with their divine nature, vision of divine life and desire for fulfillment.

This symbol reflects the state where one consciously exists within the awareness of oneness with the absolute and perfection of life, and your existence within it. One becomes aware that all things happening within the world are according to a sentient order that operates by the laws of dharma better known as the underlying order of life designed by the Divine Intelligence of the Universe. As a Buddhist philosophy it refers to the doctrine of purification and moral transformation of human beings on the path of right-us-ness within oneself and with all. One transcends the imperfections of human behavior realizing that all things are designed for all humanity to come to the awareness of Dharma.

DHARMA:
Desire
Harmony
Action
Reciprocity
Metaphysicality
Absolution

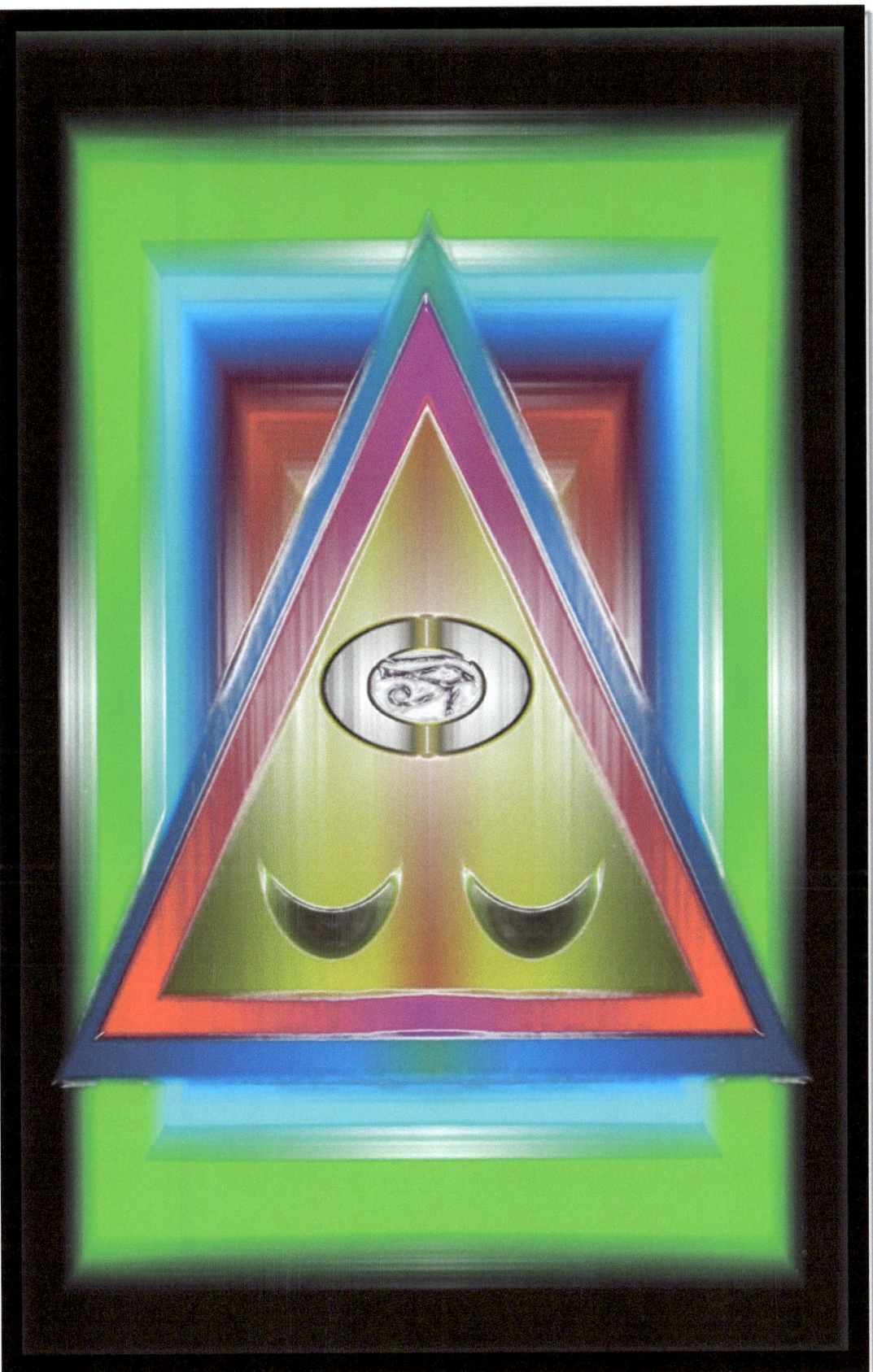

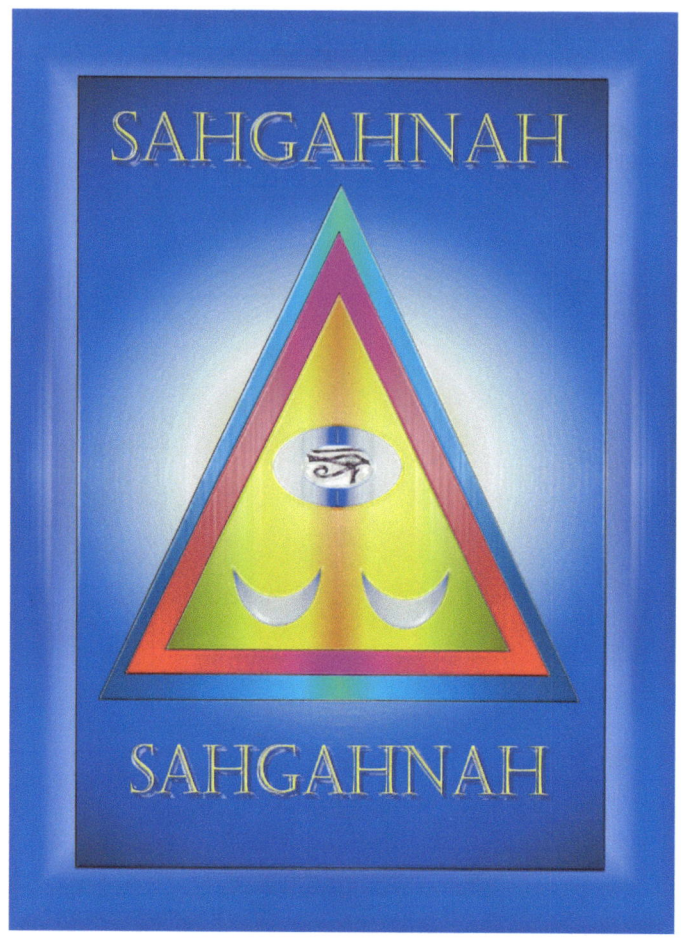

SAHGAHNAH is a symbol that represents clear seeing and is also use within the Relationship symbology. Classical Enlightenment requires withdrawal from the senses into the root of awareness and intuitive feeling; within the place of peace beyond penetration from outer events. Within this state of being one seems to float atop the current flow of life like a leaf upon the surface of river water able to ride atop of the current flow without getting caught up in or pull down underneath it. No matter how calm or tumultuous life becomes around us, the sentient intelligence of Sahgahnah enables one to flow with whatever comes, peacefully and undisturbed within yet fully aware and appropriately responsive to the reality of what is presenting itself.

This symbol represents the power of the 1st eye to comprehend the deeper meaning to the things that one encounters from day to day, along with the innate wisdom of how to respond in order to manifest the highest most fulfilling outcome. It also allows one to foresee what is to come when one is clear with what they've chosen and/or are choosing to create and is committed fully to the fulfillment of a thing regardless of what life brings momentarily. In this state, one's focus is continually on the chosen path of their divine expression. One trusts fully in life and all that it represents to bring about their fulfillment. One is not attached to how and through whom one's fulfillment comes but remain continually open and receptive to the signs that indicate the directions, the persons, the opportunities etc. that reflect your desired intentions or soul's desires that present themselves in order to move towards one's fulfillment of purpose in joy, harmony, and peaceful anticipation.

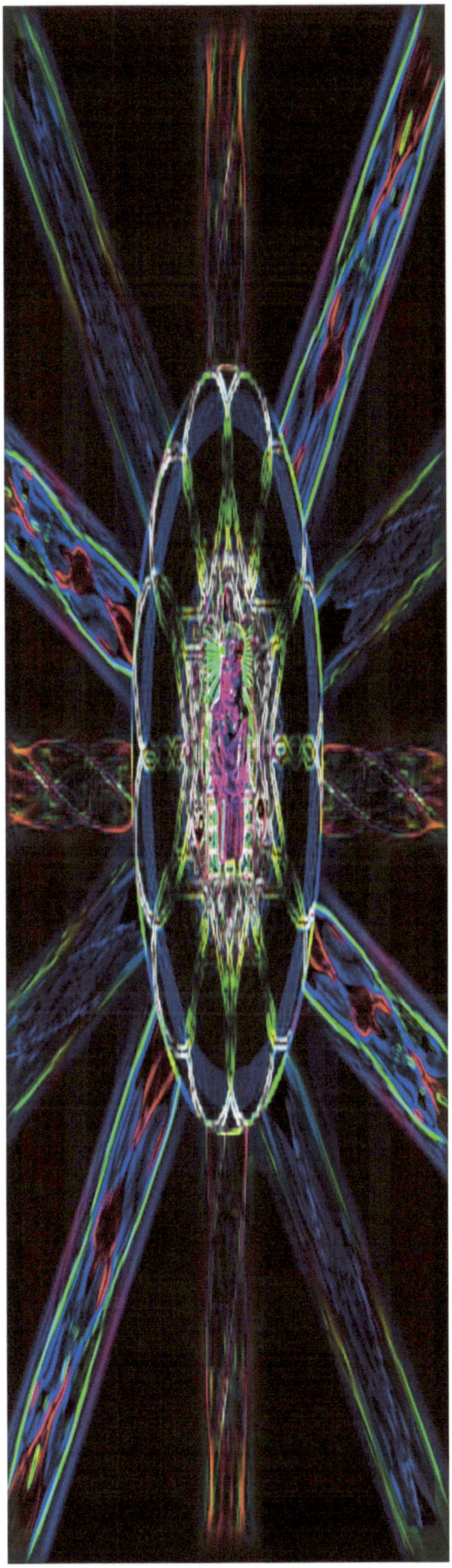

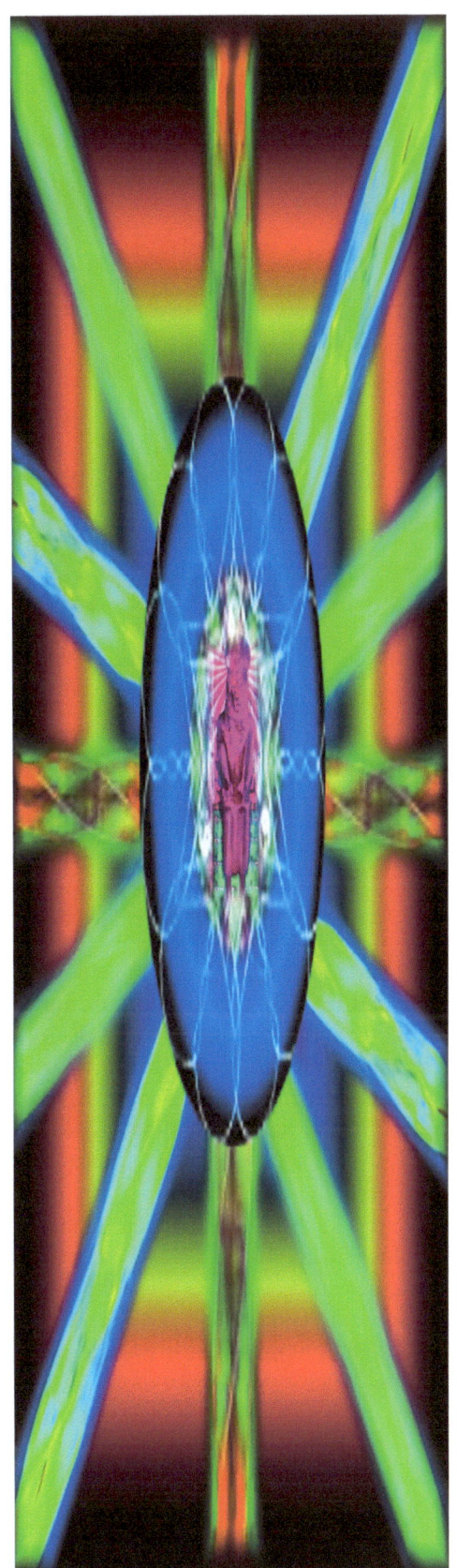

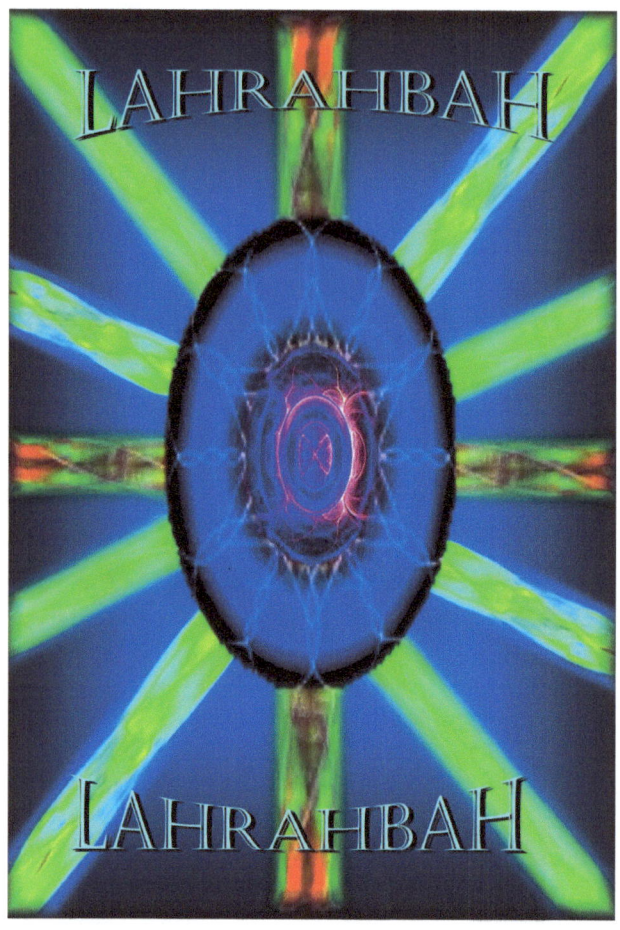

LAHRAHBAH represents the embodiment of Zen Enlightenment (seeing into one's true nature and living it as one's purpose for embodiment). This is the embodiment of perfect free expression and one's freedom to live anyway that one chooses, free from moral restraints, yet remaining basically good and kind in nature. Lahrahbah empowers us with the Creative freedom to be genuine in our expression of self honestly without sensor or filters knowing that it is the Greater Self channeling truth of life and infinite creativity through us in each moment for the raising of divine Self-awareness and its activation in others.

Persons such as Michelangelo, Albert Einstein, Prince and Kirk Washington Jr. are just examples of the ways in which Divine Intelligence and Infinite Creativity of the Divine Source expresses our true nature through our desires and internal values. When one has dedicated themselves to commune and merge with everything without filters as an open channel within one's mind, Divinity is able to express Itself in infinite ways through us as the inspiration of cutting-edge evolutionary ideas, arts, inventions and developments for the betterment of humanities evolution into divine existence.

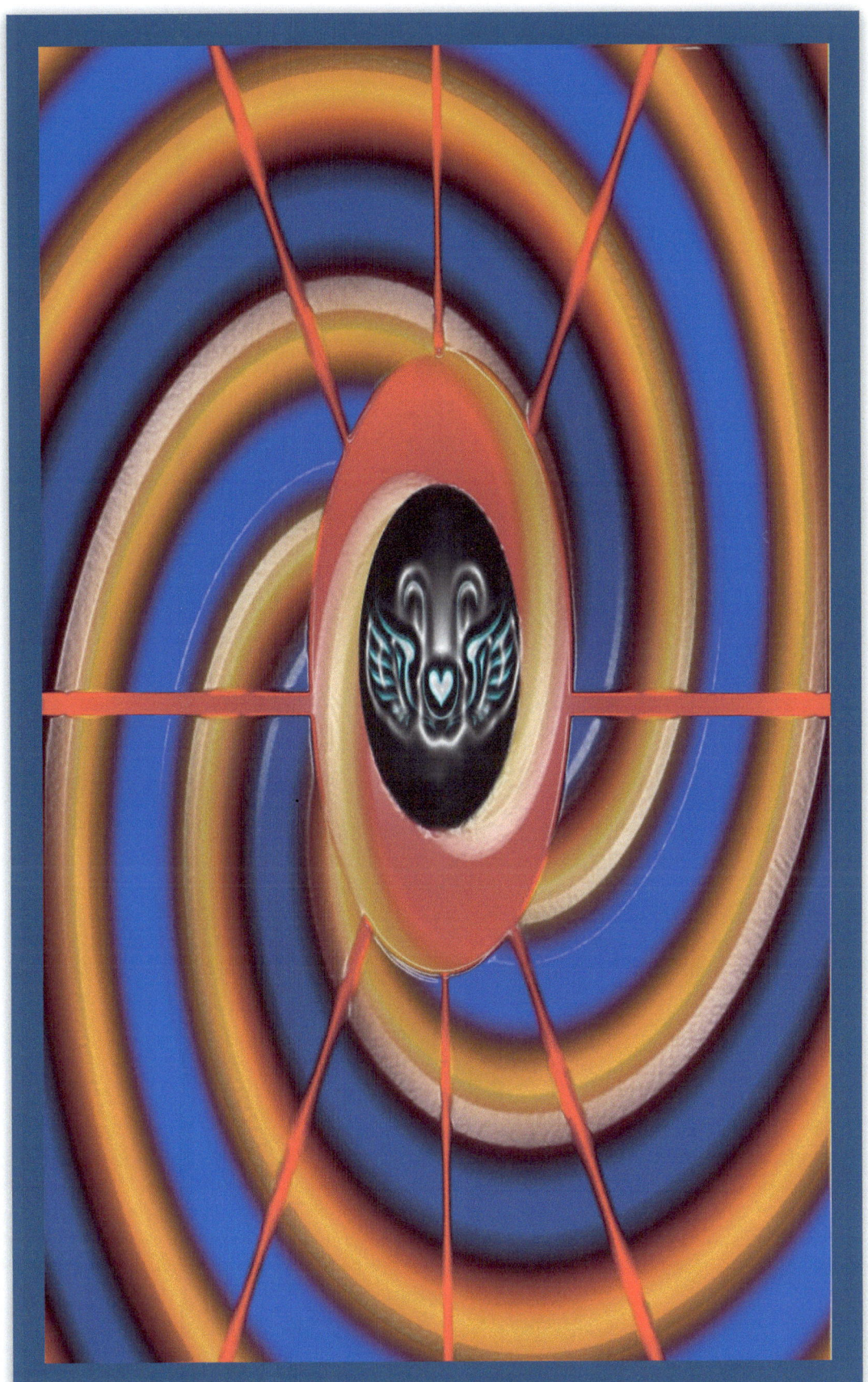

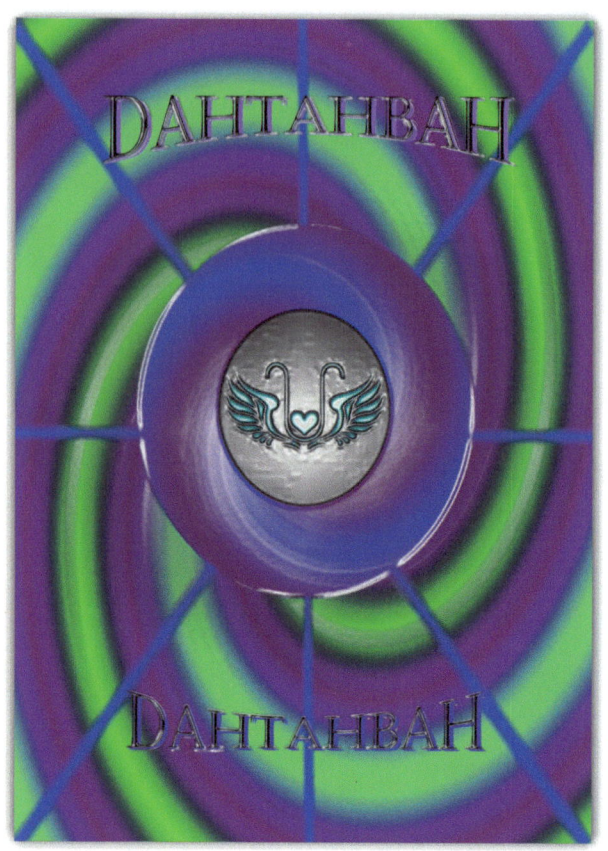

Within the Eternal Set, **DAHTAHBAH** takes on the divine aspects of Unconditional Love. It has been passed down within the Mystical Christian, Sufi, and Hasidic Enlightenment teachings as the energy that radiates acceptance of everything that is as it is with love for versus fear of the opportunities to learn and teach how to master life by healing through loving and the purpose and self-lessons learned. The lines stand for the radiance of love, oneness and innerstanding that ebbs and flows into and from the heart of others simultaneously when you have embodied loving unconditionally. Its emanation extends towards all that exists in the infinite spans of each direction peacefully without judgment or force and without the necessity of other's innerstanding or their capacity to relate at this level of loving. Its radiation inspires that same love in those within its field of influence.

As one meditates on this level of enlightenment one comes to experience a deeper sense of being present in each moment that allows them to open up to their truth with no need for reasons or responses from anyone including oneself. Dahtahbah provides a sense of grounded centeredness within one's Divine Self that one exists in when attuned to the energy of unconditional love. There is no attachment to the outcome of one's expression knowing that whatever the outcome is in the moment, it is only of temporal nature versus the higher purpose of sharing this ultimate expression of loving and basking in the comfort and power of sharing right-us-ness and honesty of one's truth that this level of Self-awareness and openness provides to oneself and to others.

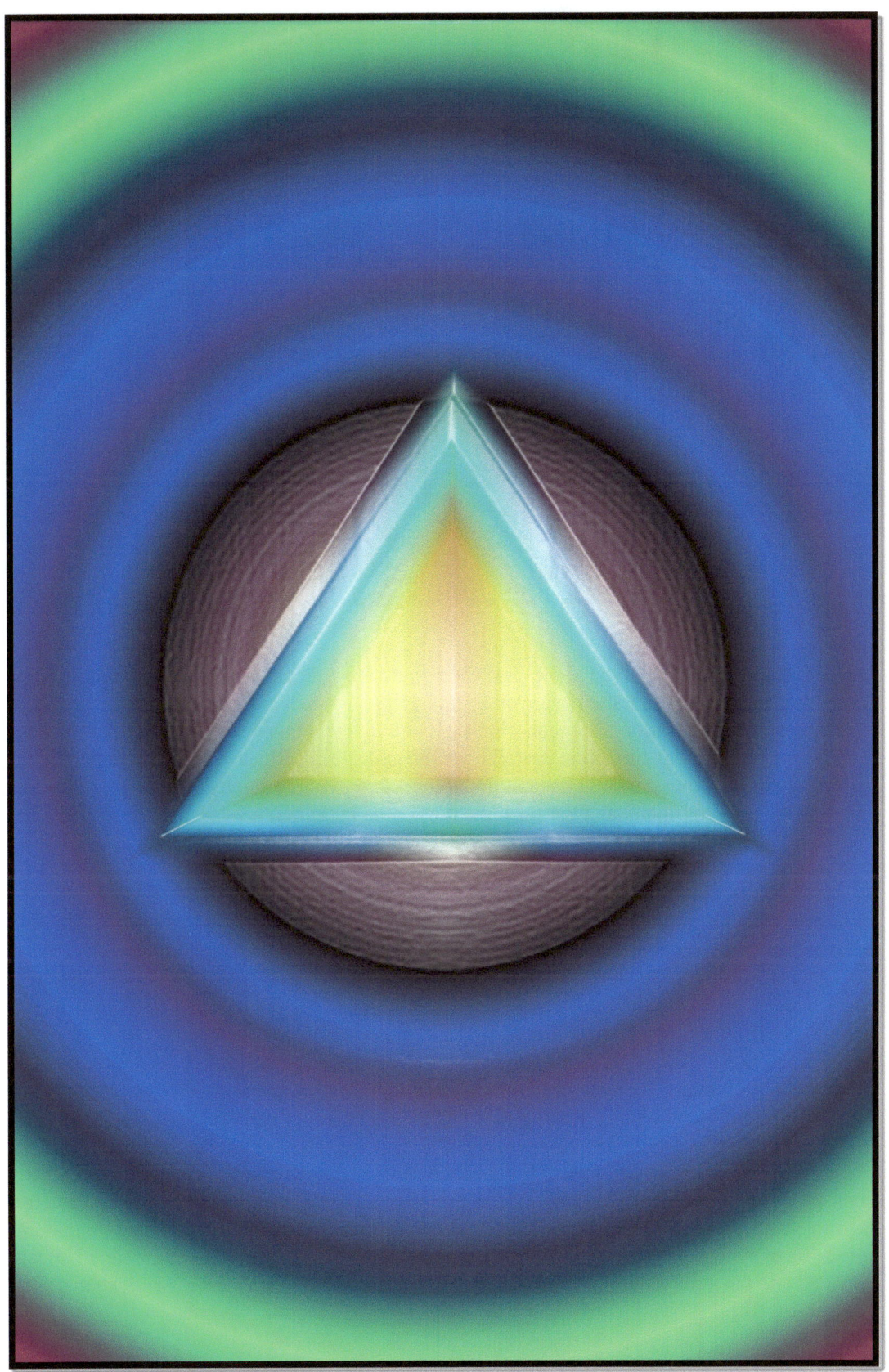

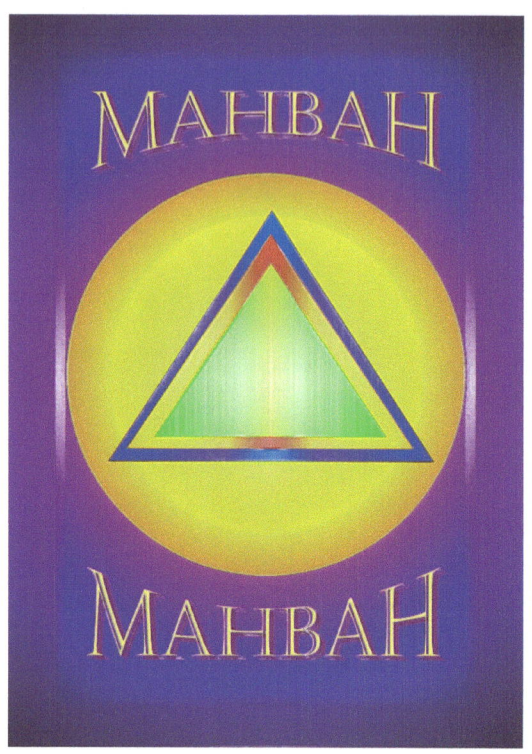

MAHBAH symbolizes sacred aloneness where there is perfect contentment with not needing anyone, not getting enmeshed in anyone, and having no attachment to material things. As Mahbah embodies within one's consciousness one finds that their values change from ego based desires for things like fame, material wealth and social affluence to the more intangible desires of true happiness, having unconditional love, and peace of mind and soul. One comes to find the bliss of simplicity and the fulfillment of being in the moment without meditating on the potentials the future presents.

Being at peace with living alone, dying alone, or being immortally alone even recognizing ones aloneness when with others provides a freedom and fullness of being present with oneself and an ability to respond completely and openly in the moment with no thought outside of the present and what is being shared in it. This is the state of Sacred Oneness and is what Mahbah activates within oneself.

Mahbah awakens your awareness that whatever you have truly needed has been provided you throughout life; that there is no need to need anything, as they are constantly being provided the opportunity to receive everything in truth that they need. One becomes aware that need does not bring about fulfillment, want does not bring about fulfillment, but knowing and being centered in the sense of fulfillment brings about fulfillment. Within the energy that Mahbah symbolizes one lives the realization of no clinging, no negativity, no delusion and no addiction to anything because one innerstands that there is no need to need anything; that within our conscious communion with All-That-Is, all things that we are truly in need of are automatically provided and the innerstanding of the difference between what is truly a need and what is just a want.

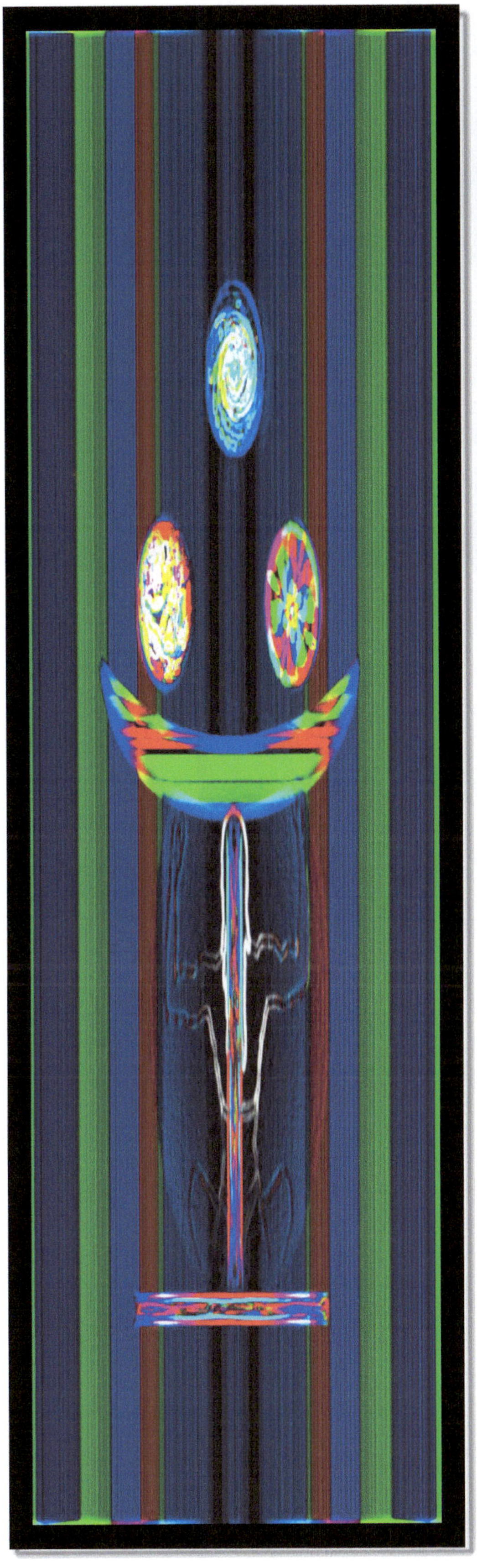

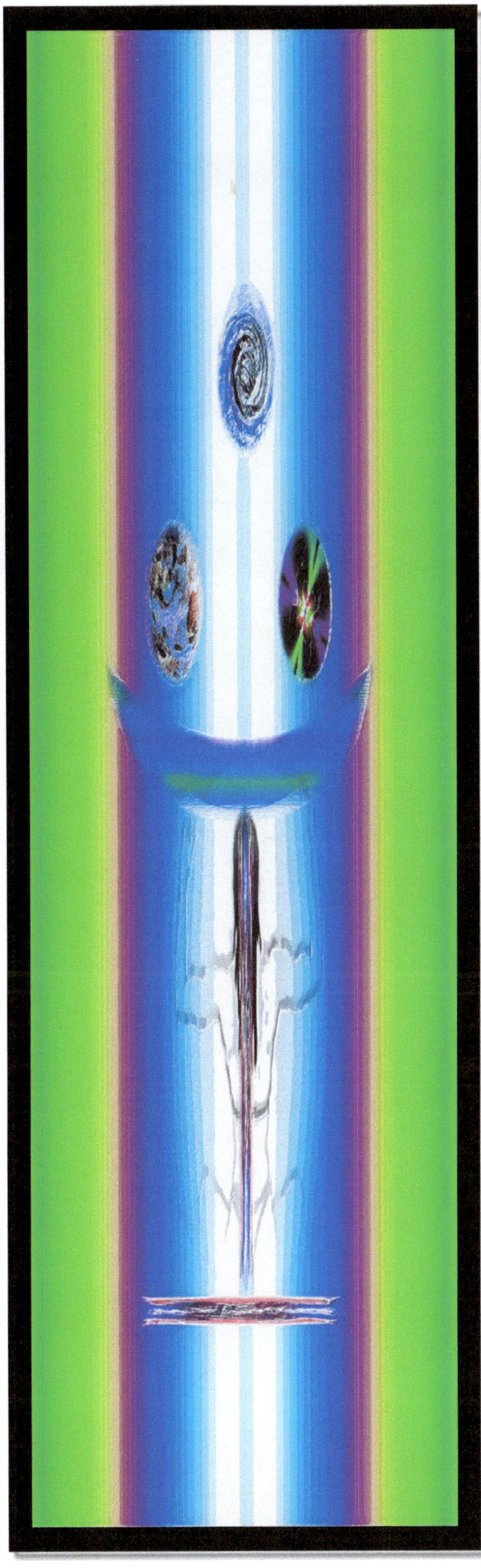

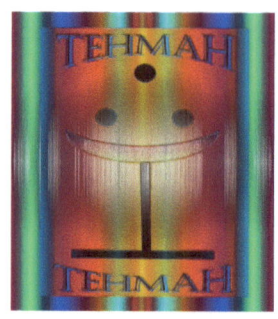

TEHMAH represents our unadulterated innate trust in Mother Earth, Her sentient intelligence as our provider and protector and the sentient intelligence of the Universe. It is within her intuitive nature to produce, provide, and protect us through that which comes from her. We are given through our intuitions the guidance that is necessary for us to survive and thrive thru the mastery of our environment. How to respect what is and live in harmony with each other and all that exists. We are also given the freedom to choose our actions at will. Tehmah re-awakens this level of pure trust within us along with the guidance and wisdom of how to live this way within the confines of modern society. It re-establishes and deepens the trust we must have in one's own spiritual nature to manifest our focused desires and intentions that serve the greater good of all of creation and one's Self.

There is abundance in and an abundance of everything imaginable and everything necessary for all to live life true to our natural desires of divine love, divine health, and divine wealth (which is not centered around monetary or material wealth but the wealth of spiritual embodiment and Oneness with life and being in harmony with it). That we may experience the joy of living our dreams. Our thoughts about self and the nature of God are the keys that determines what we receive in life. If one thinks that one must do something to deserve their desires… that they are not automatically worthy of experiencing the best, then that is what one will create in experience. If one believes that one must struggle to make it or use manipulations or compromise themselves in order to get what they desire, then one will find themselves living the charade of their own deceptions. One is limited only by their thoughts of unworthiness, lack of vision, limited thinking or by clinging to outdated beliefs that contradict their personal truth and innate desire for freedom. These things are what keep one from discovering or creating unprecedented means of living life, generating wealth, healing oneself and fulfilling one's dreams and purposes as well as their piece of the collective puzzle of ever evolving life.

TEHMAH helps one to rediscover and trust in our divine nature and our abilities to create infinitely from nothing; to embrace the opportunities that arise without being attached to the how, who, and when of it. When one is centered in the energy of love and the vision of their desires, one begins to notice where life is opening the doors to experience the fulfillment of those desires, needs, goals and intentions which is our divine purpose and divine nature. One comes to the realization that faith in our vision and desires of life and our gratitude for opportunities given fuels the manifestation of what we are envisioning. By acting upon these opportunities, one becomes one with the divinity within life and its willingness and desire to give us that which we desire especially when it serves the well-being of everyone and everything.

The principle of sowing and reaping are based on this truth. Whatever one plants into the Universal Mind as imagery and desire with faith (good or bad), will in turn, be returned to them as experience in material form. This is enlightenment in many spiritual and religious traditions and the mythical Holy Grail revealed.

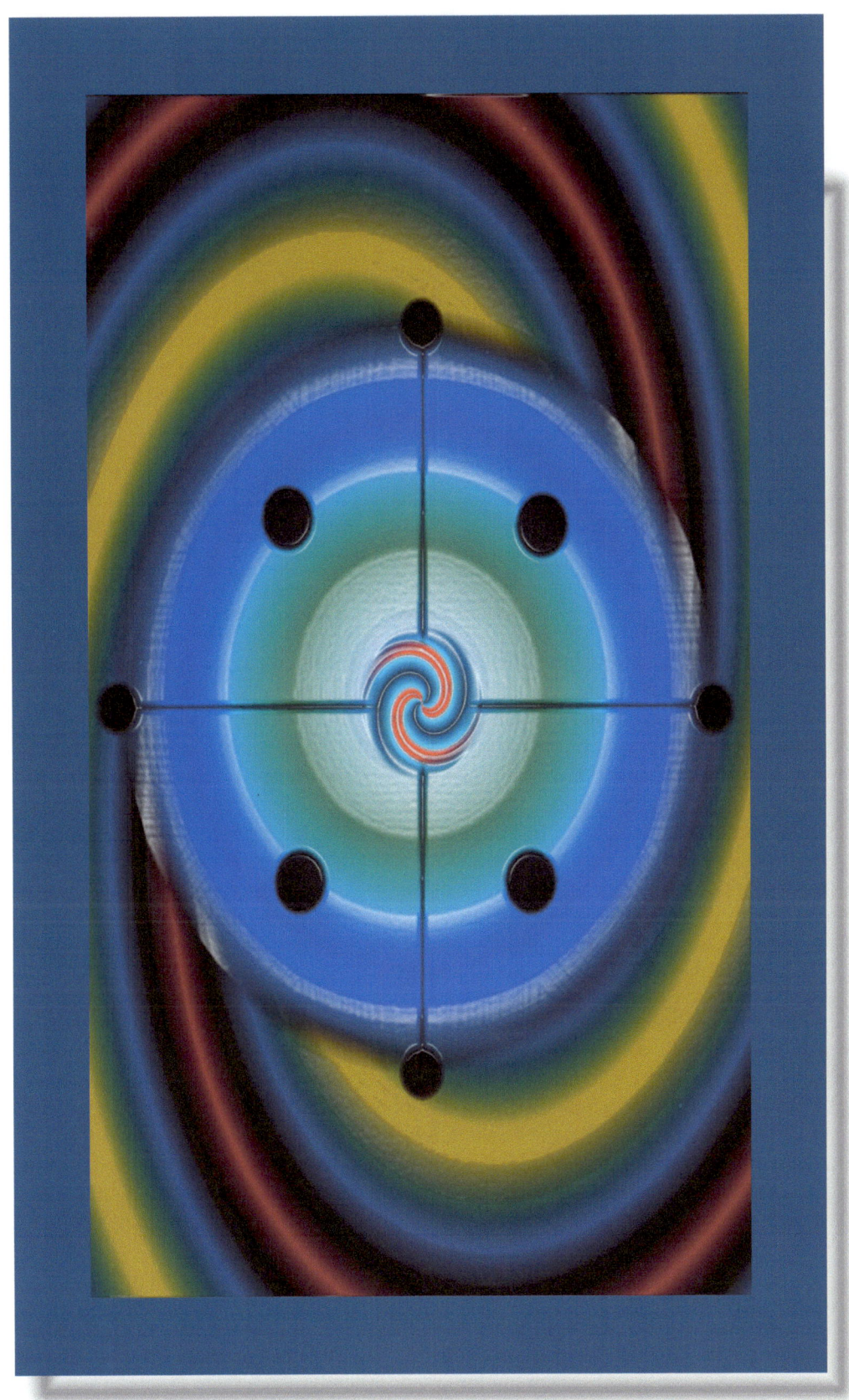

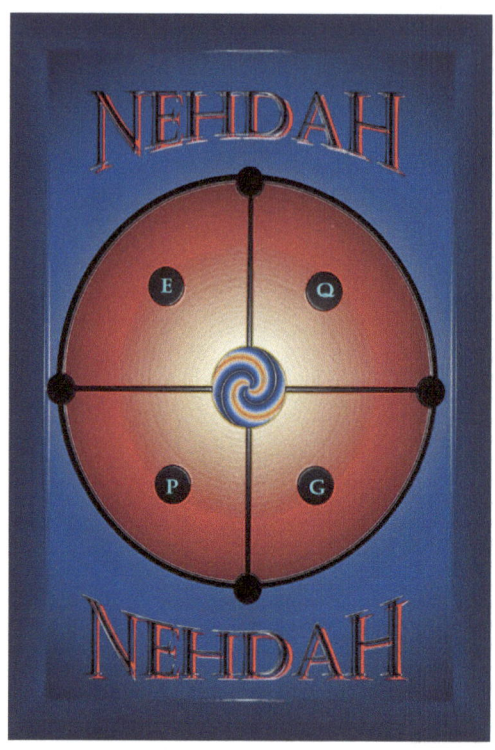

NEHDAH (No Death) stays within the subconscious continuity as we flow through all the phases of life on earth and beyond (birth, living, death, the bardo), whether physically, metaphorically, or metaphysically speaking. It's easy to distinguish this as referring to the various transitions of the body however, birth, living, death and the bardo (phase of existence between incarnations) happen multiple times within one's life and within various aspects of living it. For example, when a person experiences a divorce and carries on with their lives after having gone through the ending of the relationship they will have gone through the life, death, bardo, and re-birth of a way of living and a way of being. This not only relates to the dissolution of a marriage relationship but the metamorphosis of re-creating oneself anew with new relationships, new goals and a deeper awareness of one's true self and personal values. It awakens the ascension process of evolution from operating according to one's institutionalized nature to operating in increasing alignment with one's divine intuitive nature.

In recent scientific revelations science has come to understand more concerning the dimensional forces of dark matter that all of creation derives from. These quantum elements have been penned (The God Particles) in the realm of physics. These particles (Electrons, Quarks, Protons, and Gluons) are now thought to be the creative life force energies within the cosmos. On a macrocosmic scale the skies portray the same interactive dance of particle that are made of the same life force dynamics that make up our own cellular matter and that everything in existence is made up of in differing arrangements. On a microcosmic scale, the way our cells are designed reflect the same dance with the same cosmic dynamics that planets, suns, and star systems do.

The letters for these elements that represent these quantum particles have been added within each internal sphere of Nehdah as a reflection of the way they relate to the evolution of conscious awareness of what makes up the Universe within ourselves and outside of ourselves macro and micro cosmically.

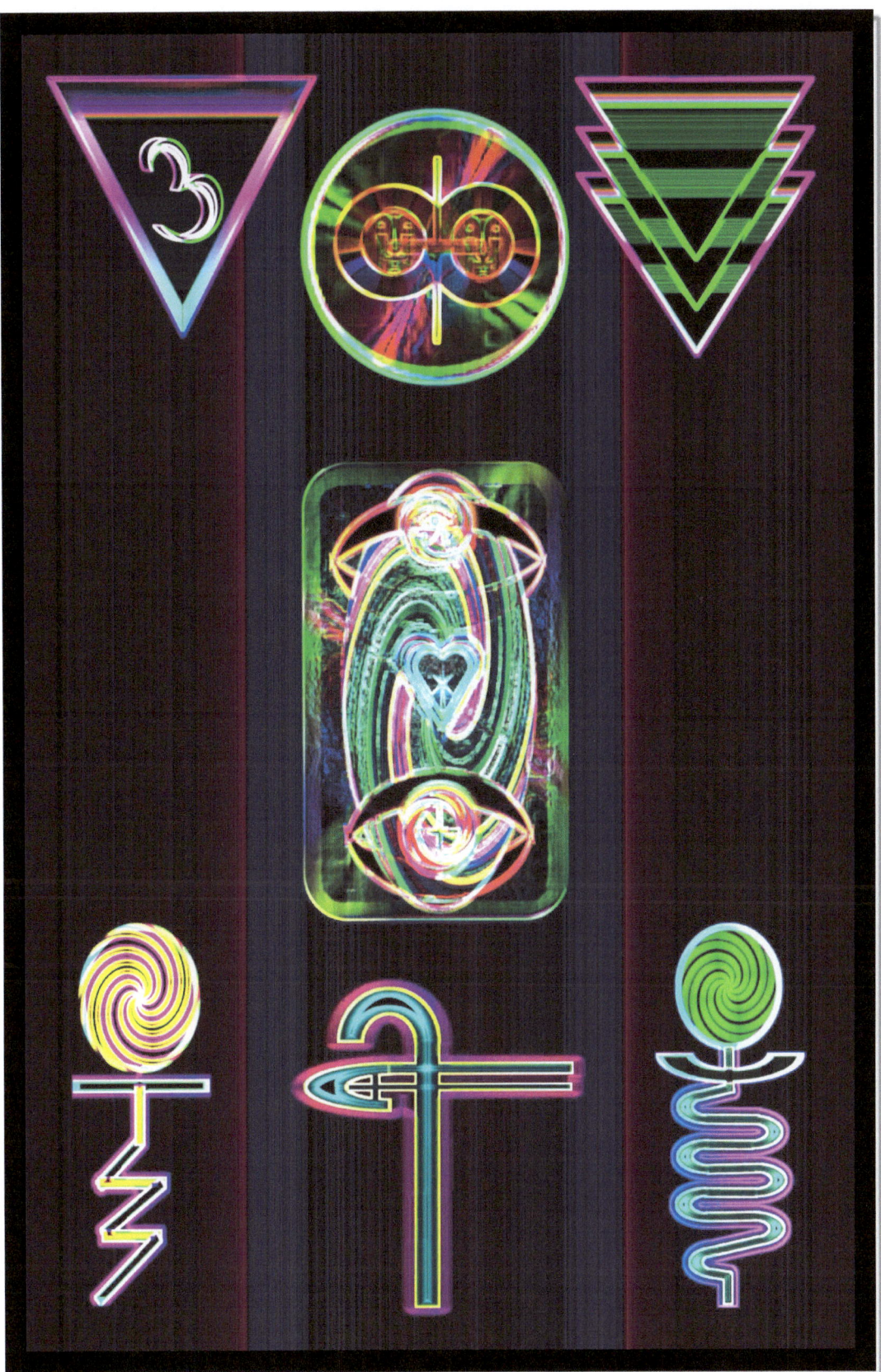

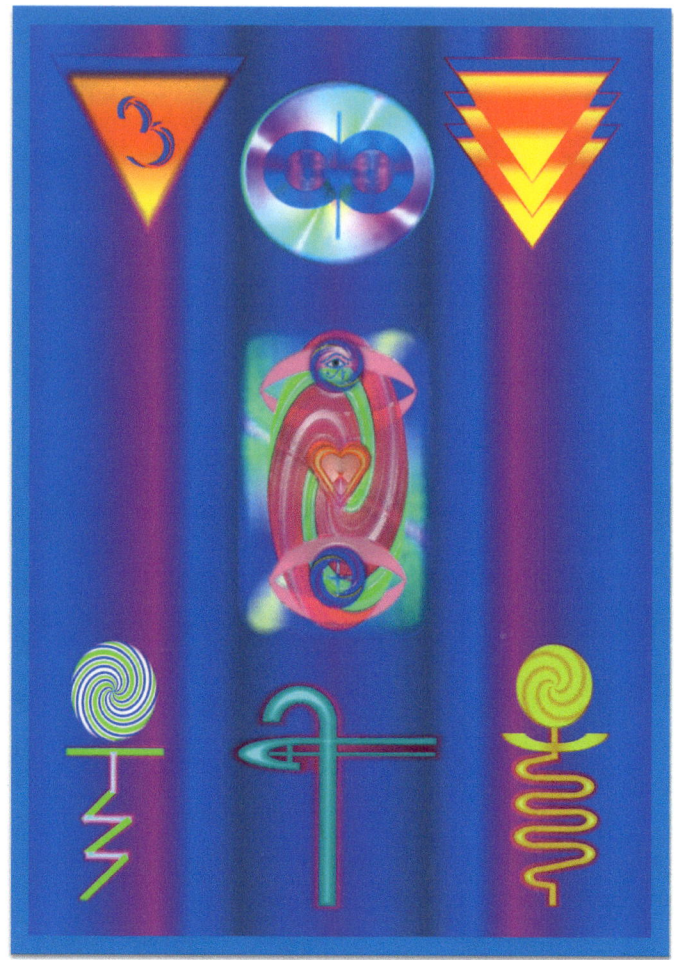

TANRAN REIKI ENERGY MATURITY SERIES

The Tanran Energy Maturity Set is the last of the Tanran symbol sets that correspond to the Chakra system that forms the Tanran Reiki Mandala. The information concerning each of the energy maturity symbols also indicates their chakra association and aspects of Universal Life Force Intelligence.

The Basic set and the Pure Eternal Life Set go together as a polarized pair that represents the mind of enlightenment. The mind of enlightenment speaks to the internal transformation and evolution of thought that transpires from seeking to innerstand the universal soul and become one with the spiritual truth and revelations of God within all of life seeing through its eyes and innerstanding through its mind the human and spiritual dynamics of our souls.

The Long Life Empowerment Set and the Energy Maturity Set also complement each other by polarization representing the body of enlightenment. What is meant by the body of enlightenment is the various self-disciplines that becoming conscious of one's responsibility to act upon the insights to what it means to live in love, harmony, and respect with all sentient beings as an embodiment of universal oneness and as a reflection of the pure essence that we as spiritual beings exist as when living in complete embodiment as our Higher or Divine Self.

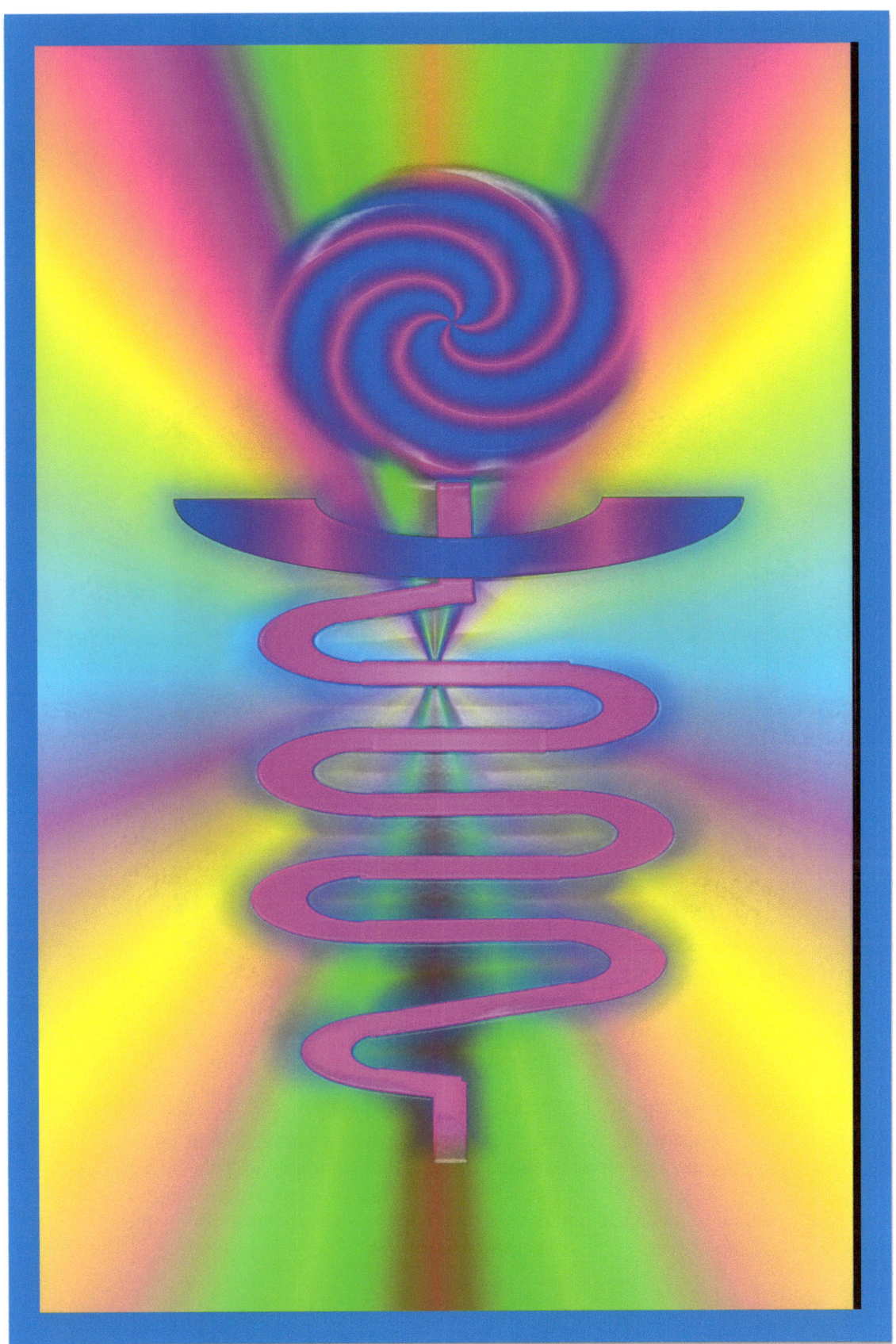

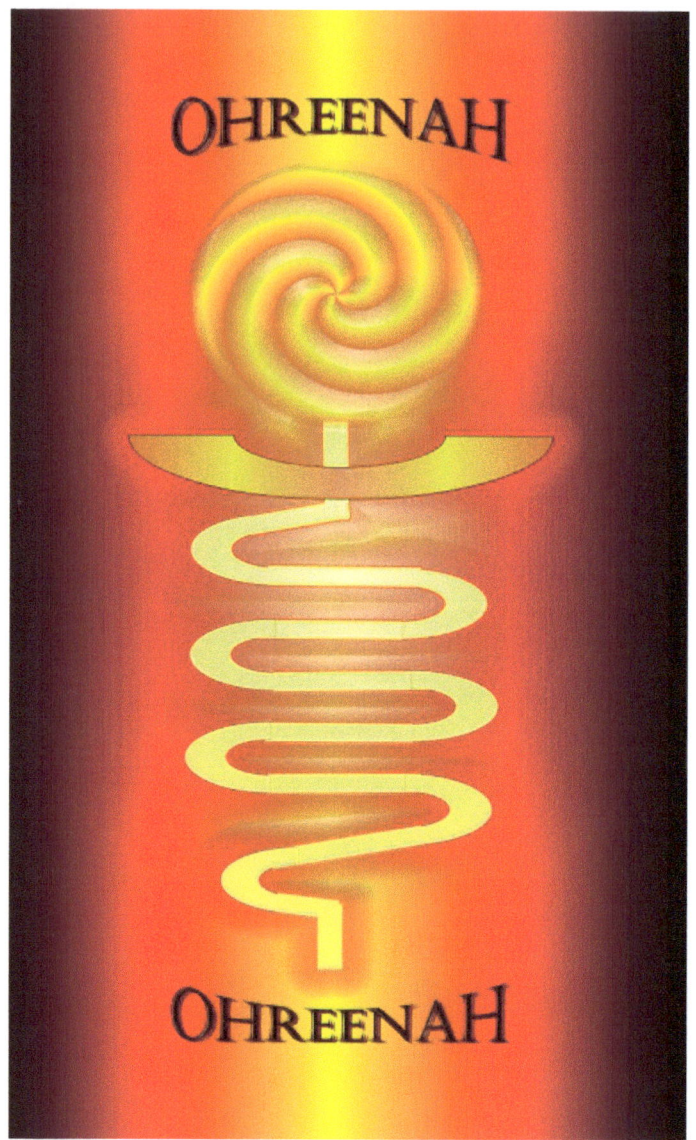

OHREENAH works within the Crown and 1st Eye Chakra's simultaneously. The symbol is visualized at the 1st eye point with the sphere visualized above the head. The symbol is about activating the ascension of one's spirit/soul from out of one's body that is experienced in astral travel, death, and "out of body experiences".

When accessing the energy of Ohreenah, one does not have to strain to connect with higher dimensions one can link with the pre-existing energy and surrender to its upward pull or momentum. This activation allows kundalini to feel natural rather than the hardship of swimming upstream against the current of gravity. It allows one to access higher realms of metaphysical information and quickens one's ability to comprehend and apply the knowledge that one receives.

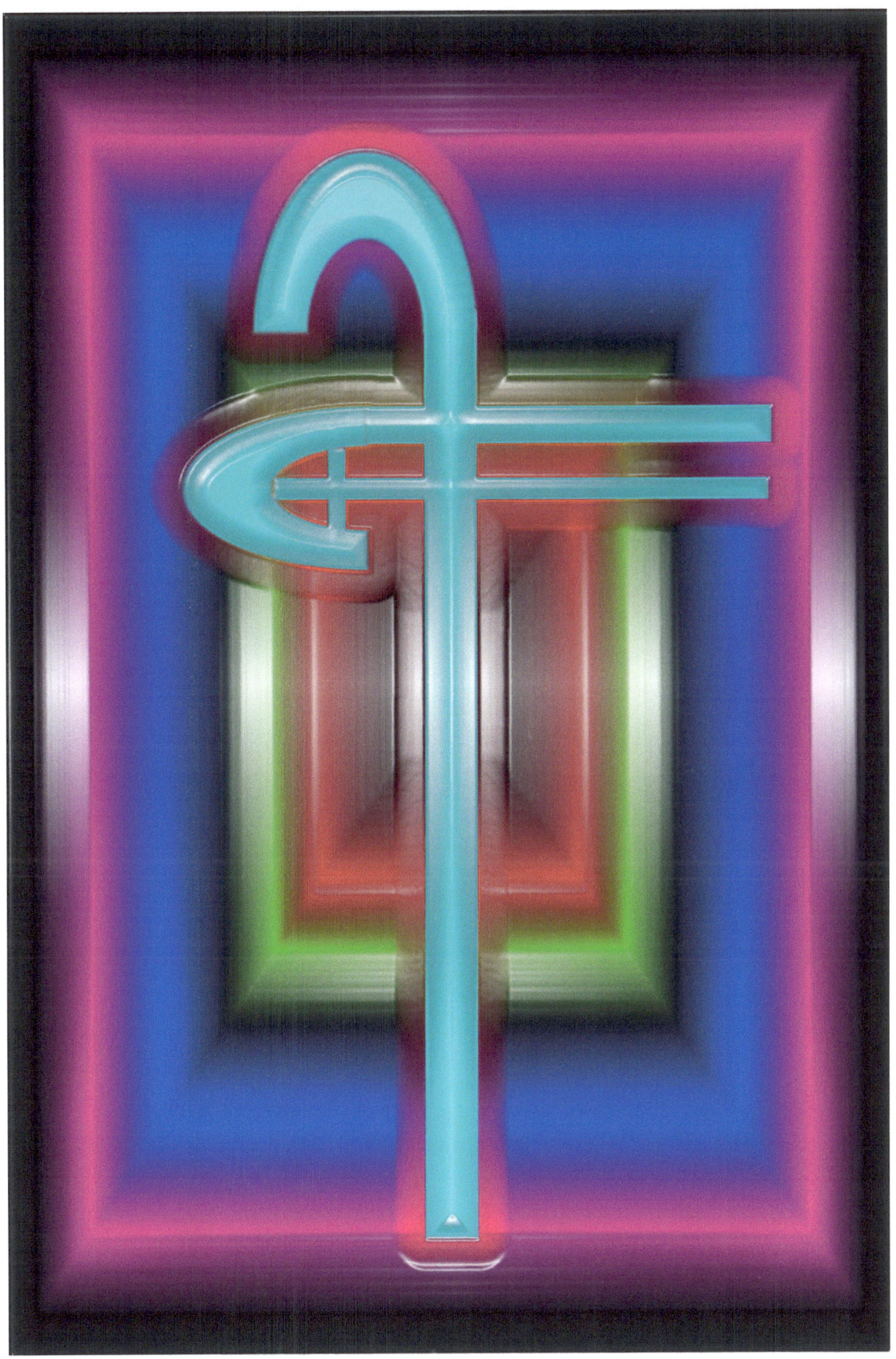

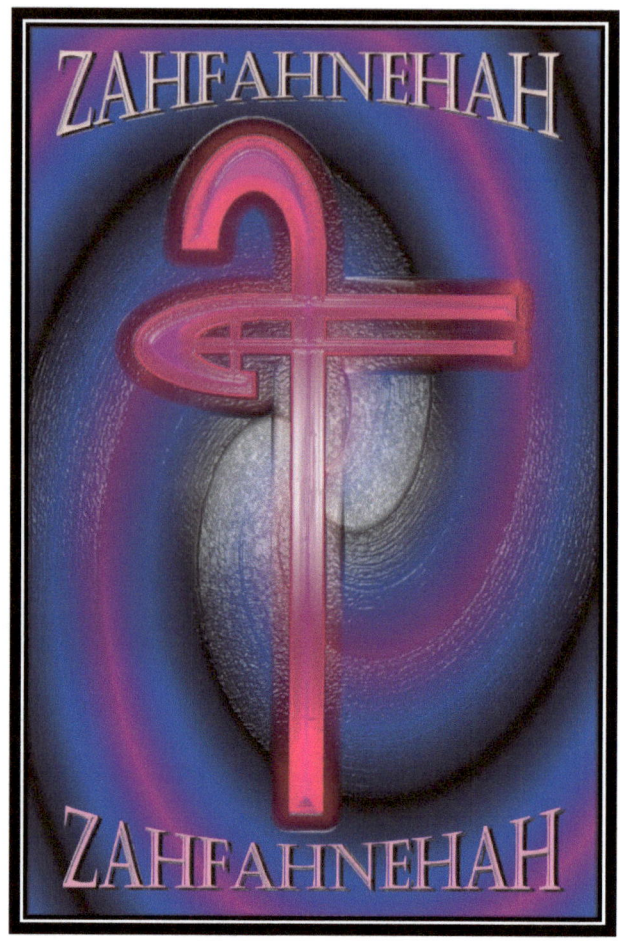

ZAHFAHNEHAH relates to the throat chakra and that of the 1ˢᵗ eye. Zah Fah Neh Ah is about removing energies that are not from one's energy system such as negative descriptions or associations about one's character during childhood that were meant as a means of controlling or manipulating one's behavior in order to keep them subservient. Its purpose is that of cutting cords with outdated or negative thought forms and negative or false things said about oneself in the past. It synchronizes with your 1ˢᵗ eye vision to assist one to disassociate from identifying oneself with negative labels and projected personifications and redefining one's self based on one's inherent goodness and Divinity.

Through the energy of Zahfahnehah one is able to identify and envision the times, (past, present, and future) where one was given honor for speaking or living true to one's true and divine nature. Through this, one is able to redefine one's sense of self in a more positive affirmative context and establish a sense of rightness and oneness with one's truth and transcend the feelings of needing to justify one's self for being who they are.

As with Tibetan Buddhism, Tanran Reiki works with the throat chakra more than other traditions through the use of visualization, invocation or chanting. These spiritual tools are quite powerful and can be used to dissolve and transmute energies that have been projected into your energy field by others and have become stuck there.

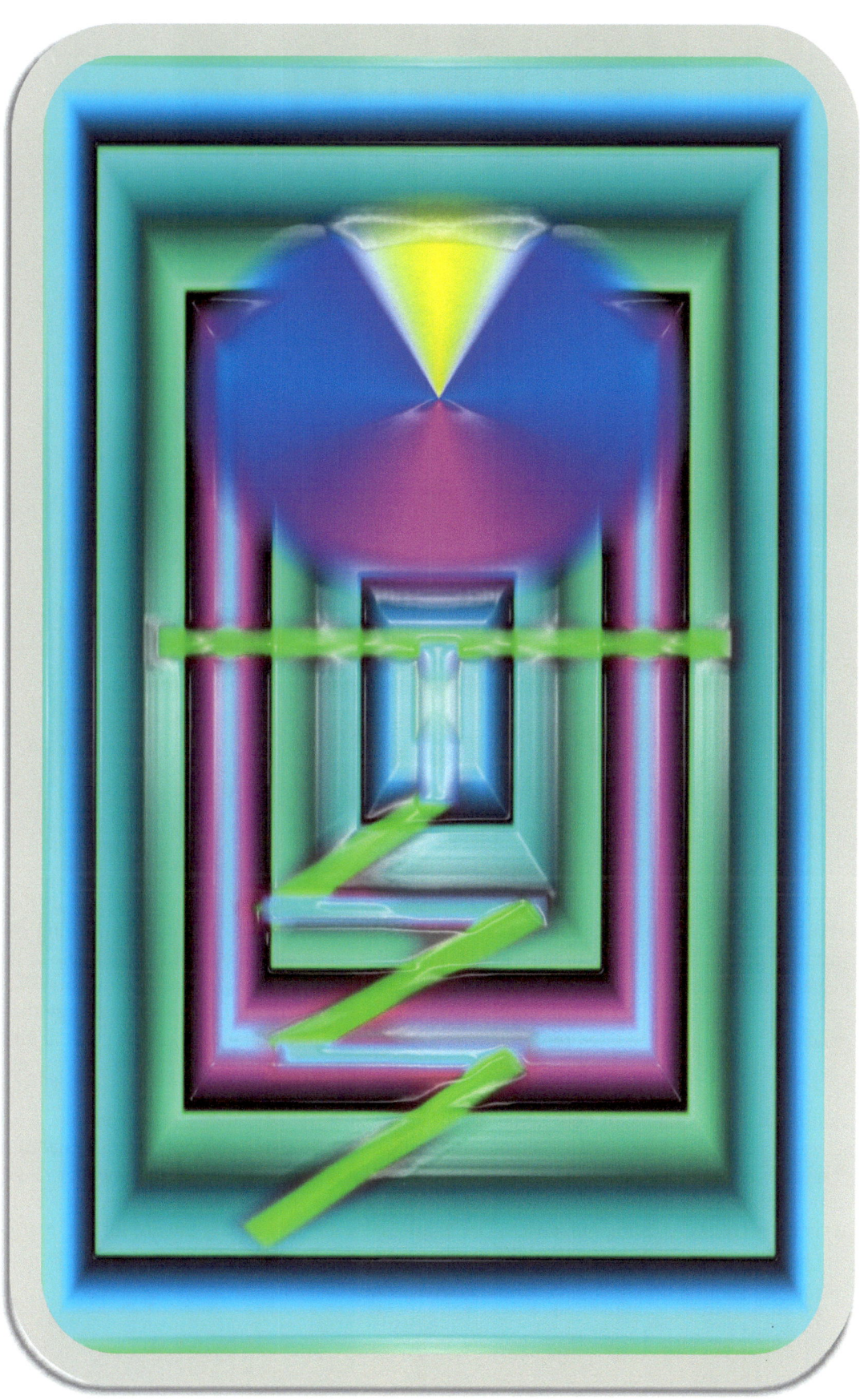

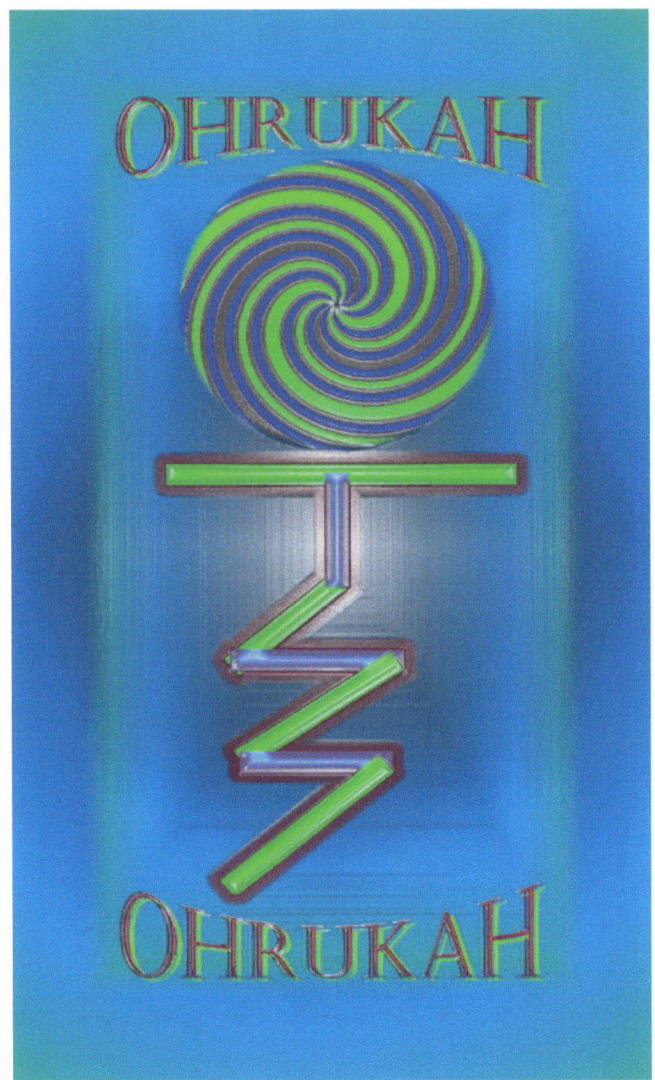

OHRUKAH resides in the throat chakra at the back of the neck and regulates the opening and closing of one's psychic gate. In most humans, this is a place within us that is vulnerable to the negative thoughts of others. The circle represents a hermetic or airtight seal of protection that envelops one's being. The lightning bolt represents the highly focused protective energy that anchors in this gate. The "T" represents ones standing in open dignity or divine pride at all times when its energy has been embodied.

Guilt is a mental practice, or belief, that causes energies, emotions, and beliefs about one's self and negative energies surrounding situations to get stuck inside of you. Guilt is a false belief of responsibility for someone else's chosen actions or conditions that one was not meant to take responsibility for. One may regret their actions and need to apologize or reconcile, but we are never meant to regret being ourselves. This particular gate is a crucial juncture for our energy to flow upwards so that we may be at peace with our own choices and sense of truth.

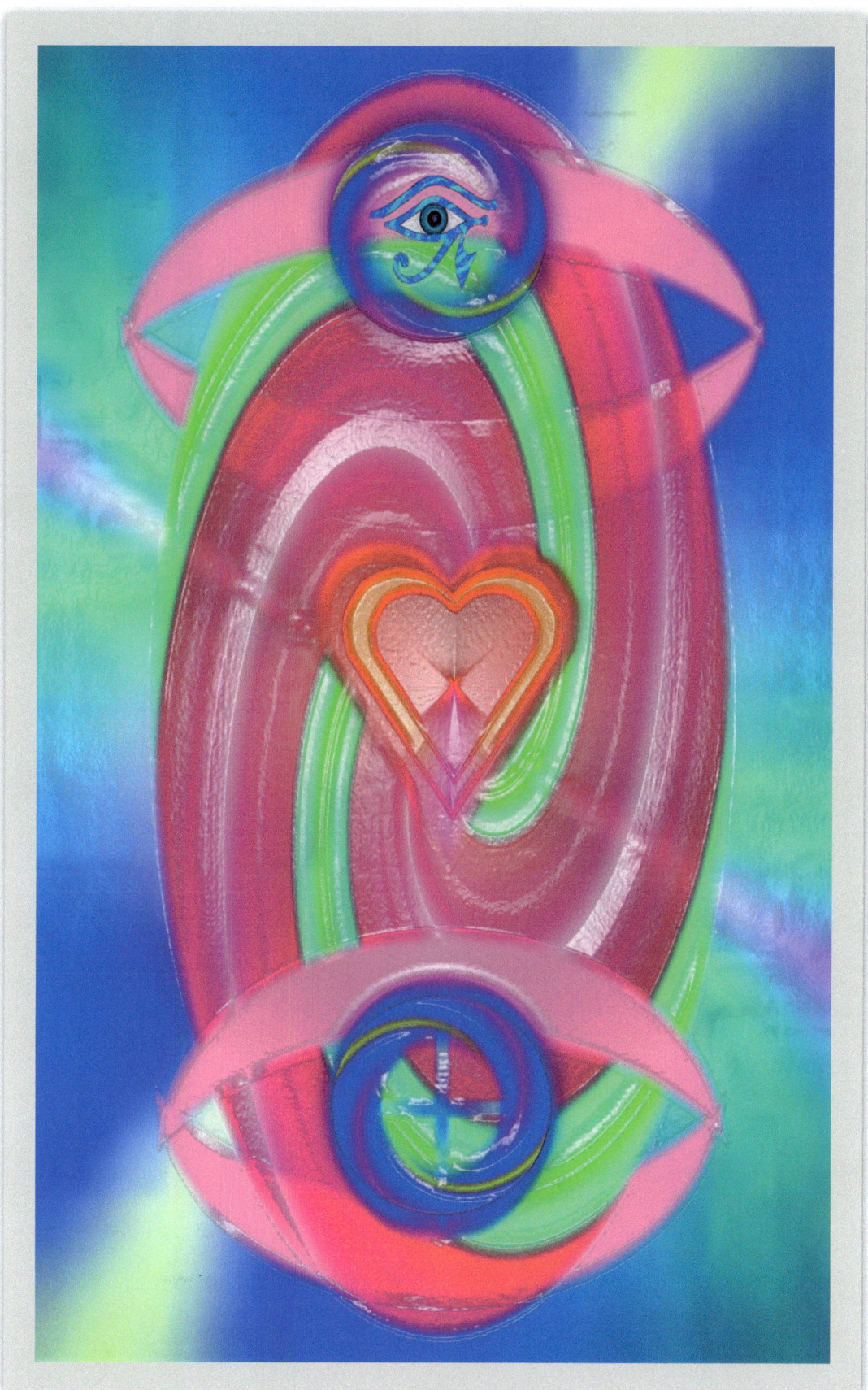

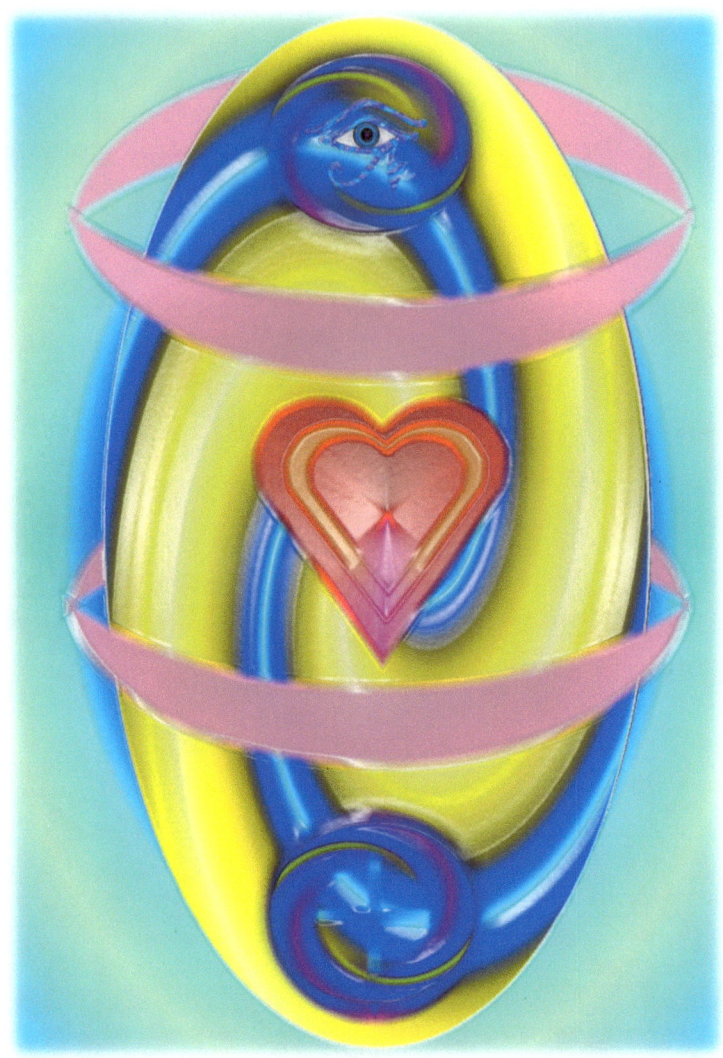

Within the Energy Maturity Set **TEEYAHNAH** resides within the Heart Chakra and reflects our choosing to experience life from the center of our energetic heart space. The Eye of Ra symbol at the top reflect the way in which its energy awakens one's 1st eye to the wisdom of one's own heart bringing to light within us our behaviors that are blocking us from love. The radiating heart symbol in the center represents the alive feeling that grows inside of one's heart as one becomes centered in the power of their heart to love. The circle cross is the lower belly of the symbol of Teeyahnah represents the harmony and balance that attuning to the four elements of fire, air, water, and earth creates. The two horizontal circles represent two consecrations. The upper circle of consecration is about one thinking thoughts consistent with trusting life. Jesus teaches this attitude in the Be-attitudes and Buddha in the Sermon on the Thousands. The second circle of consecration is about protecting one's self from getting enmeshed in the energies of others.

"Tee" is stronger than "Teh" as it reflects more of a commitment to purpose versus momentary involvement.

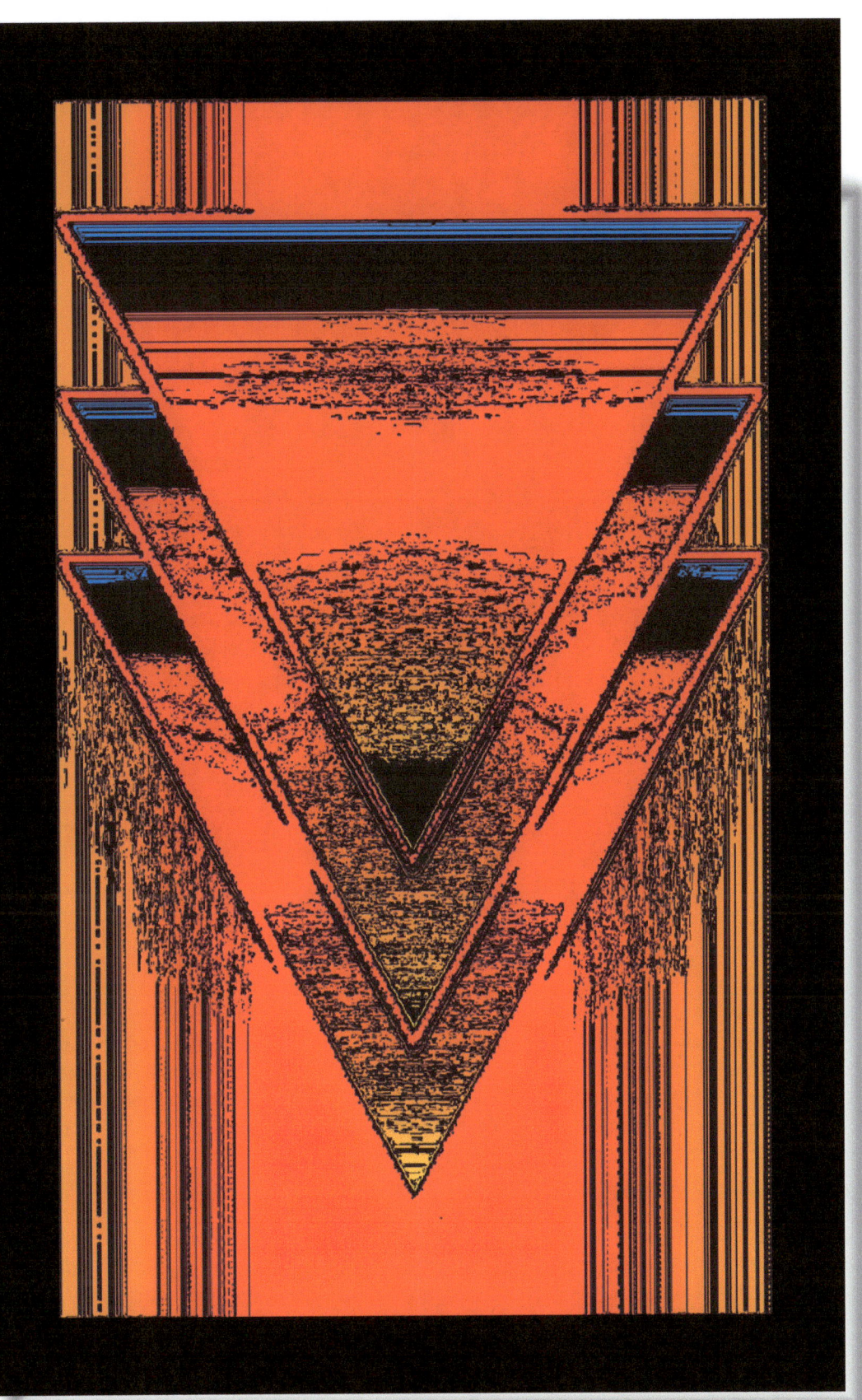

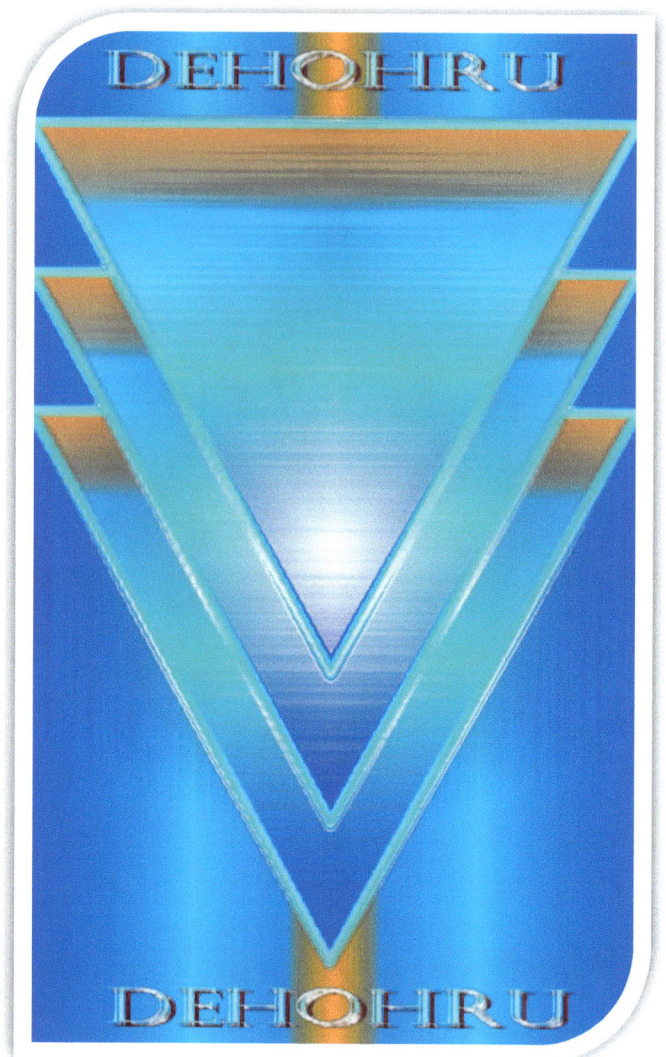

There are processes of transmutation of karma that are important to be aware of. **DEHOHRU** helps to unblock karmic issues so that they may be recognized, transcended and released. When it comes to negative karma one best serves its purpose by evaluating what one learned concerning the subtle body effects of one's past actions what actions or responses better serve the highest good to transmute and release the karma without necessarily having to relive its effects. Karma related to one's spiritual purpose is better to be moved through as a process of actualization.

Dehohru also activates along the spine to assist in postural alignment to allow energy and emotions to process congruently in a way that one's divine sensitivity is able to communicate and operate within one's own conscious and subconscious responses. This is where the blessing of divine wisdom and healing are able to change the energy and manifest within one's self and those whom were involved.

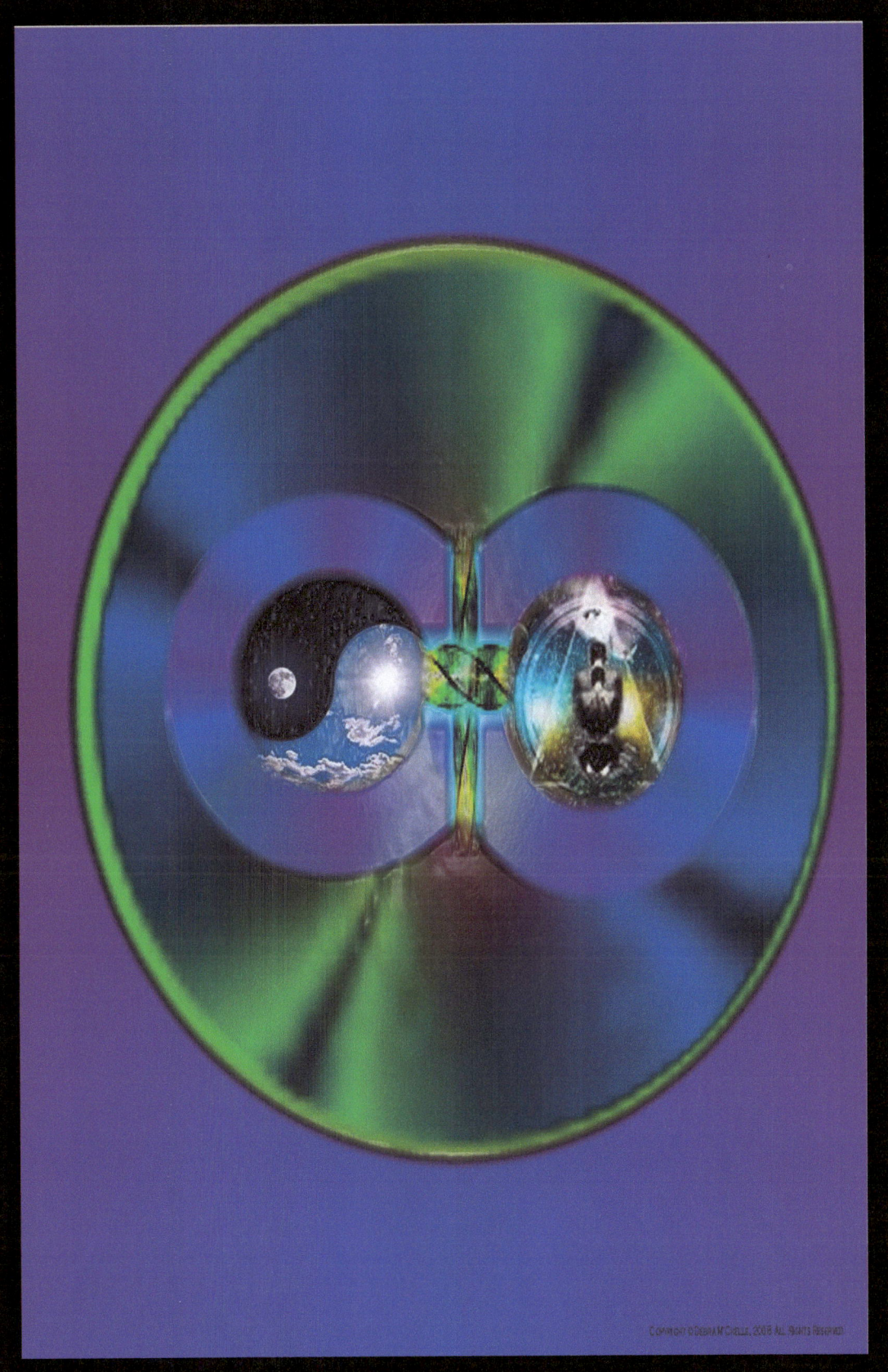

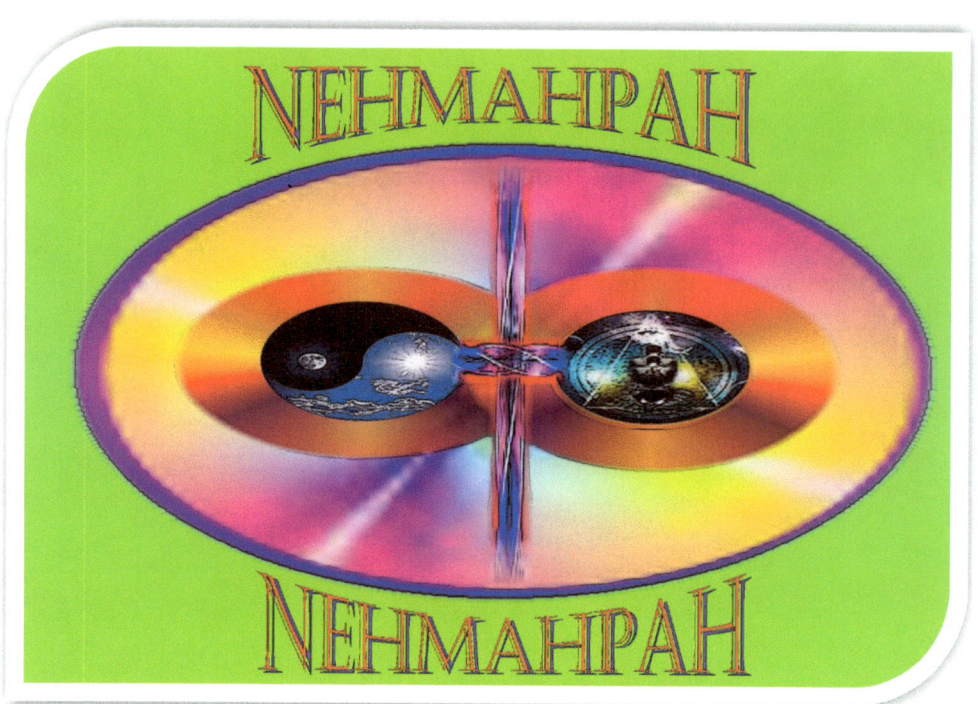

NEHMAHPAH

NEHMAHPAH

NEHMAHPAH resides in the belly or navel Chakra. In the Itanamic language it means "Choosing to Experience the Essence of Innocence." Restoring the memory of living as One with Mother Earth and Mother nature as we were designed to by living in harmony with her ways and naturally within the nature and abundance of their provisions versus living selfishly without consideration of Her well-being. Nehmahpah is a breathing symbol that resides in the belly correlating the importance of breathing from this space, (also referred to as rebirthing breathing) versus shallow breathing from the lungs. According to traditional Chinese medicine and health practice this area is known as the Dantien which translates as the "sea of qi" or "the energy center" where our life force Essence and Spirit are stored and regenerated. It is the centering of one's mind in the lower Dantien one is better able to control one's thoughts and emotions and achieve higher states of awareness thus the ability to tune into the power and healing intentions of the symbol. During the developmental phase within the womb it is this area where all of nutrients that are transferred from the mother through the umbilical cord build and disperse from this space. It is the processing center of all that we ingest and this energetic reservoir remains accessible to us through meditation and inner contemplation.

The outer oval represents consecrated space created within and around us, the infinity symbol reflects the continuous breathing flowing and smoothly switching at the center crossing between the exhalation and inhalation, the spiritual and the physical, the immortal and the mortal. It is designed to cleanse one's self and ones vision of life and how they are meant to live it and return us to the innocence and bliss of having all our needs met for you versus by you, returning you to working to live versus living to work, returning you to the simple essence of life and its fearless, peaceful, harmonious flow effortlessly. It requires one to make a choice to focus in this way at every moment. By choosing so one then makes the process of creating one's experiences of life conscious.

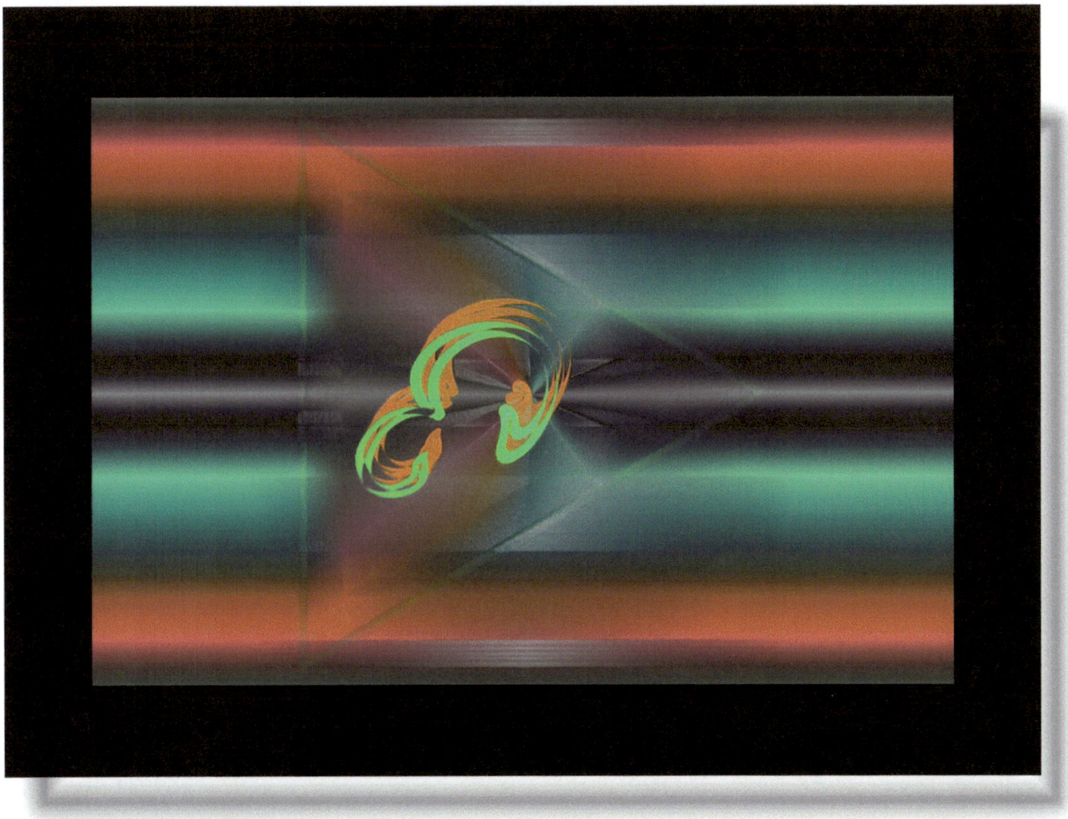

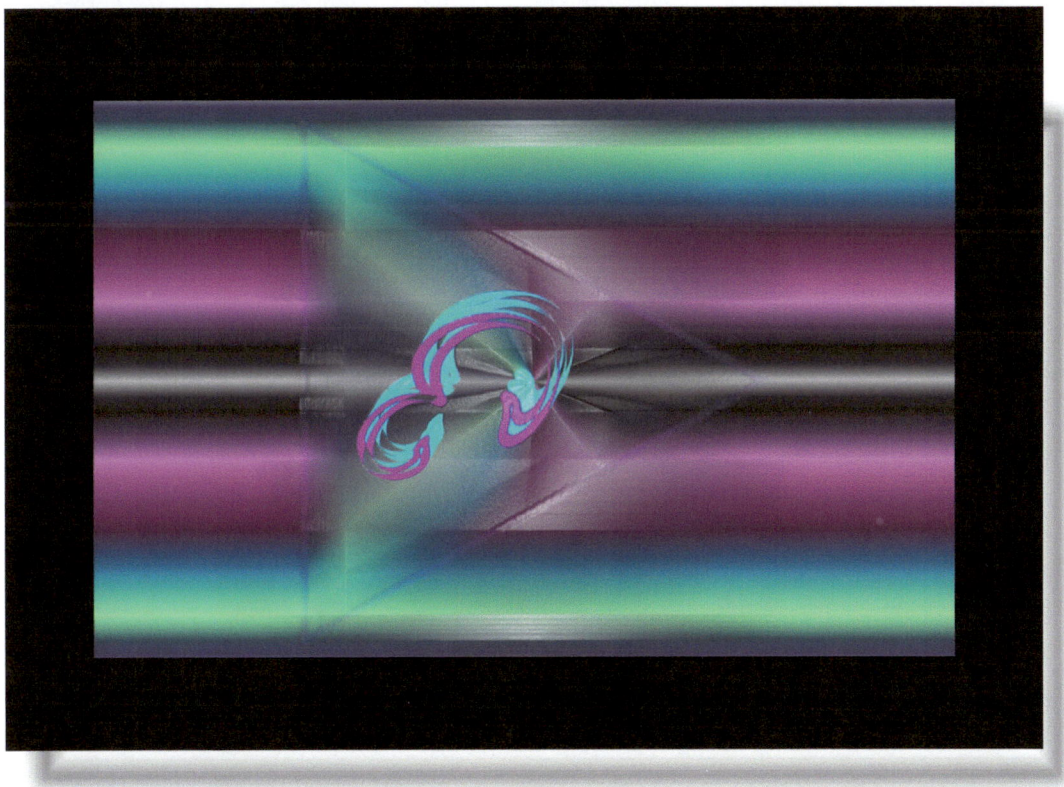

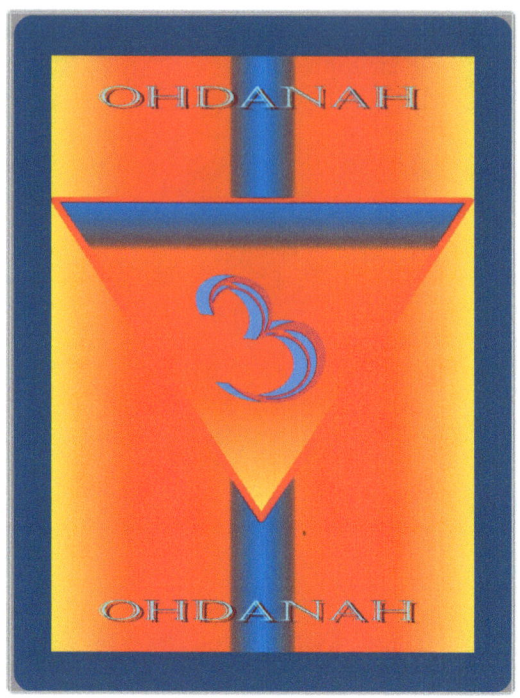

OHDANAH corresponds to the root Chakra. In Itanamic language, there are two basic realms. These are the Ohka (The realm of the material experience) and the Anka. (the realm of eternal qualities) The root of this word "Dan" represents the "experience of letting go". Through the experience of letting go one is able to transmute the heaviness of the material realm into the lightness of its eternal qualities opening themselves up to the innerstanding of the correlation between the two and the eternal purpose for the things we experience in human form. This changes matter into thought and brings it under the control of one's divine individuality. One key that my master teacher William Bagley was given by the Itana Sohra was, "Visualization IS Materialization". Feeling the truth of this heals the heaviness of matter.

The heaviness of matter is the belief that it is a substance that one cannot control or create with their mind. In this culture, reality itself is considered a substance that is "objective" which cannot be influenced by our mental imagination. Yet, the truth of life is that everything is a mental creation or the effect of a mental creation. Therefore, the very word "reality" as it is associated to the material realm is a mislabeling. The symbol has a short ah" at the end which derived from the Tibetan traditions; it symbolizes Vajra Yogini which is the Master of Psychic Heat or Tumo. The Reiki Guide continuum includes her as well as other great beings from all religions.

The angles of the triangle represent the mind, heart, and body; the center represents intent. It also represents coordinating visualization with prana or breath, and body sensation. This is called "hooking into the energy" so that one can again, influence it without their mind. There is a paradox here… Our control of matter, which is our natural right, has to be done within an attitude of complete surrender or letting go. When one is surrendered to becoming "One" with their Ka body or divine Self then one will have the power to transcend pain. The total surrender of Yeshua to his eternal "Ka" body beyond his flesh allowed him to resurrect his body from the Cross and beyond aging and death. The short "ah" is the mustard seed that grows into this kind of faith.

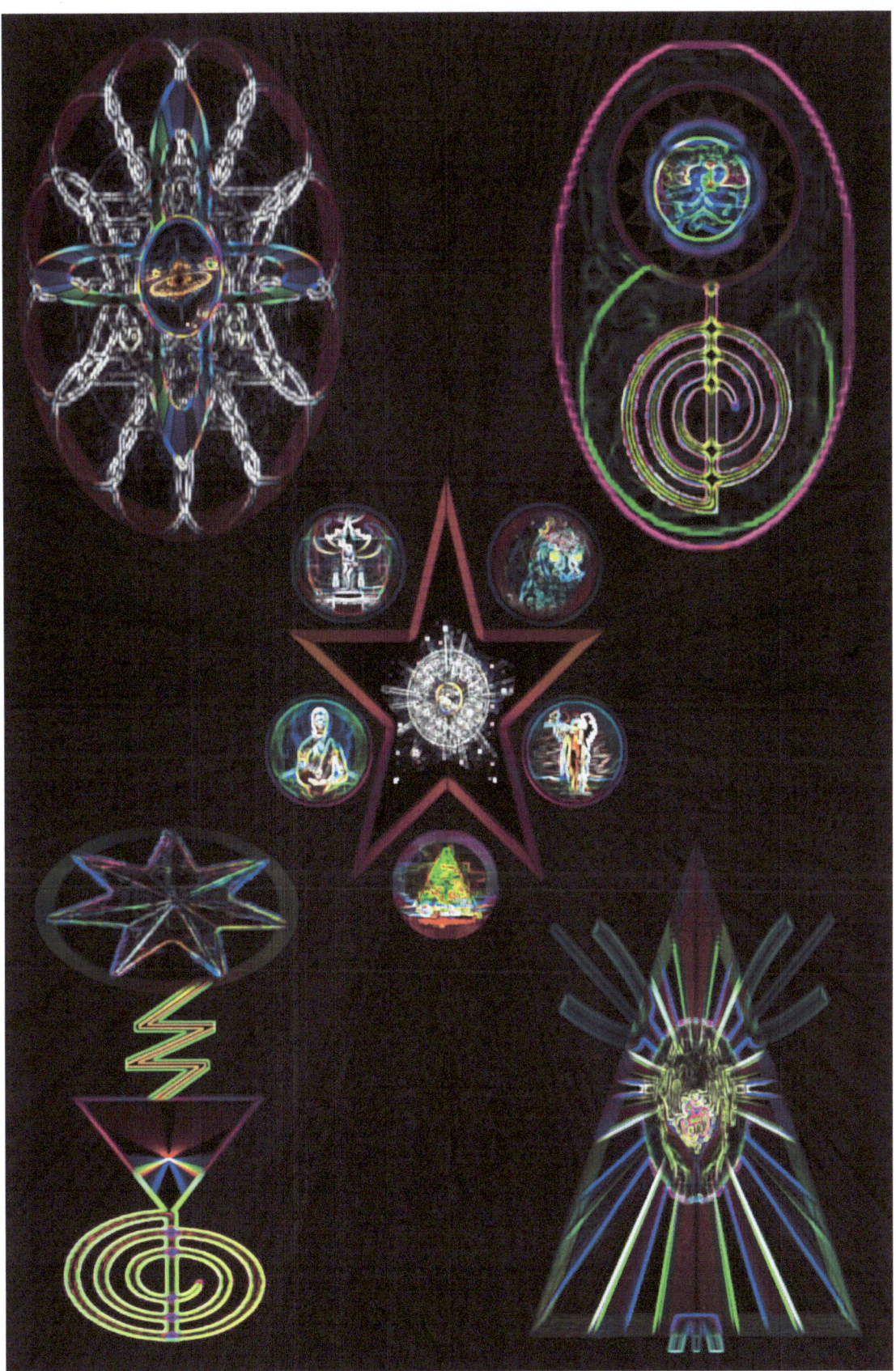

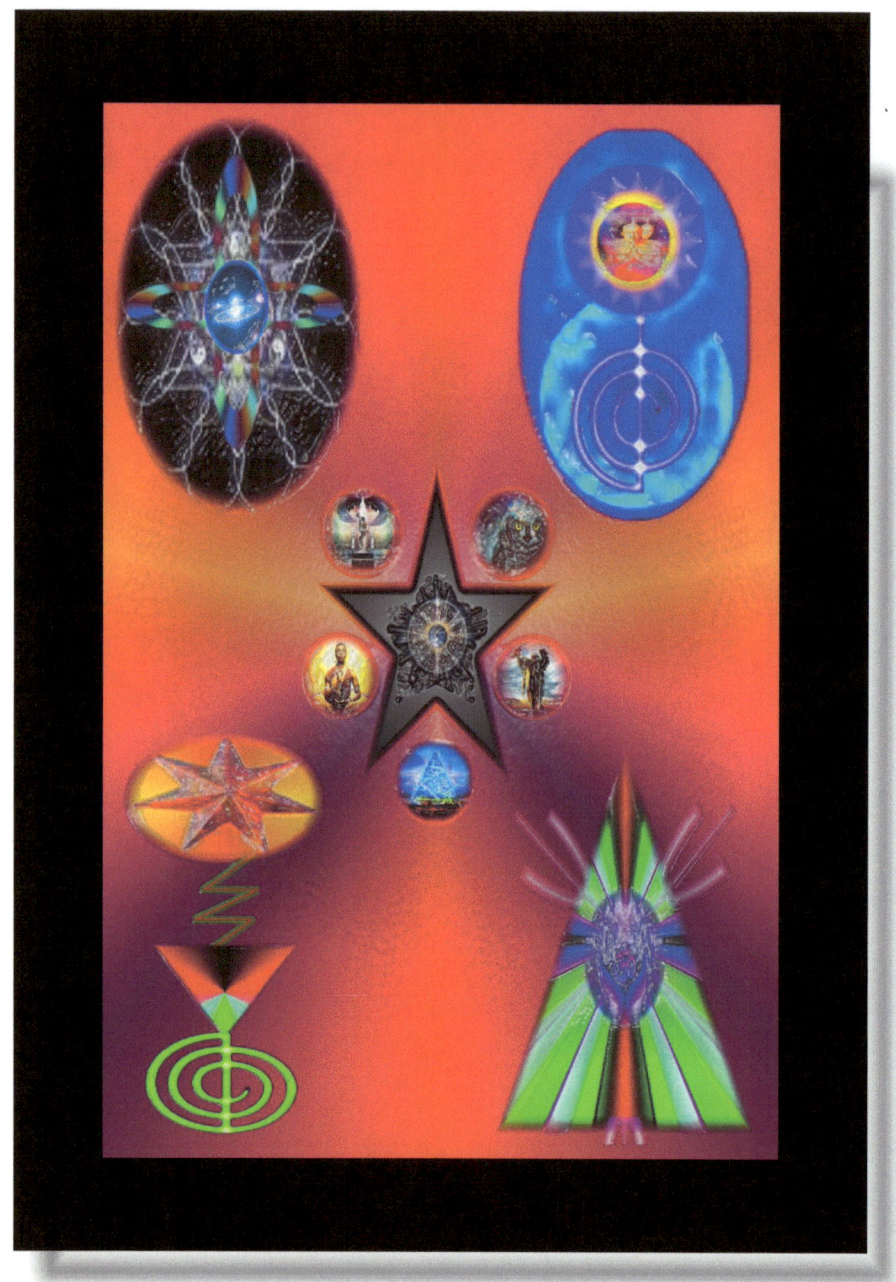

TANRAN REIKI 5 SPECIAL SYMBOLS SERIES

Within the Tanran Reiki Mandala are Five Special Symbols. These symbols do not align with the chakra system but are special initiations within their own rights. Each represents a sacred initiation into deeper levels of conscious awareness of one's own wholeness within oneself and within all of creation. Also, each symbol of this set imparts the innerstanding of that particular symbols meaning with the ability to recognize the roles each play within life itself.

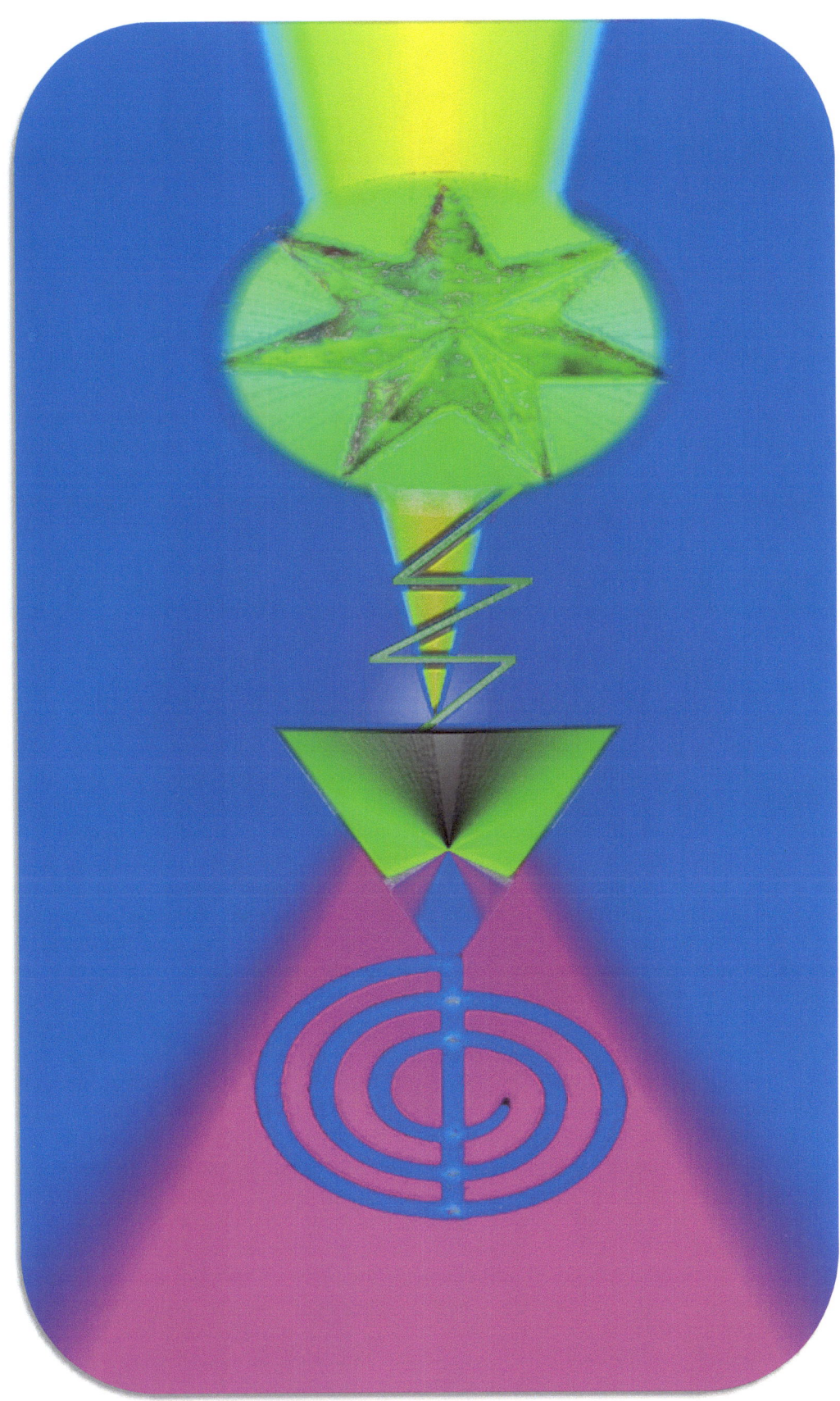

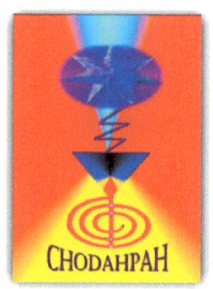

CHODAHPAH

The **CHODAHPAH** symbol is a gift of White Tara, the Dakini of Alchemy, who is part of the Tibetan Trinity of Physical Immortality along with Amitayus ad Unishavijaya. Amitayus calls back and integrates the energy we have lost to others. Unishavijaya burns away one's karma so that nothing can bring them down. Tara transmutes painful emotions into blissful emotions. Long ago, The Goddess Energy of Tara incarnated on Earth in various forms to influence the development of Buddhism, such as inspiring the Chod Rite. The Chod Rite teaches the path of accelerated evolution. The key of this path is facing every fear and embracing one's own shadow side within oneself and within others without judgment.

The bottom spiral is the kundalini unfolding from the root chakra and flowing upwards to bring all fear as anxiety sensation, emotional shutdown, and mental resistance into one's Spiritual truth. When we move through our fears 3 times, by choosing to let ourselves fully experience what comes, we break through their illusion enabling us to see that sensations, emotions, and thoughts come and go and do not define us. One comes to realize that these 3 phenomenon are impersonal; they float through their subconscious minds like clouds through the sky. The triangle represents the 3 demons or negative thought forms which relate to 3 root fears of pain, punishment, and rejection that we meet. Pain can be related to stress, aging, and death or any diminishment of our abilities. Punishment is related to guilt, fear of reciprocity for negative things we've done, ones judgments around past failures and the feeling of not deserving to live. Rejection is related to shame, feeling that just being oneself is not sufficient or acceptable and the worry that one will not be approved of or loved. The deepest of these 3 is the shaming, because it's through shaming that one learns how to repress parts of themselves and the emotions within them. The 7 pointed star with the lightning bolt represents the star nature from which we as spirit beings came from. Our connection to the stars is our true spirit selves and the flow of their light essence transmutes these 3 thought forms by dissolving them into the light of our spirit body.

A visualization that has been used is being guided by OYA & Shango the Guardian of the Dead and the Fire of Transmutation, to a cemetery, where you strip off all clothing to become naked in body and soul. The body and soul then make the offering by playing whatever wants to come up from within on a drum and offering the body to be eaten by the 3 demons of fear. By this offering you empower Oya & Shango, (The Orisha of Fire, Lightening, the whirlwinds, and the cemetery) to protect ones soul while dissolving their attachment of defining themselves as their flesh allowing them to re-member that they are a spiritual being designed to remain attached to their awareness of the spirit realm and are able to correspond and communicate with both the spirit realm and the essences of universal and earthly elementals whenever one chooses. As we operate in this knowing that our body is only a shell, a vehicle that we chose to allow us to operate on this earth plane just like one's car is the vehicle we choose to transport us from place to place.

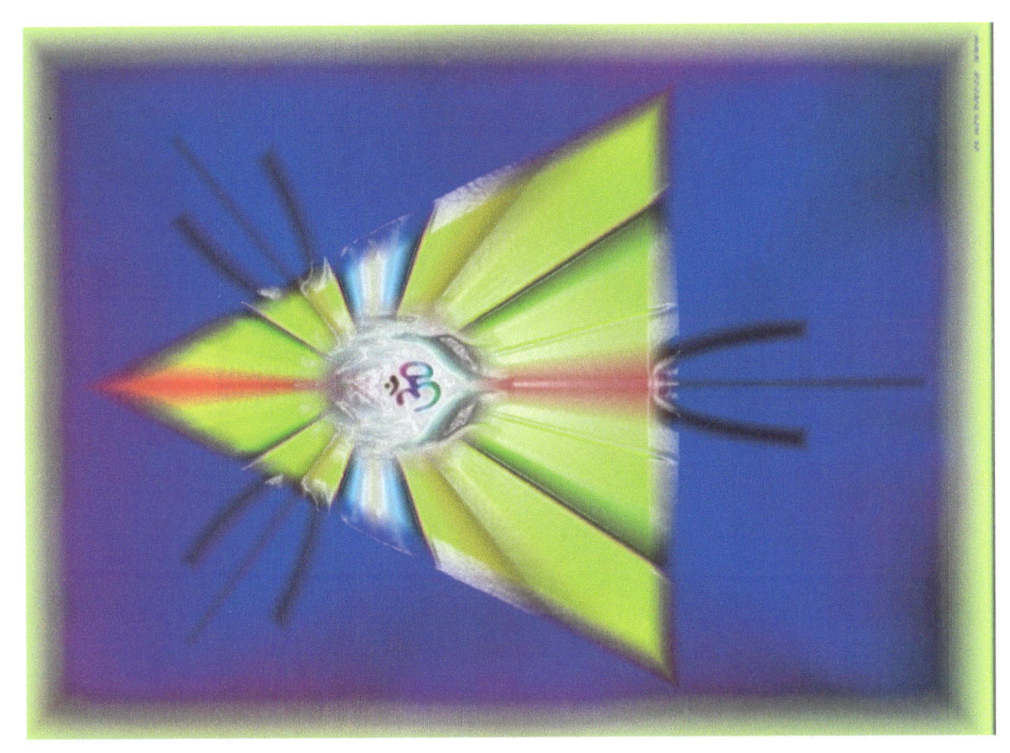

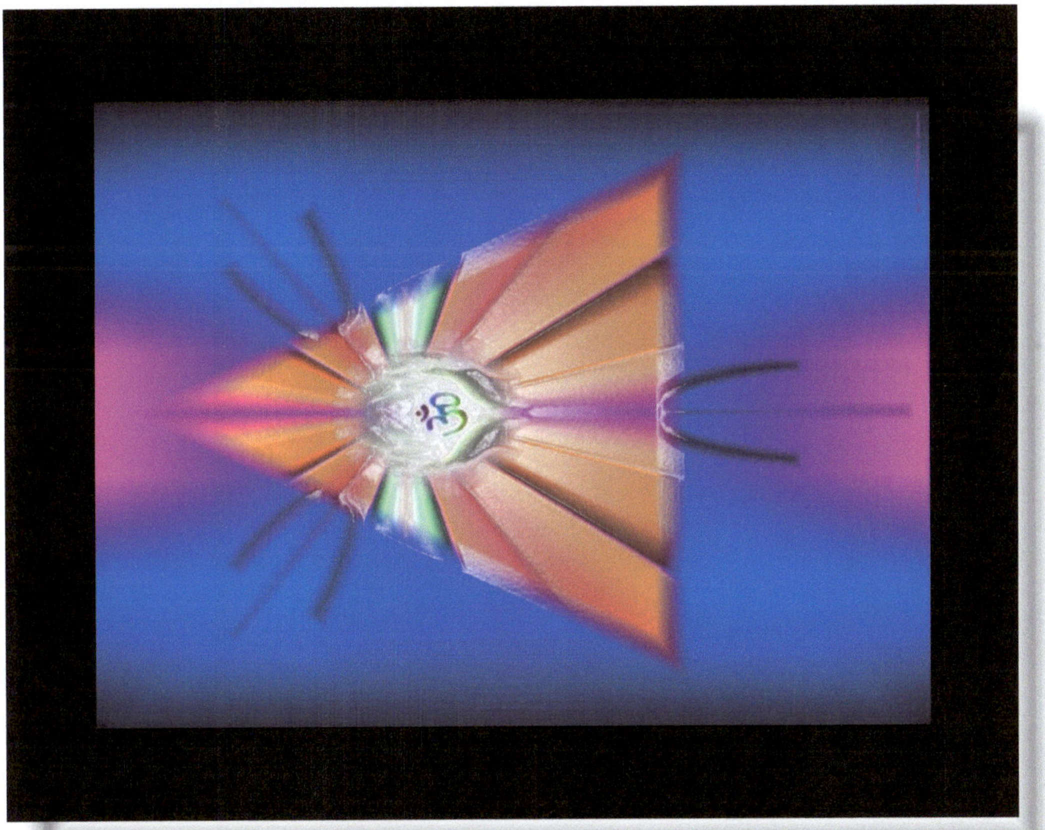

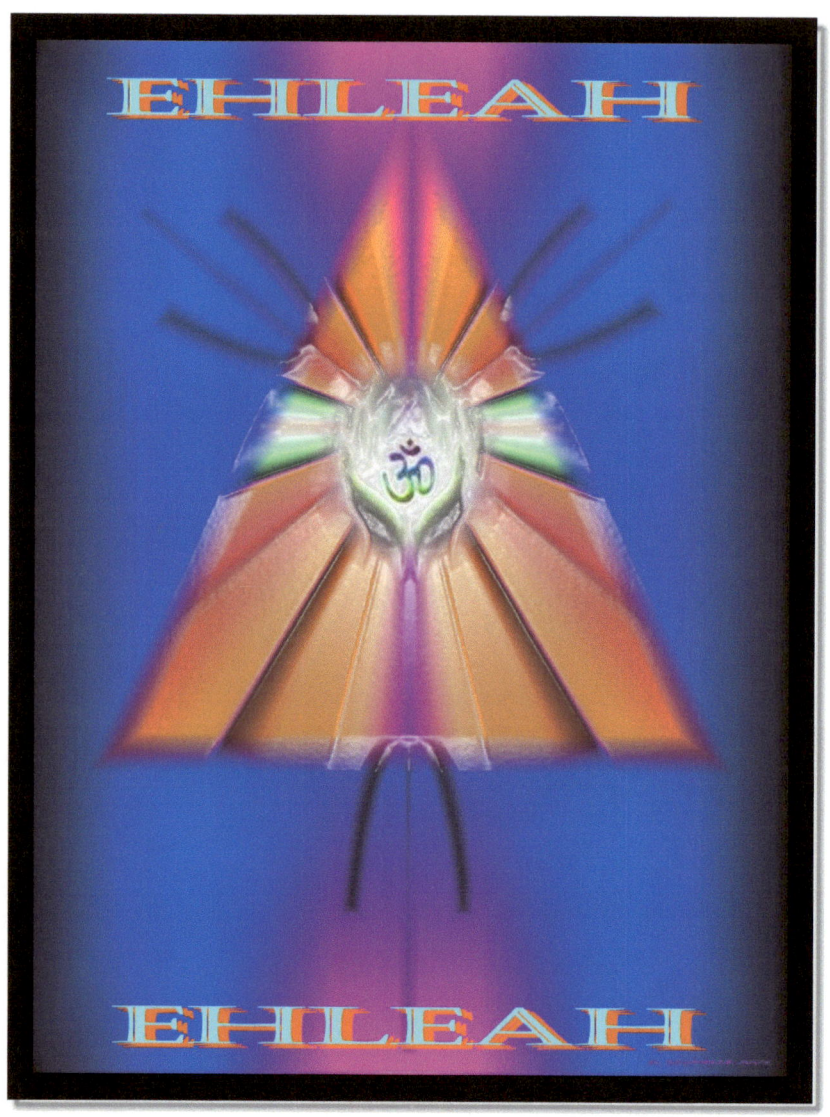

As a soul retrieval symbol **EHLEAH** is good for both getting pieces of oneself back and also for grabbing and removing energies that are not one's own from within them. It is also good for retrieving aspects of one's cosmic origins and past life energies that one needs in order to evolve into their divine attributes, characteristics and associations consciously. It works well with all the other symbols but most especially with Zee Gah Nah. This symbol helps to accelerate and make more peaceful the soul retrieval work that is being done on the planet at this time. The Shamanic version of this work can be more intense and more risky. There is a whole section on this symbol in the Tanran Reiki Training Manual written by William Bagley. However, the simplest way to work with this symbol is to visualize it and then ask it to retrieve the parts of our souls that have been lost to us or to remove from our soul what is causing pain and sorrow in our life or in the life of the person that one is channeling its healing energy to.

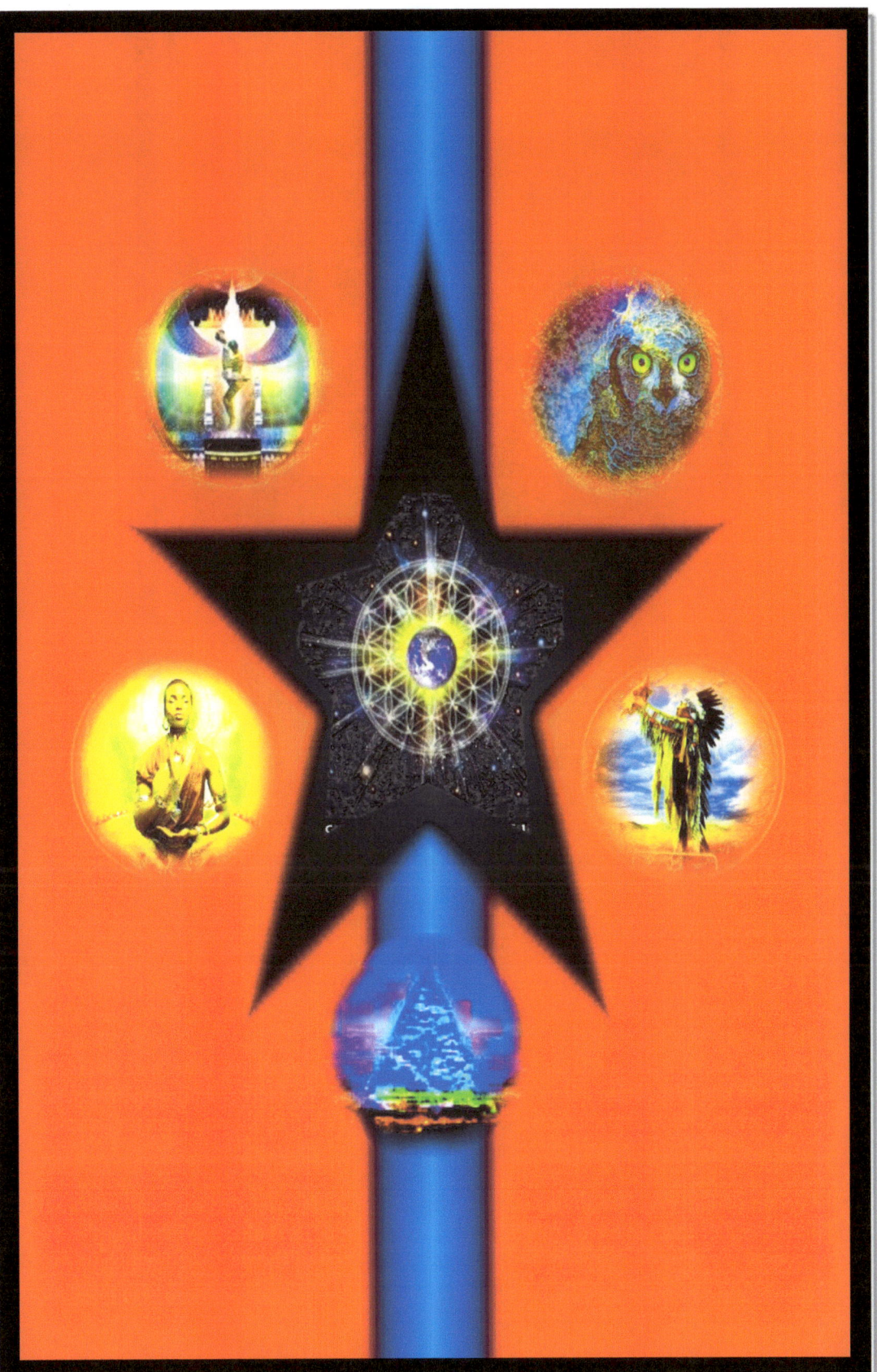

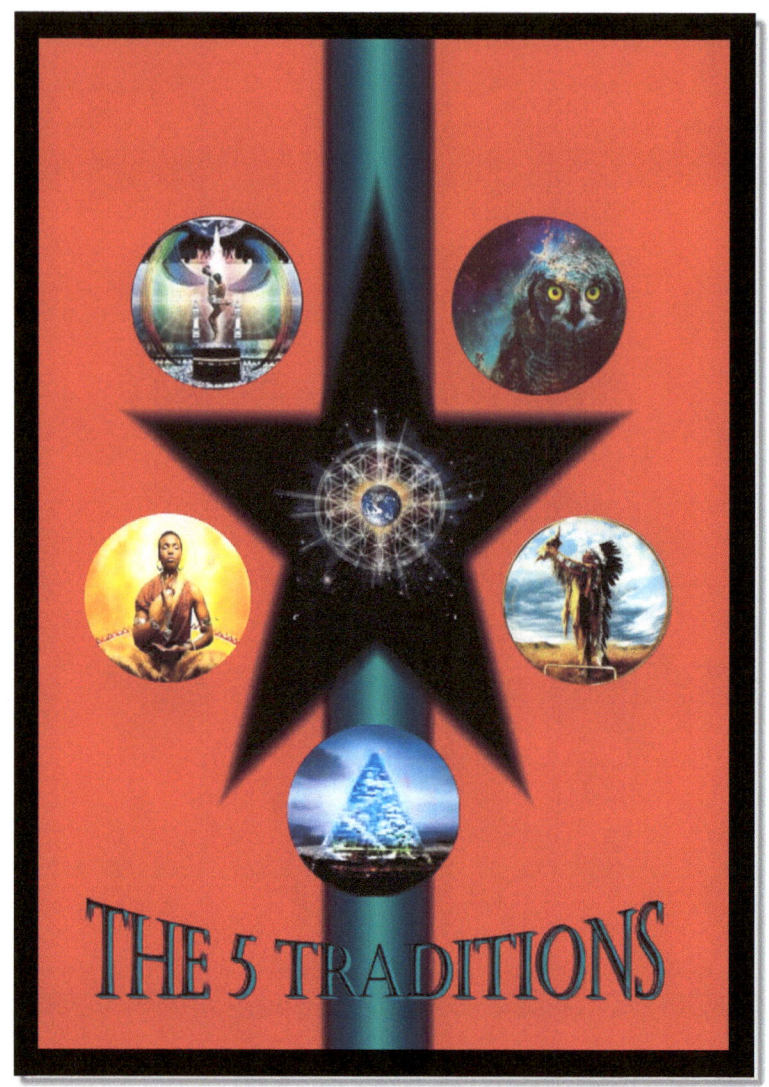

THE 5 TRADITIONS

TEHZEENAH - The FIVE TRADITIONS symbol represents the spiritual essences of Love, Wisdom, Method, Action, and Mastery. Every religion integrates the essence of one or more of these traditions teaching a combination of them in practice. For instance, the essence of Buddha is wisdom and uses the method of meditation to realize this wisdom. The essence of the Christ is love and uses the action of helping others to realize this love in unconditional ways. Hatha Yoga is a combination of body mastery, asana method and nonattached action as its path. Karma Yoga has the essence of nonattached action. Bhakti yoga has the essence of devotional love and the method of chanting.

At the center of The Five Traditions is primordial living awareness that permeates throughout the galactic center that we are spiraling around and beyond. It is also a symbol for the Syrian connection which appears in nearly all the esoteric religions of the Earth and which has seeded the Earth with an evolutionary stimulus to propel us to enlightenment and beyond. It also relates to the Sufi vision of universal spirituality.

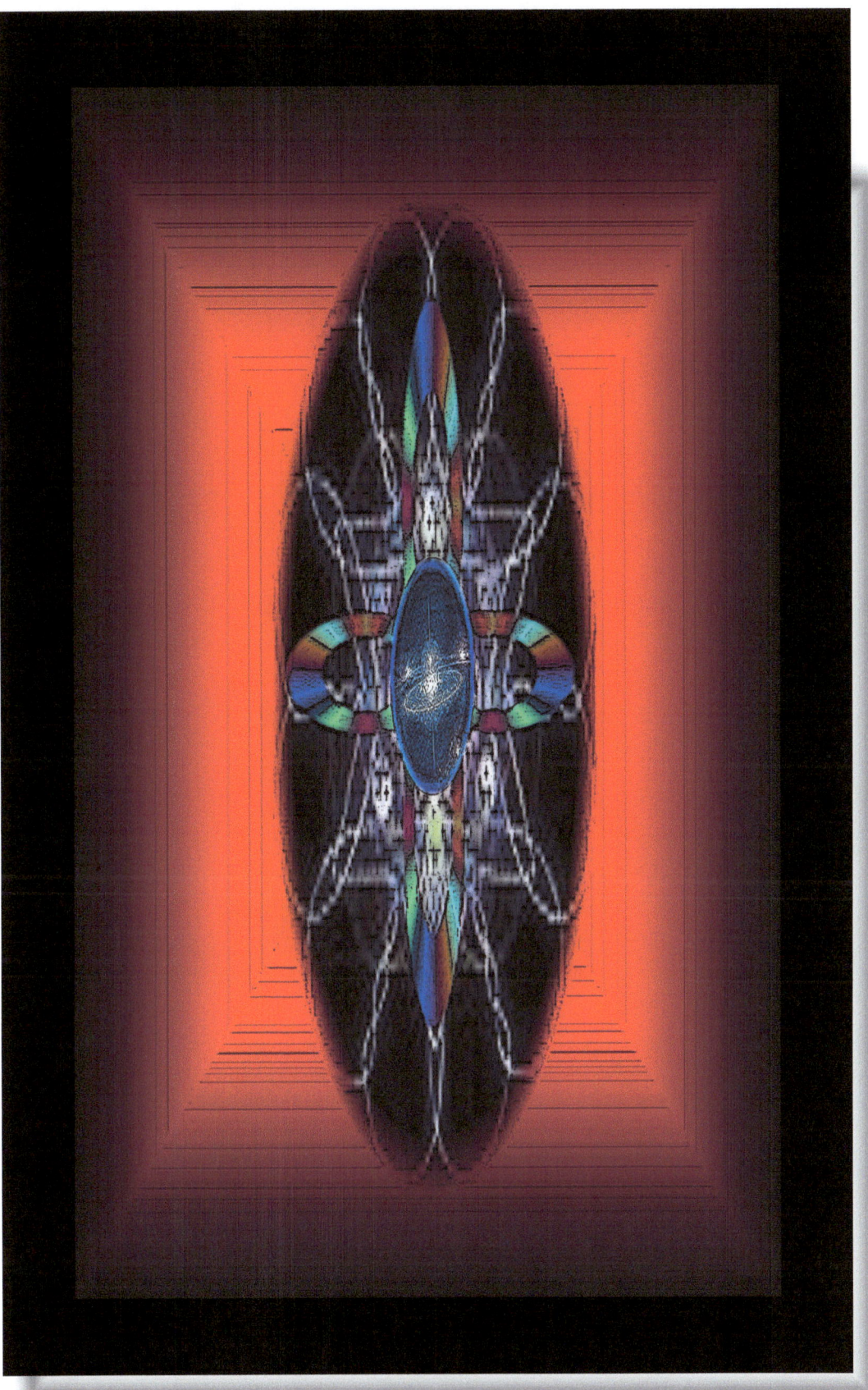

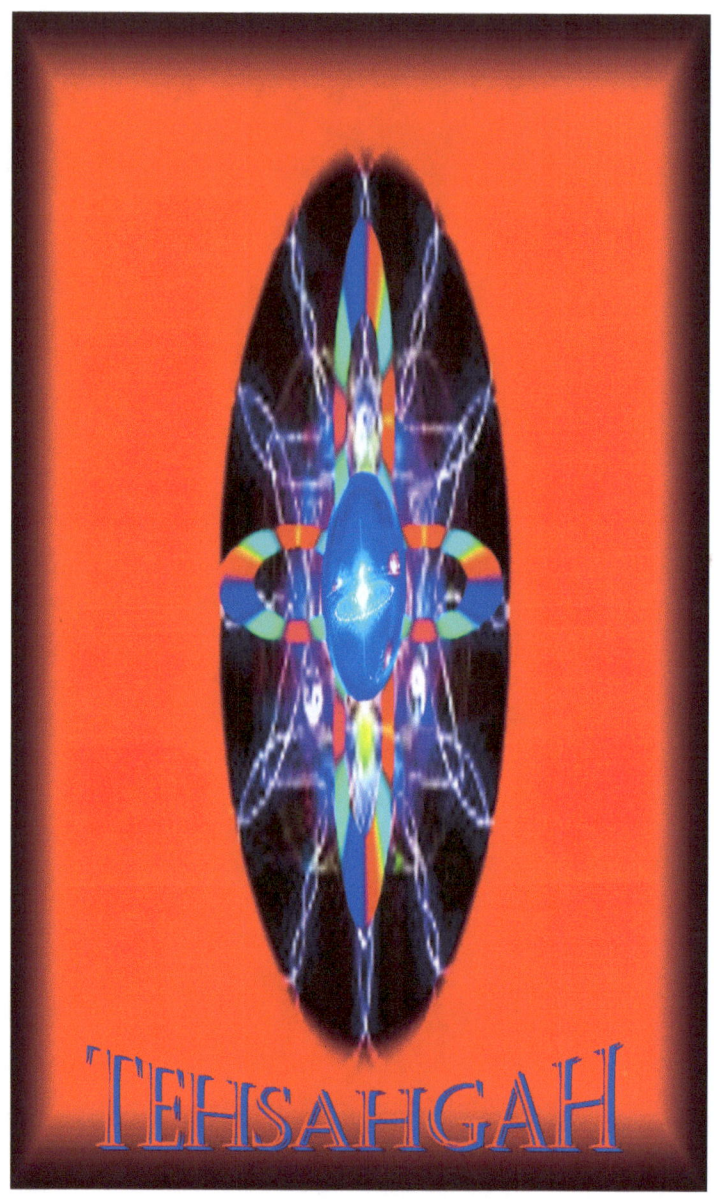

TEHSAHGAH

TEHSAHGAH is the symbol for the Reiki Breathing Community. The key lesson of the symbol is to link with all the other Reiki people within the Reiki continuum through sacred breath as in the Rebirthing breathing done with Rakira intuition. The Reiki continuum includes those who are "planet side" and those who are in transcended bodies guiding us from the invisible realms. The symbol points to the "Corpus Christi" the body of the Christ. We heal because there is only One Healer and One healing and we are particles of that One body. What lies ahead?

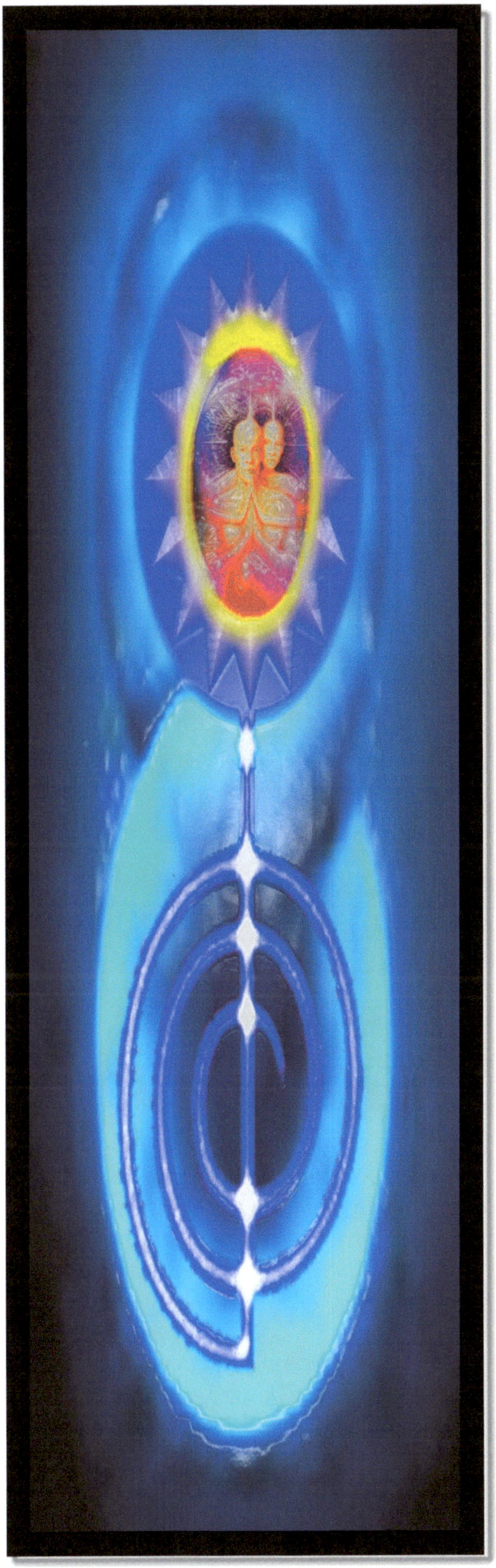

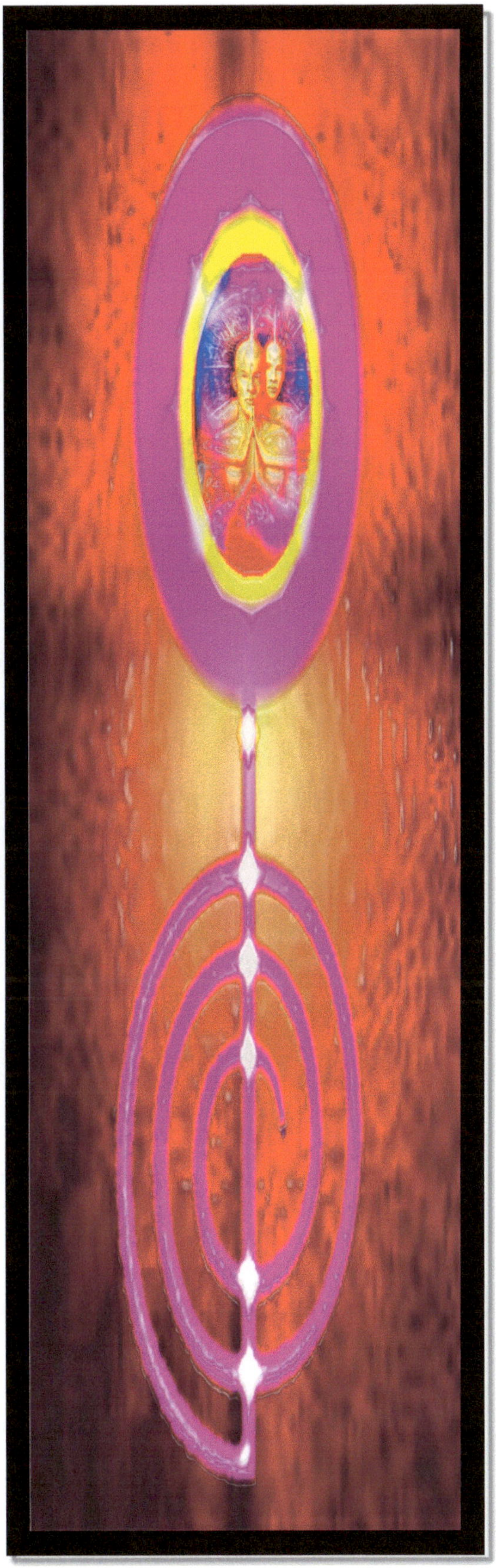

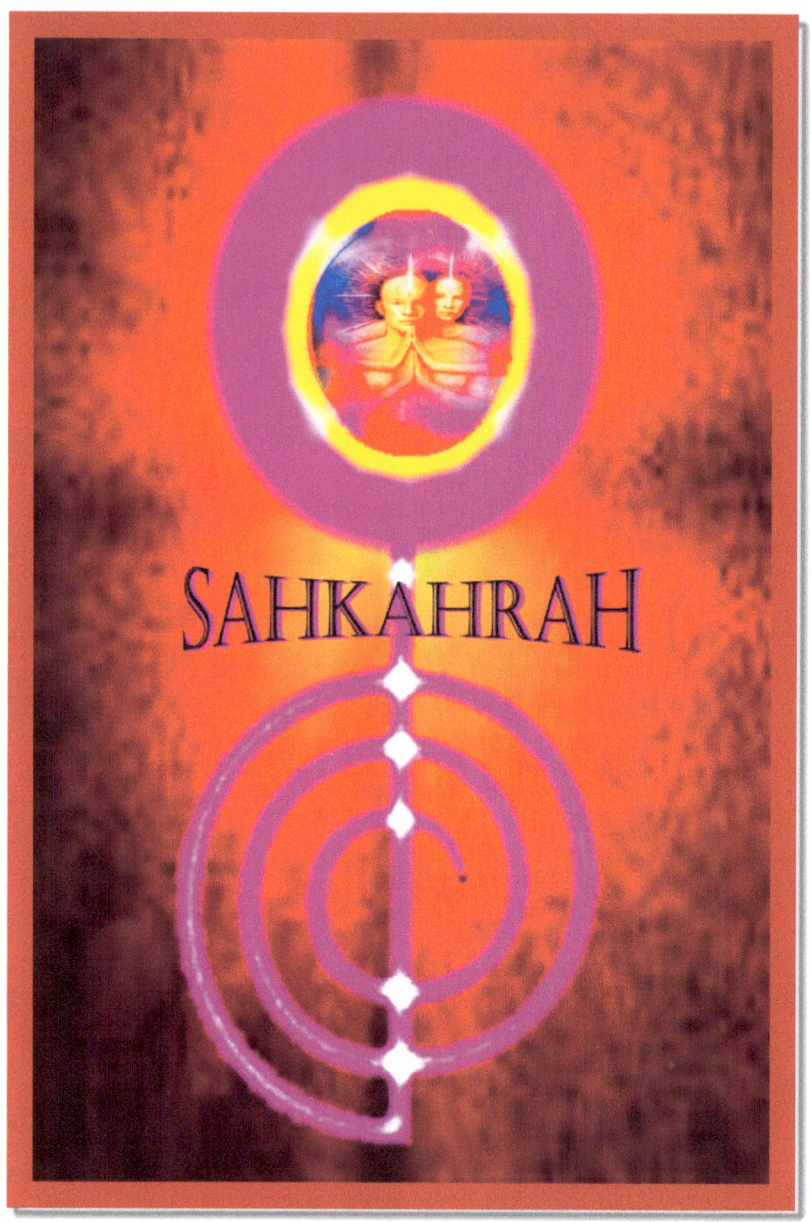

In the Energy Maturity Set **SAHKAHRAH** represents the opening to the 8th chakra which is beyond all duality it is also part of the relationship healing symbols because it transcends and includes male and female, inner and outer, self and other, order and chaos, karma and grace, front and back, top and bottom, higher and lower, life and death, conscious and unconscious, and mind, heart, spirit and body.

When this center is fully open, there is no tension between anything and anything, since nothing can oppose anything within the vast unity that we live in. The Dzogchen realization of ever arising spontaneous perfection is part of this, where all sounds are mantras, all thoughts are dharma, all sentient beings are Buddha's and Dakini's, and all appearances are the living Mandala.

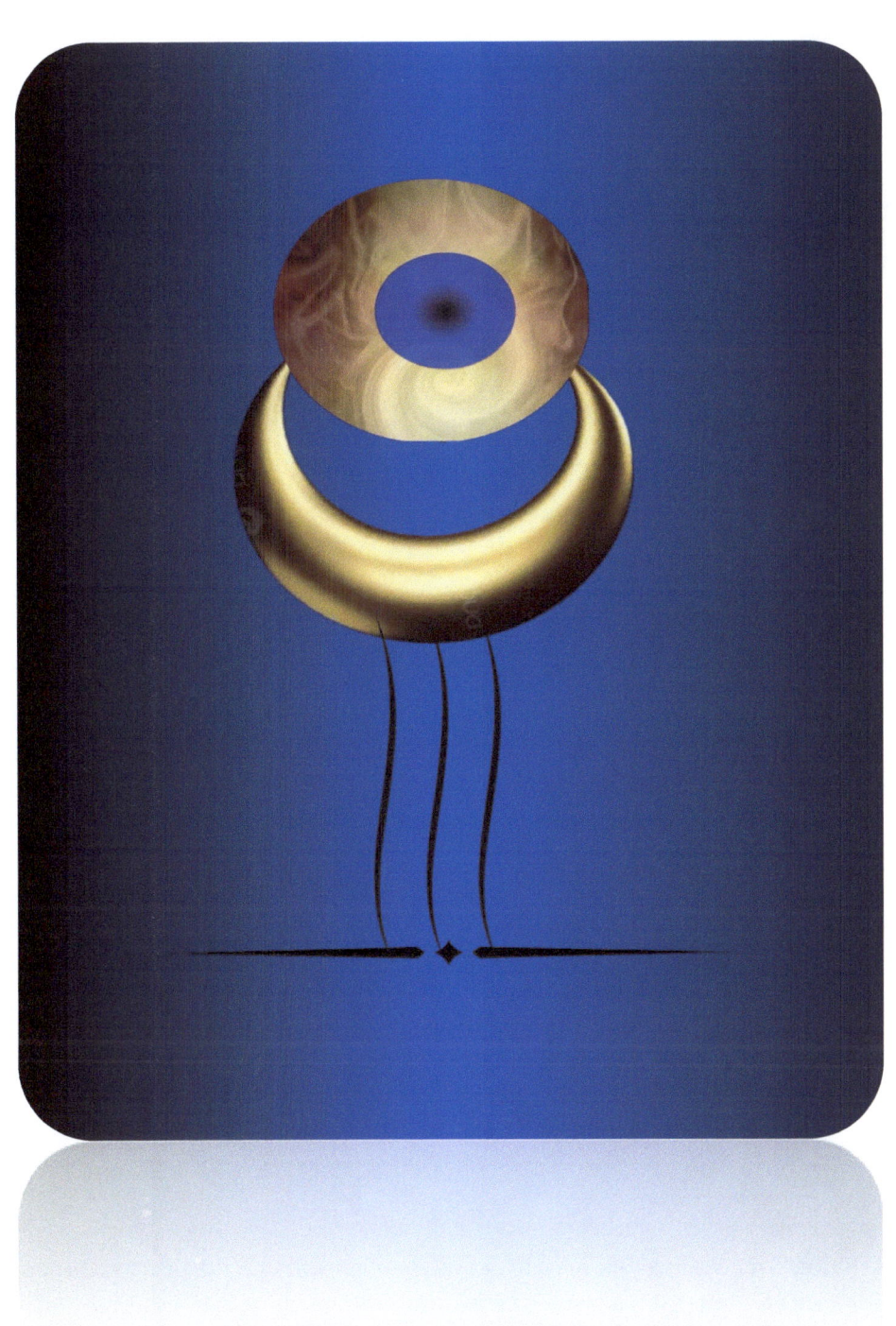

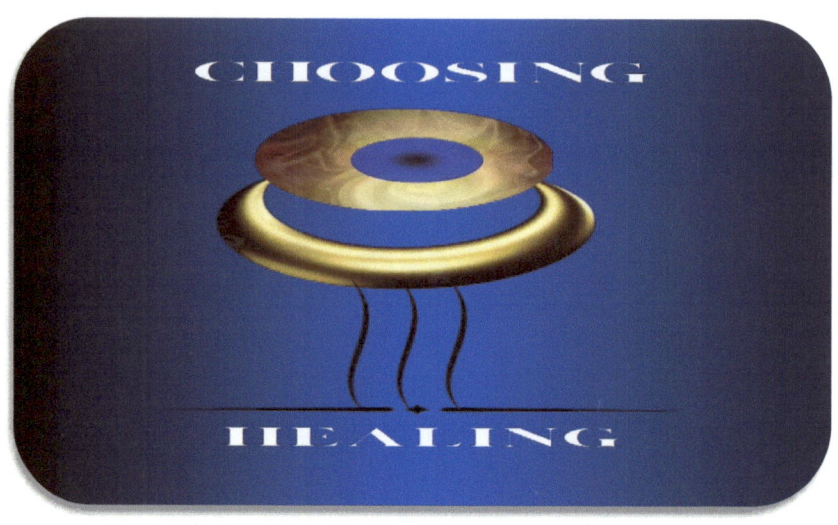

TEGANAH

This symbol is used with Dohyanoh and is the gate symbol to the Mandala. The inner meaning of Teganah is "choosing to be healed". It is the symbol that determines whether deeper healing work may begin. Its inner meaning *choosing to be healed* reflects a fundamental spiritual truth: healing cannot occur without willingness.

Universal Loving Energy, as channeled through Reiki, is non-violent and non-coercive. It does not override free will or impose transformation. It responds only to what is permitted in the present moment. To activate Teganah is to consciously allow healing by acknowledging one's own need for it—without judgment, resistance, or denial.

This acknowledgment is itself a powerful act. It dissolves unconscious barriers and opens the inner field where healing can occur naturally. Reiki, entering through Teganah, delivers exactly the level of healing the body, mind, and spirit are ready to receive at that time. Nothing is forced, and nothing is withheld.

Teganah also carries an ethical teaching for practitioners: healing cannot be imposed, even with loving intention. True healing unfolds only when consent, readiness, and presence align. In this way, Teganah affirms personal responsibility, energetic maturity, and respect for the soul's timing.

Choosing to be healed is choosing conscious relationship with oneself. When that choice is made, the gate opens, the Mandala becomes accessible, and healing proceeds through allowance rather than force.

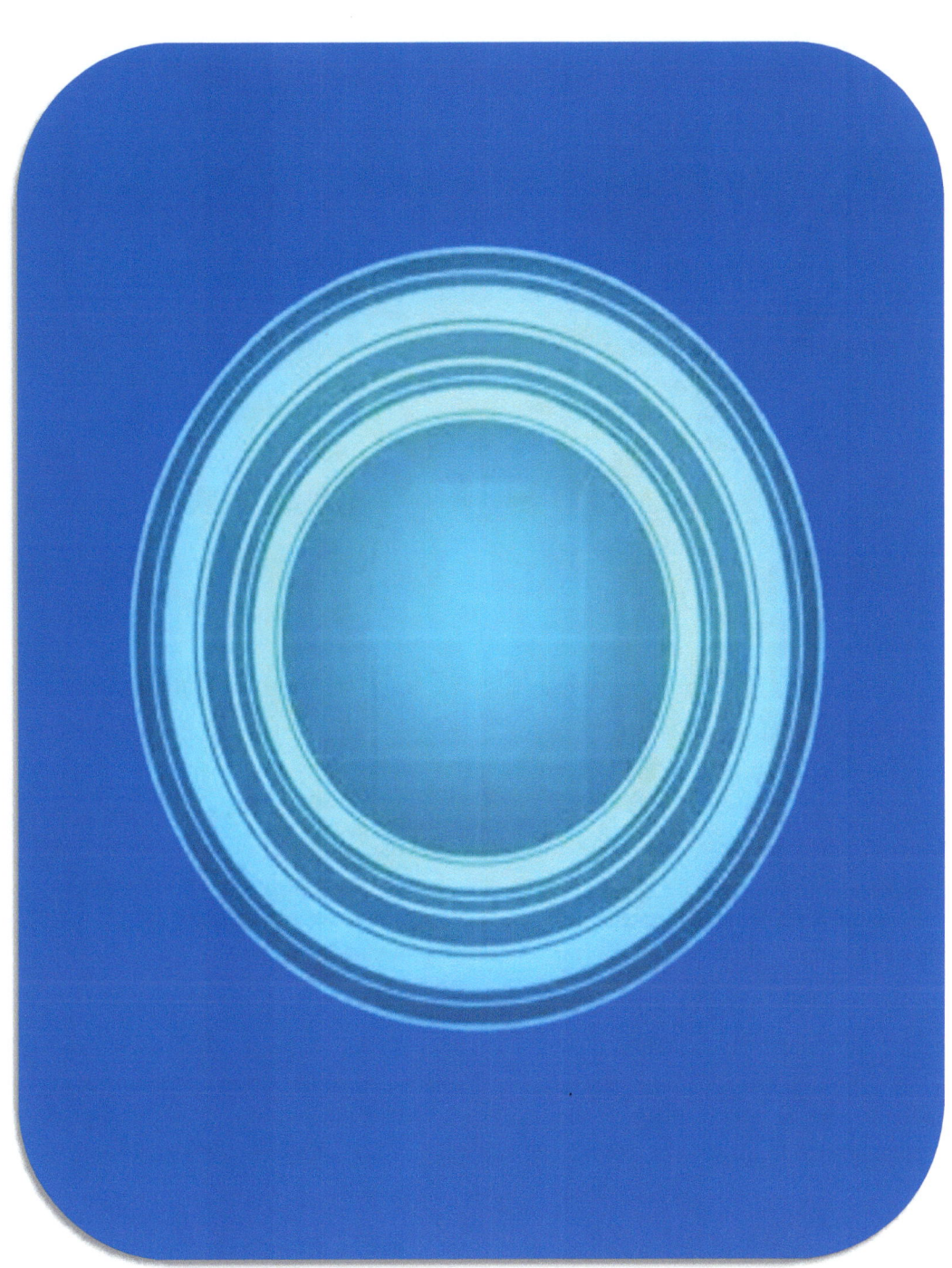

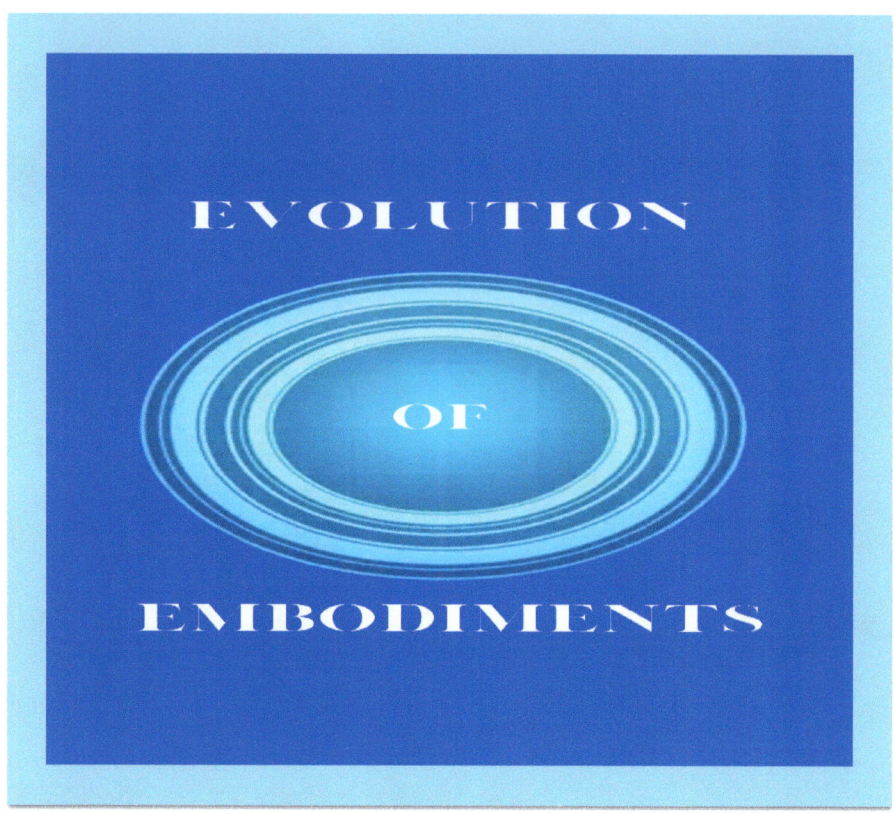

OHNEESAN

Ohneesan is a First Eye activation symbol that carries the frequency of conscious arrival. Its essence is "Welcome to the World," signifying the soul's intentional entry into physical embodiment while maintaining continuity of awareness between lifetimes. This symbol supports the preservation of the inner thread of remembrance that connects the soul's wisdom beyond birth.

The name Ohneesan holds layered meaning. *Oh* refers to the manifest universe—the visible, material realm into which consciousness enters. *Nee* represents the purpose of experiencing life on Earth, emphasizing incarnation as a meaningful and chosen journey. *San* embodies the wisdom gained through lived experience, affirming that learning arises through presence, participation, and reflection.

Ohneesan is a symbol of orientation and alignment. It assists the individual in remembering why they came, anchoring the soul's intention within the physical world while keeping awareness open to higher knowing. Through this remembrance, one is better able to stay on course, make aligned choices, and navigate life with clarity rather than distraction.

Within Tanran Reiki, Ohneesan supports conscious embodiment, helping the soul integrate fully into the body without losing connection to its greater purpose. It affirms that birth is not a forgetting, but a transition—one that invites awareness to remain awake within form, allowing wisdom to unfold through experience.

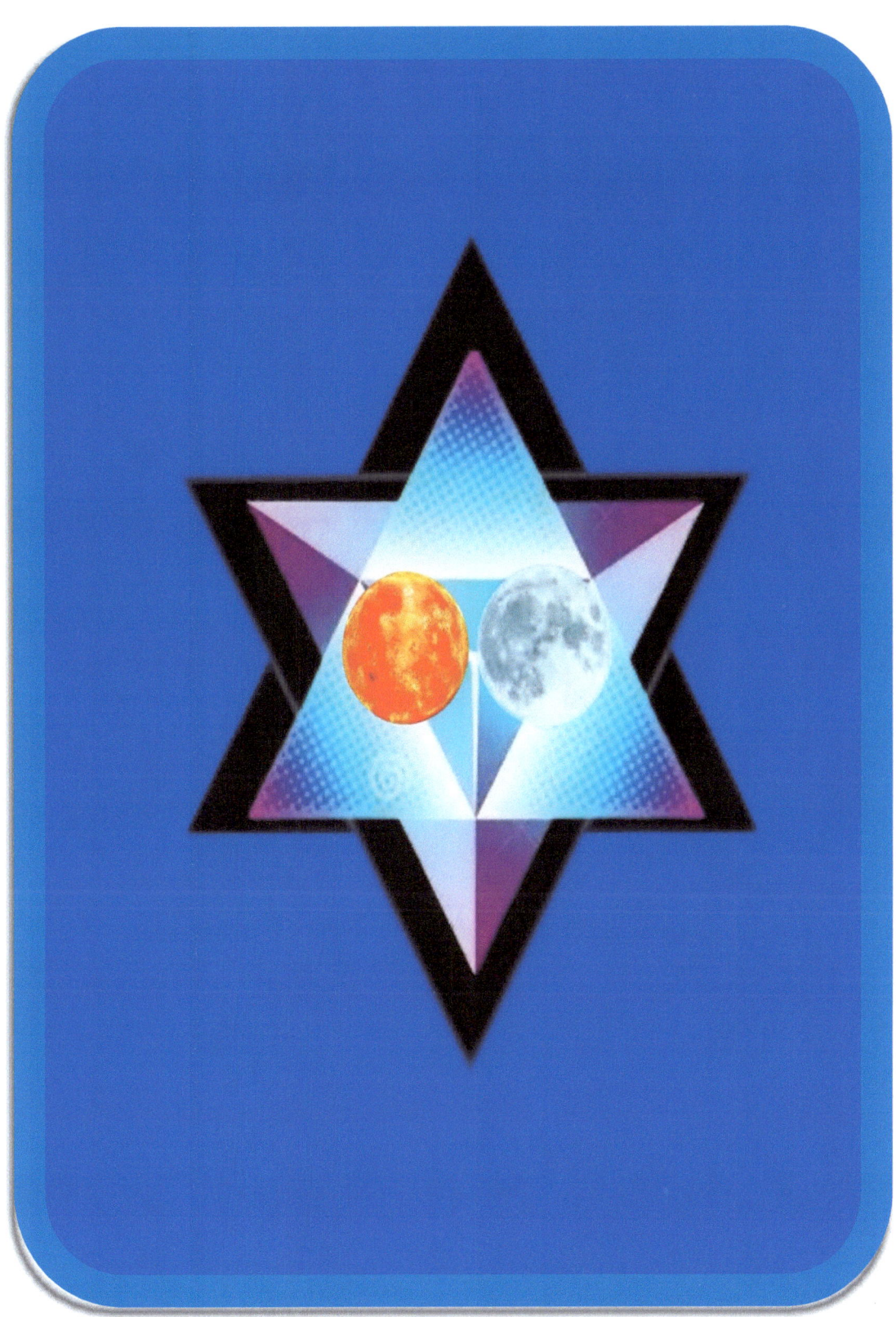

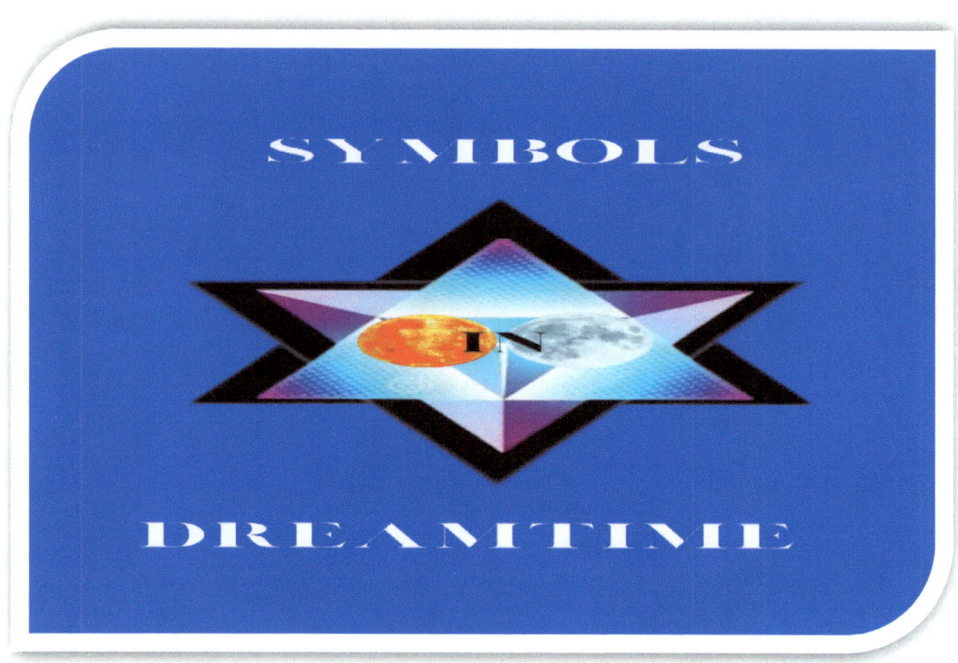

NETEEYAH

Neteeyah is a symbol of evolutionary continuity and spiritual updating. It is an abbreviated form of the Itanamic Senka mantra *Neteeyah Sangeh Ooteema Ooteema*, a living library frequency that carries encoded knowledge accessible through dreamtime and subtle awareness. When activated, Neteeyah opens a personal channel through which symbols, insights, or energetic tools may be received as needed for one's healing or service.

This symbol is used when existing Reiki applications require renewal in response to new challenges, shifts in consciousness, or emerging evolutionary needs. Neteeyah acknowledges that spiritual systems are not static; they evolve alongside humanity and the planetary field. Rather than replacing tradition, it restores relevance by allowing wisdom to update organically through direct inner knowing.

Neteeyah also supports the reactivation of Sacred Symbols from the Planetary Traditions— those ancient energetic languages that predate formal systems yet continue to live within the Earth's memory and the human bio-field. Through this reawakening, practitioners are guided to work in harmony with both ancestral wisdom and present-moment necessity.

Within Tanran Reiki, Neteeyah affirms that guidance arises when it is needed and in the form most appropriate for the time. It honors dreamtime, intuition, and direct revelation as valid pathways of learning, allowing Reiki to remain responsive, alive, and aligned with the unfolding intelligence of life.

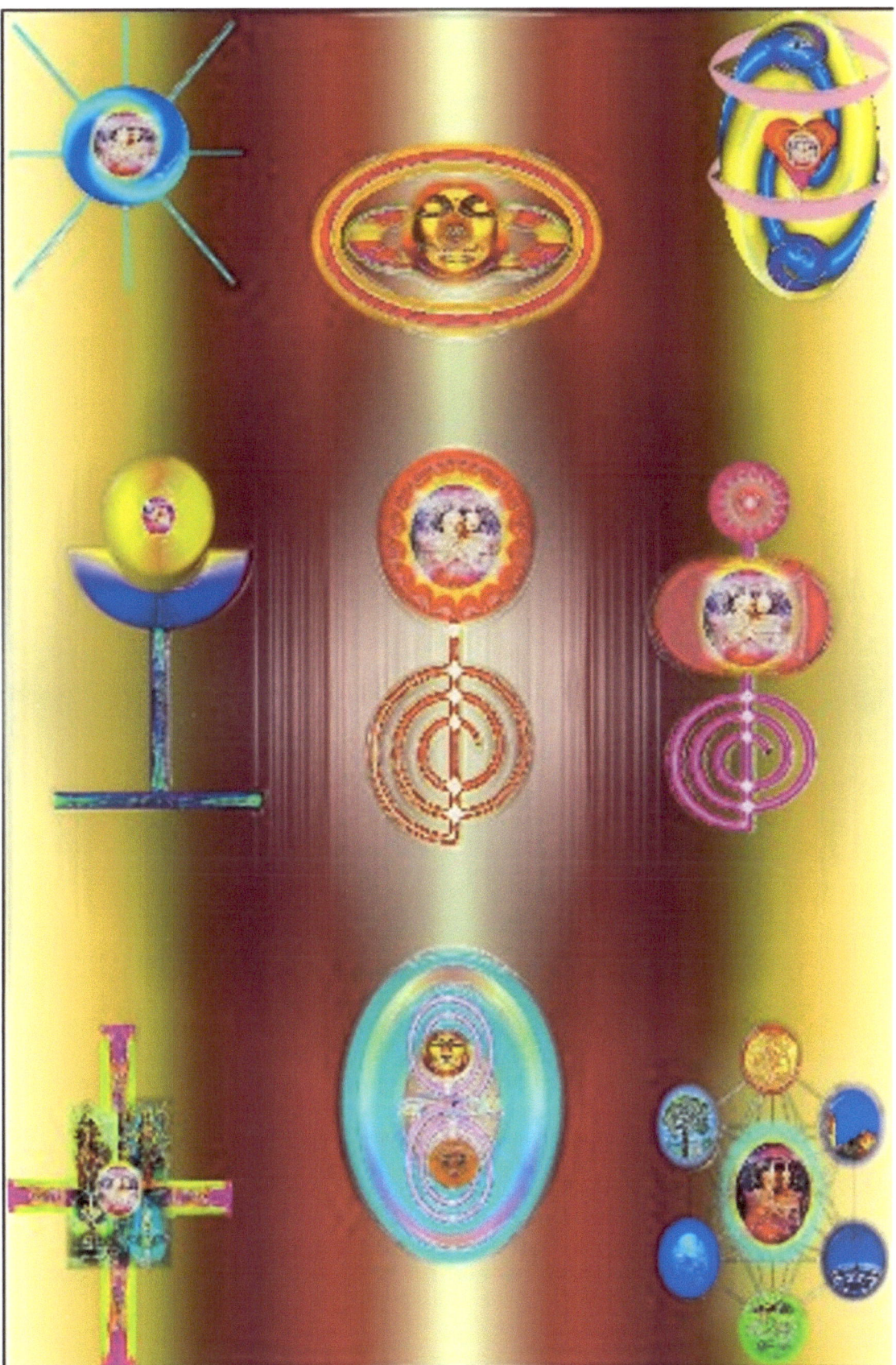

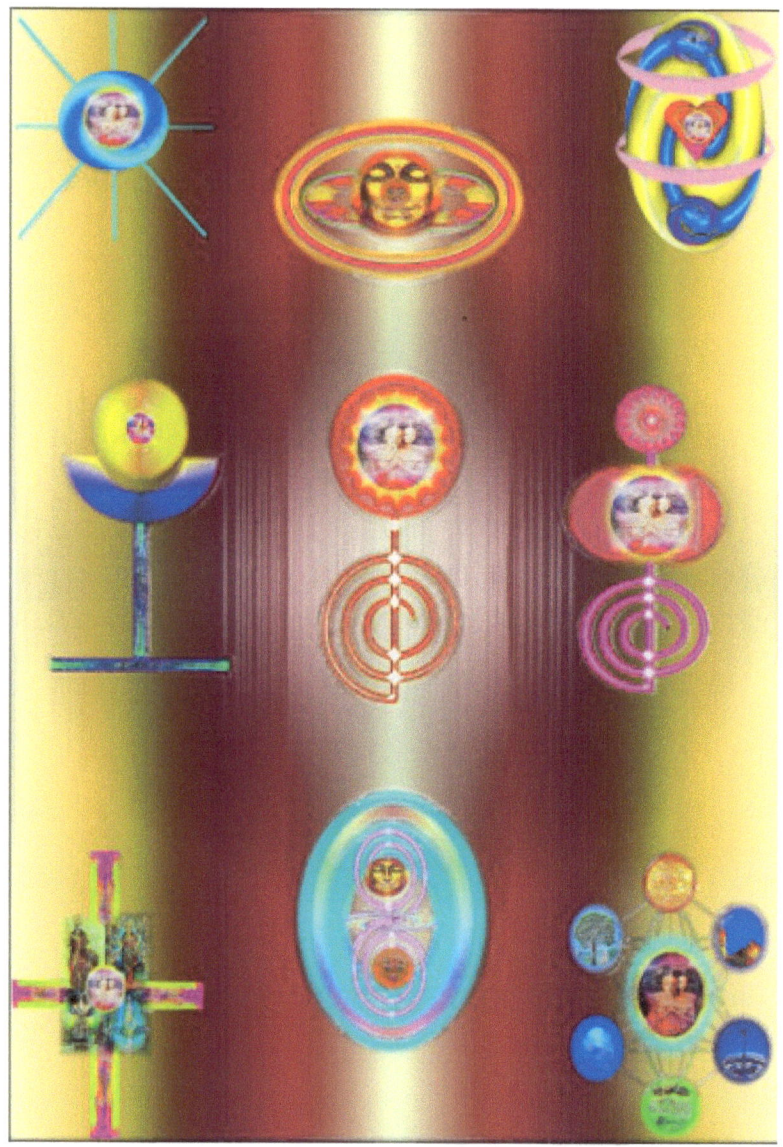

<u>TANRAN REIKI RELATIONSHIP HEALING SERIES</u>

The Tanran Relationship Series possess the symbols that are in command of how Divine relationship develops between the masculine and feminine, man and womb-man. The wisdom within them is that of how we were originally and spiritually designed to develop in relationships before the deactivation of the DNA strands. These dormant strands of DNA possess the blueprint of our immortal selves as Gods/Goddess' and are being triggered to awaken in these times. These images contain the essence and sentient ability to bring about awareness's of how one may cultivate and positively transform outdated attitudes and beliefs concerning the true bond and Divine balance of love, sexuality, divine purpose and soul balance that we were designed to operate in. From the first glance to soul commitment and every phase of love and bonding evolution that can be experienced in between are represented within this series.

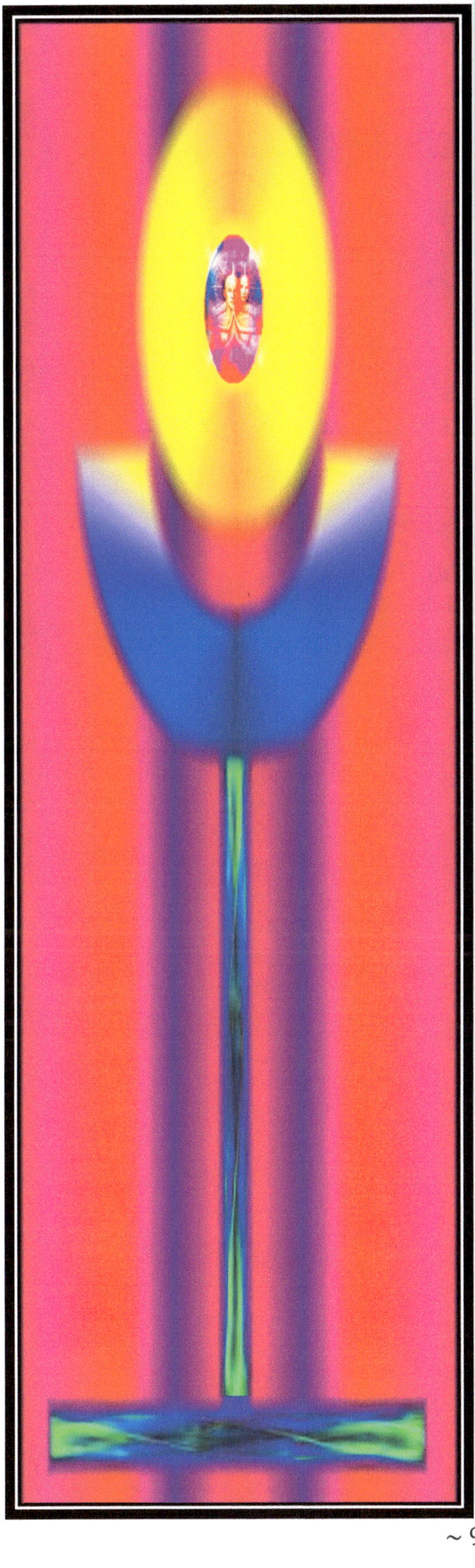

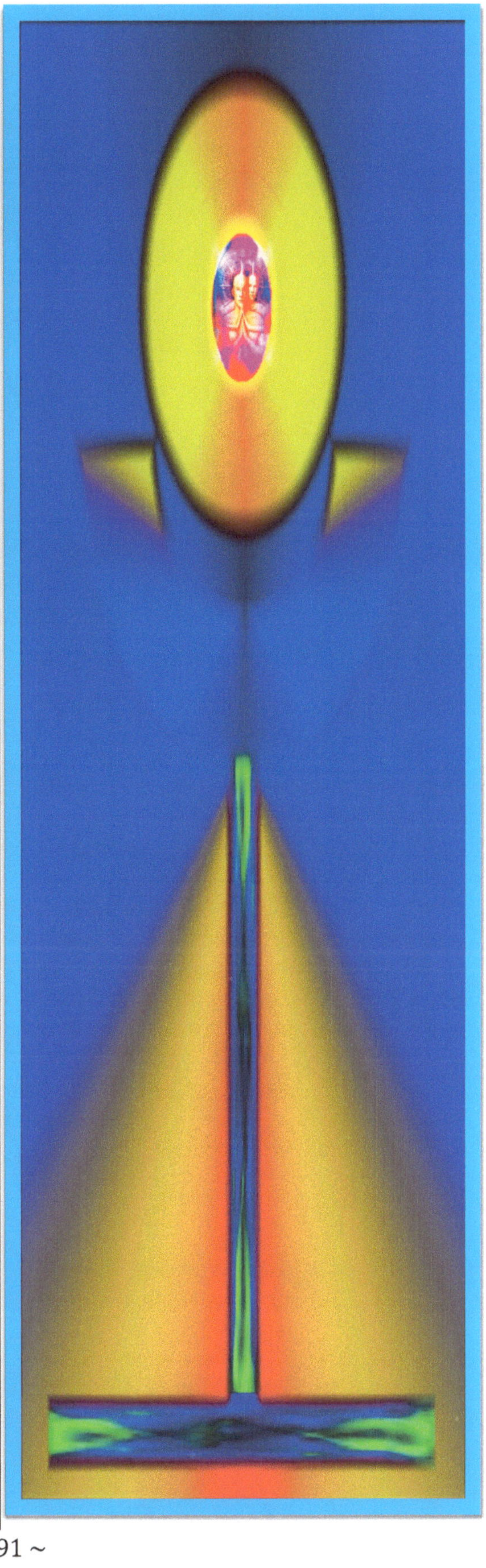

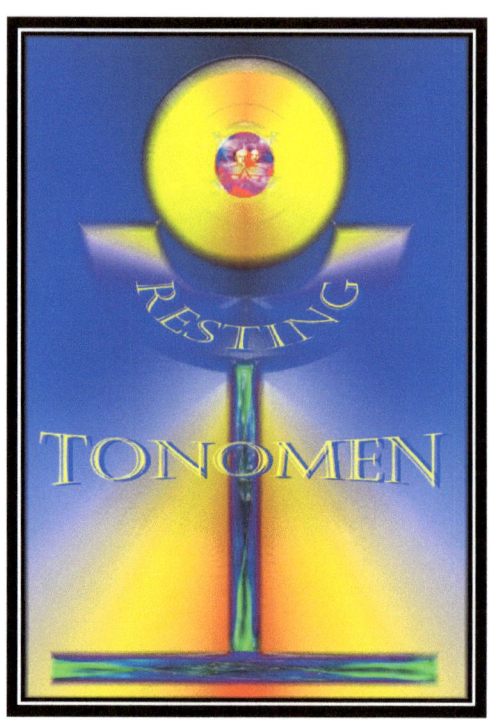

TOHNOMEN
"Choosing to Like Another"

Males and females flourish when true equality is present and the deepest levels of unconditional love, respect, and divine trust are completely embraced within both partners such that even the thought, need, or desire of one gender or energy to control or manipulate the other does not exist in consciousness. These principles are true regardless of gender and only in this atmosphere of unconditional love, divine trust and mutual respect can a relationship reach its highest level of evolution. In this image the masculine and the feminine are resting in each other. The word "Tohnomen" means to choose from our essence to experience liking another person. There is a very powerful importance to this statement in that the love learned from relating within a family is not based on choice but expectation. To like someone is in a sense to choose to see and accept them for who they are with no expectations or presumptions.

The curve in Tohnomen represents the embracing, nurturing hold of the divine feminine and the flowing essence of lunar energy that inspire women's moods and menstrual cycles. The swirling vertical line represents her sense of dignity and the gentle, loose, yet empowered support of the divine intuition reflected within a woman's kundalini energy that flows along her spine. The platform symbolizes her rootedness and sentient connection with the nurturing life giving character of mother earth. The circle symbolizes the solar energy of the masculine and the need to be centered in its own nature and individual radiance. It also reflects the concentrated energy of the male within his purpose as a central magnetic light figure that provides the methodology necessary to sustain life. The center image of the male and female reflects the radiant power that this type of union represents where the feminine is the foundation that naturally supports the centeredness of purpose of the masculine and the masculine naturally supports the feeling and intuitive rootedness of the feminine.

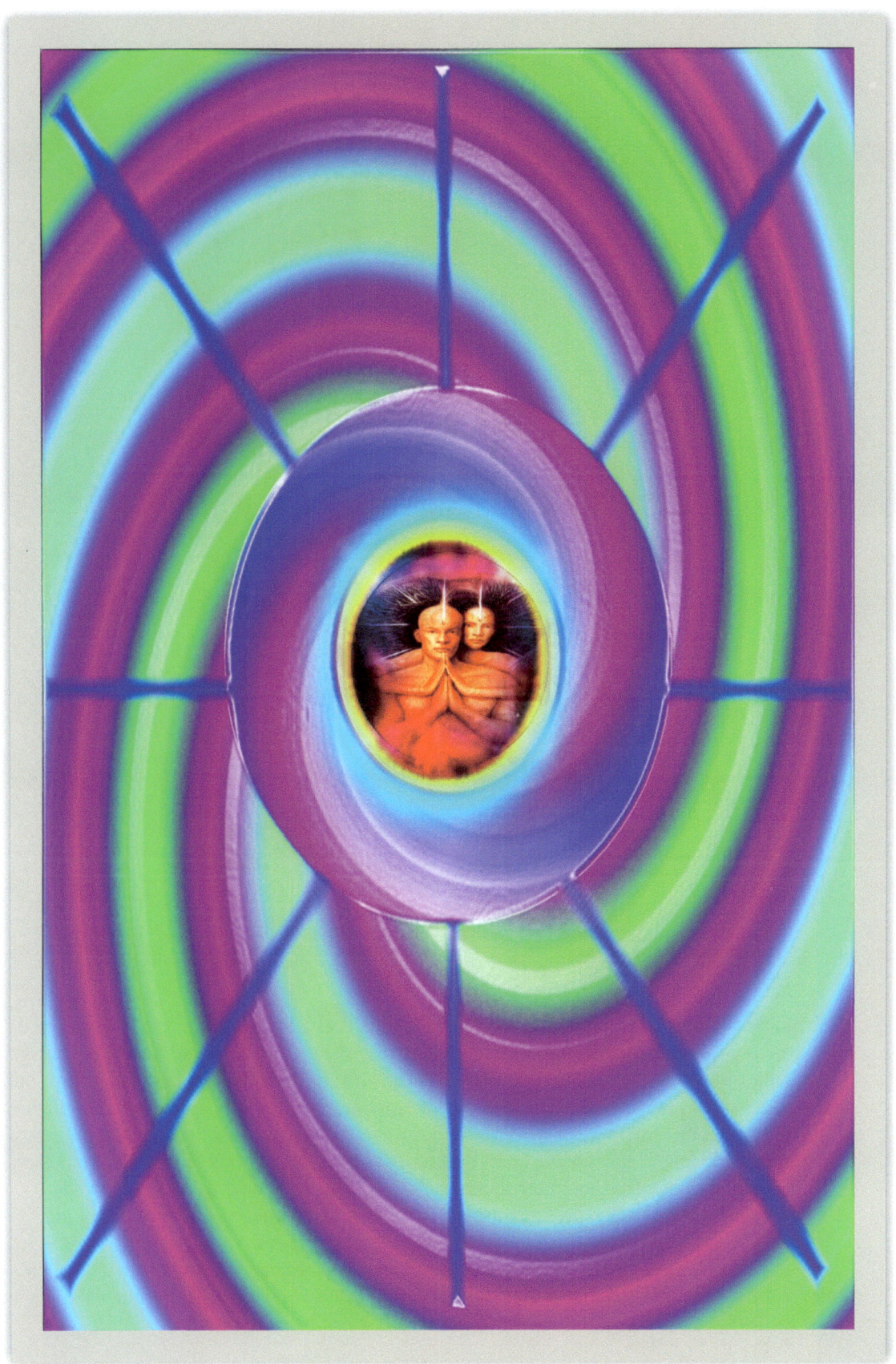

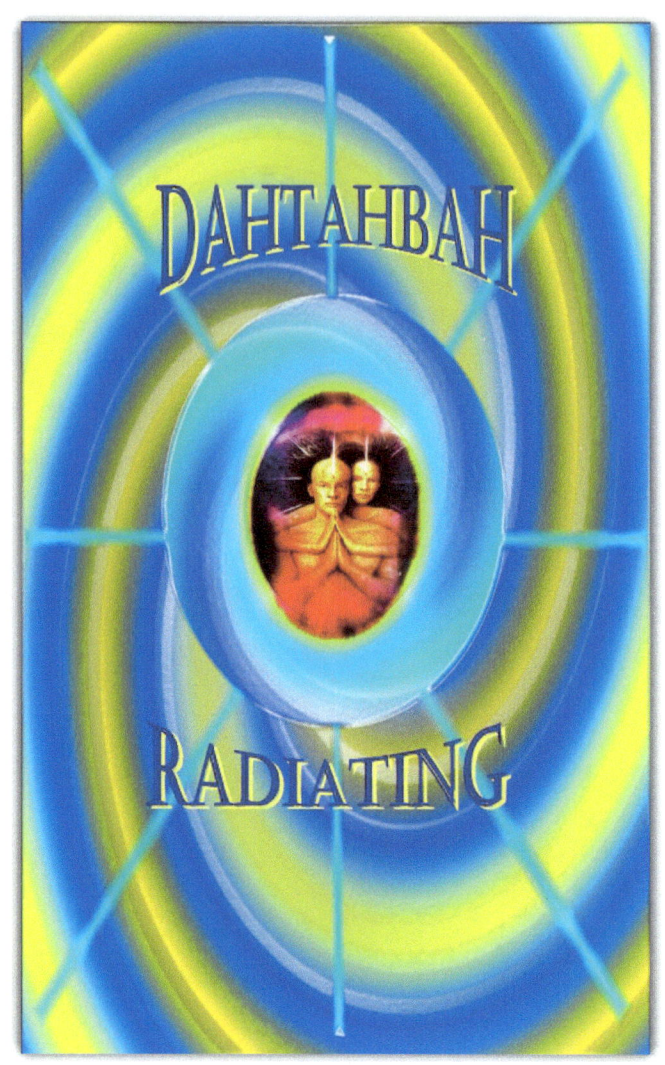

DAHTAHBAH
"Radiating"

"Dah" means letting go and relaxing into the hearts natural attitude, "Tah" means heart, and "Bah" has to do with centering and fully being oneself. We are not fully our Selves unless we are radiating truth and love unconditionally to others. It suggests that love is not an effort, but a relaxation into what we always want to do when we are not reacting from the need defend ourselves from being wounded, or the fear of repeat woundedness. It is between the phases of Tohnomen, (choosing to open one's heart to liking another and wanting to know them better) and that of Tehgah, (the soulmate feeling of sharing likeminded dreams, desires, and expressions). Dahtahbah represents the phase of love that comes after the free-flowing exchange has diminished and the tension of relating in an imperfect world starts to arise. It helps us to stay loving, open to seeing the good in our partner and willing to work through whatever difficulties present themselves so that the love and connectedness continues to grow and evolve.

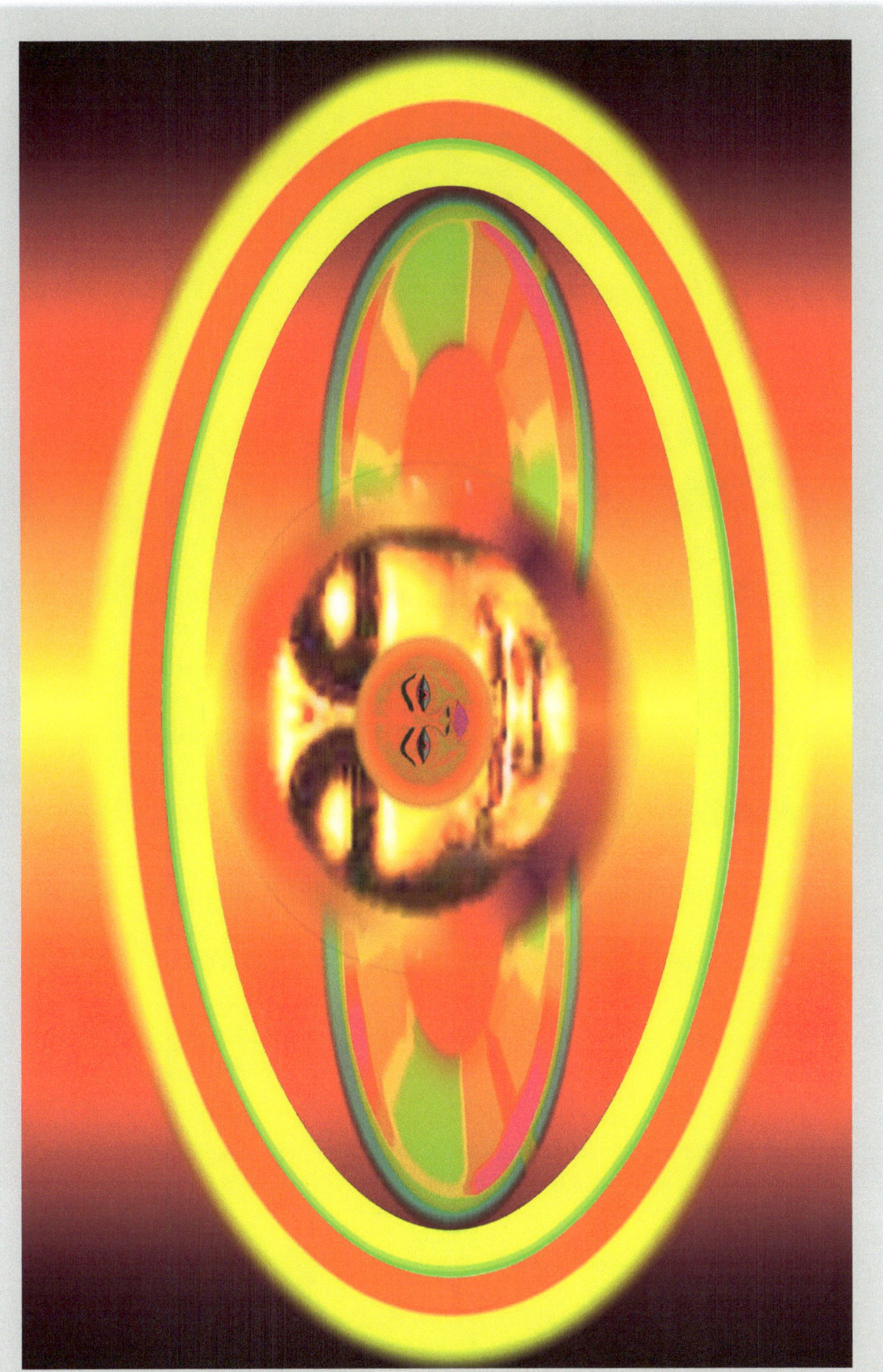

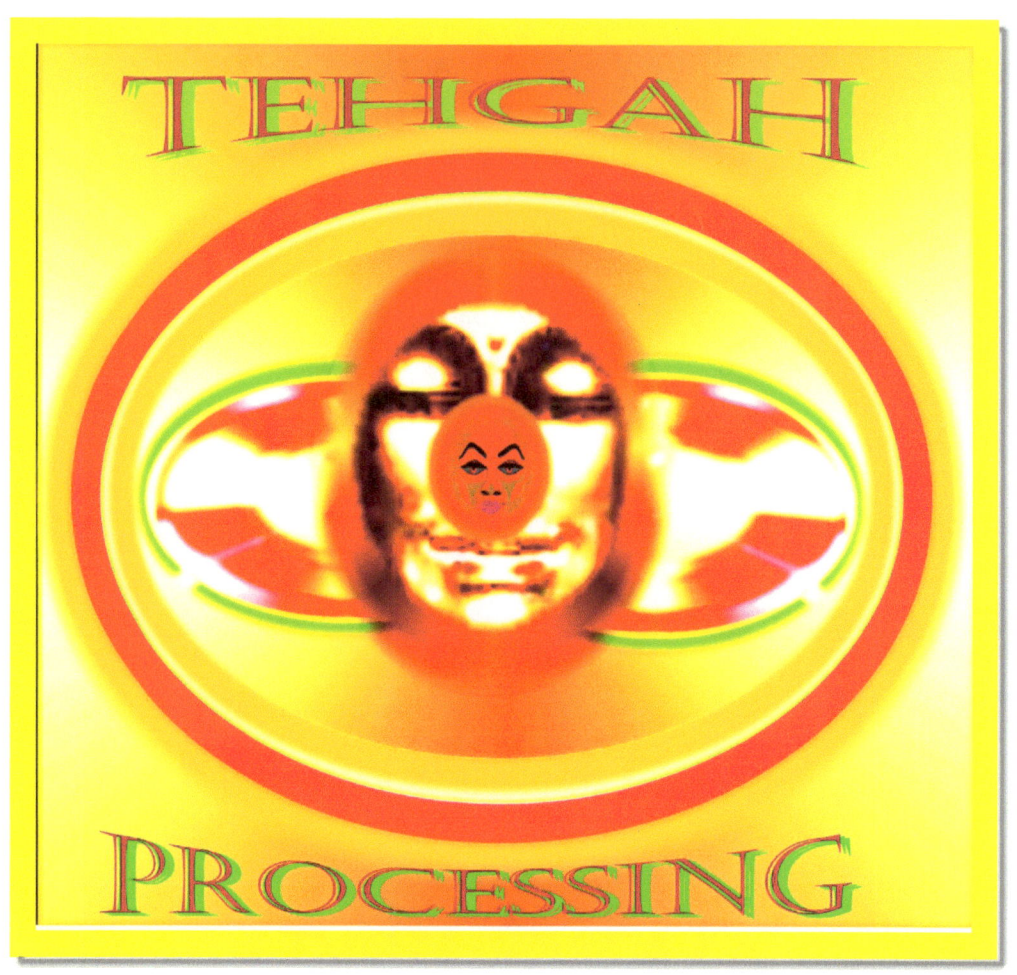

TEGAH
"Heart Choosing Wholeness"

The feeling of internal unity, an all-inclusive oneness with life, and the feeling of being Completely innerstood, that is the essence of Tehgah. It symbolizes the process of intermingling, meshing, and enhancing the masculine and feminine energies that begin with the first inviting glance and the propulsion of hypnotic magnetism that cause a us to want to inquire further, to share their sense of self and connect deeper with each other. This is the healing innocence that when pure in its intention creates the essence of divine love, joy and excitement that being in love generates. This exchange whether fleeting or leading, triggers a subtle energetic recollection of the non-dualistic unity of masculine and feminine energy that resides within us and the completeness it re-creates. Tehgah can be performed as a unifying meditation between couples based on its sacred design. Partners, while facing each other, hold hands left in left and right in right reproducing the infinity symbol within Tehgah. While sharing breath in
synchronized unison, (one exhaling as the other inhales in one synchronized rhythm) they envision a circle of light surrounding them which creates sacred space around the couple. As they breathe in unison the synchronicity of their energies brings about a state of oneness where they are able to feel each other as one eliminating all energies of disagreeableness, or separateness between them.

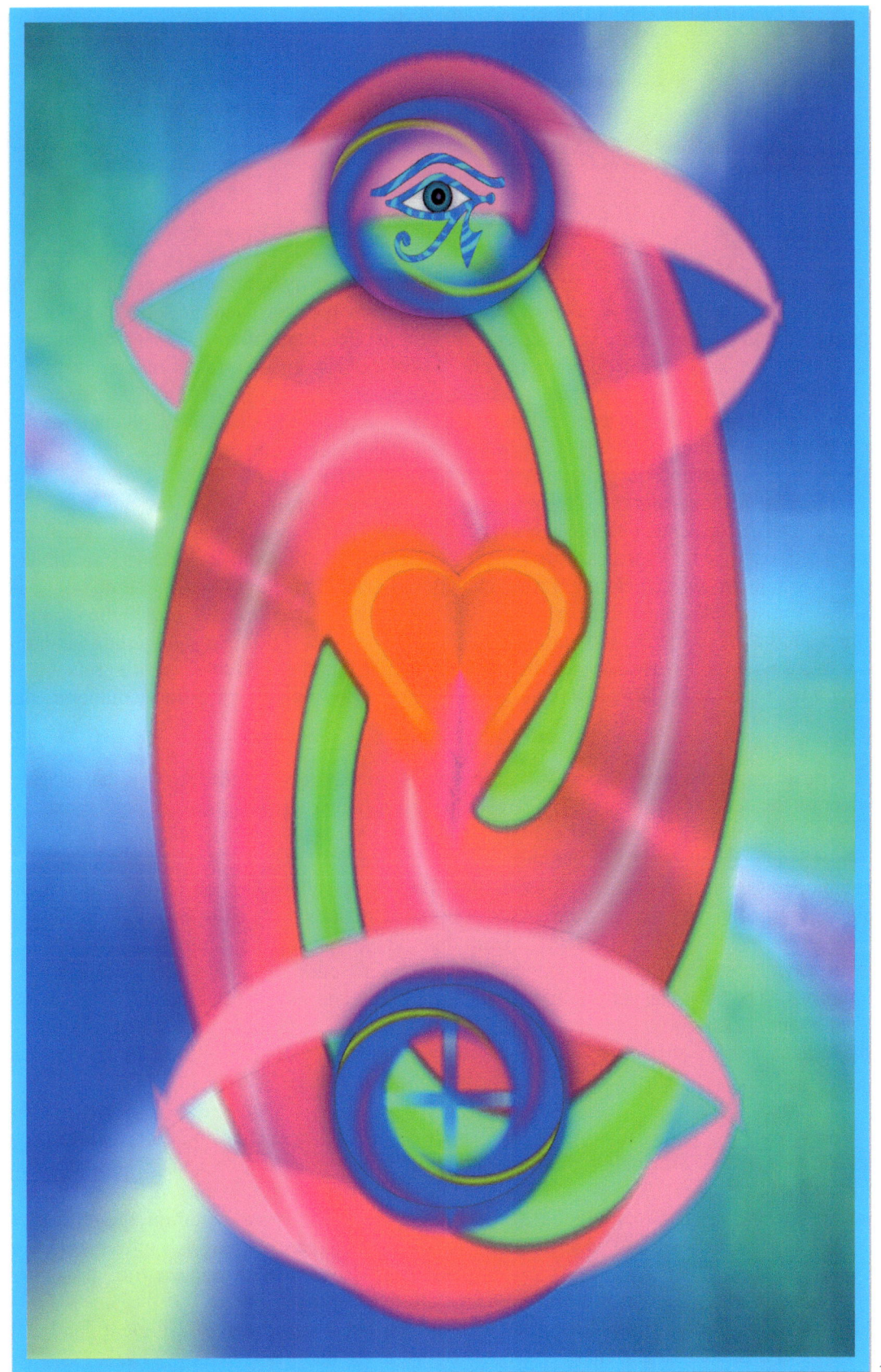

1

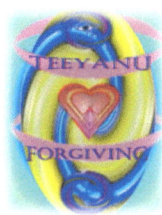

TEEYANU
"Blamelessness and Forgiveness"

TEEYANU is a holographic symbol from the Energy Maturity Set that represents the many internal parts when the 1st eye is open. It links the 1st eye, the heart, and the soul so that one's attunement to the true nature of things can register in one's perceptions allowing the radiant love of Dahtahbah to cause our observations to become wise and skillful. Teeyanu awakens one's ability to keep their hearts open and loving at all times yet not be ignorant and undiscerning of negative or pessimistic people. It is important to see clearly the negative or debilitating tendencies that beings succumb to and yet be able to stay in the chosen energies of love and peace and not succumb to it oneself. The 1st eye opens more fully as one's desire to recognize and confront these dynamics of the sacred and the shadow of the soul within themselves and others becomes realized. It is through one awakening to the power of unconditional love that one is able to alter the ways in which they relate to that of a healthier, more harmonious way of relating. And unconditional love is the only way that humankind is able to transcend the consciousness of punishment for transgressions and trust in the laws of truth and karma to correct another's behavior nonviolently. By this one is inspired to judge ones deeds with the innerstanding of their soul condition and the infallible law of karma and to respond with calm truth, love, and honesty the unlimited possibilities for positive outcomes and change.

The heart inside the heart symbol is a reflection of the way in which the heart of the 1st eye supports the heart of our being. The circle plus in the belly region of the oval, represents the necessary balanced and centered state within our lower chakras. When we are balanced and centered in our lower chakras, our spirit and soul become aligned and our intuitive nature is able to operate properly. Therefore, we are not likely to be subject to manipulations and power plays designed to prey on our weaknesses. Centering in our solar plexus, our personal power center, allows us to protect ourselves from this. The two rings above and below the heart center symbolize the protective boundaries that are set around the heart when we honor our intuitions. The heart can stay open without being hurt when we are centered and balanced in our lower chakras; when we are "not led into temptation" by false perceptions of lack and longing our first eye sees things as they are and our heart accepts them without rationalization or self-fulfilling motivations.

For the 1st eye to be fully open we must recognize our part in choosing every painful experience entered into and on this basis let go of blaming and forgive. Once we can accept that we had chosen this experience as an opportunity to learn the lessons of self and life mastery we can shift to becoming thankful for their role played in our evolution into our higher sense of self and purpose and what we learn from forgiving becomes the basis of our service to others. The word "Tee Yah Nu" is the strong heart purpose to fully experience life. It helps us to innerstand the dynamics of what it means to follow our joyful passions and to know that though we are meant to live in happiness with our desires of success and fulfillment there will be challenges and sacrifices that we must make in order to achieve them.

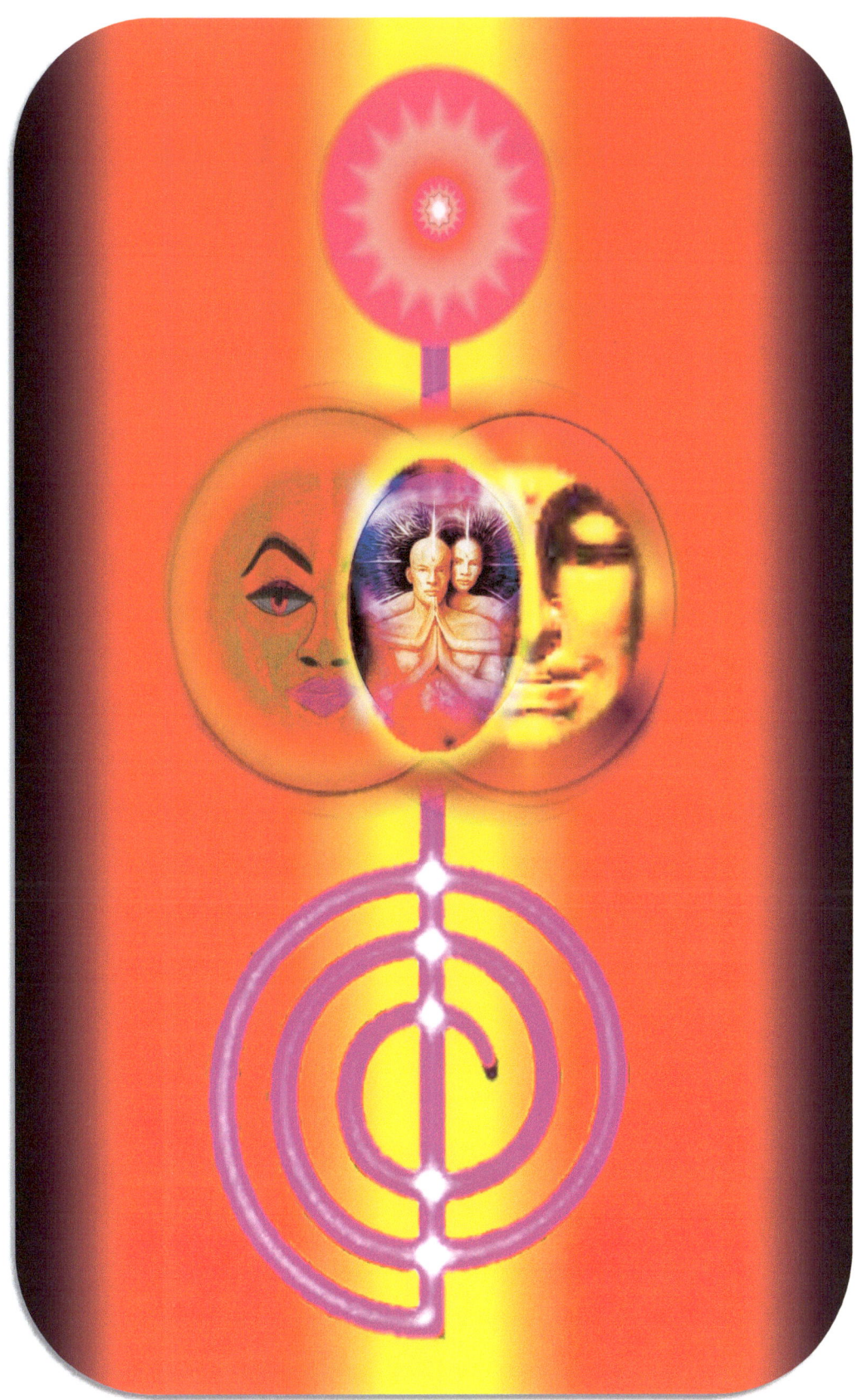

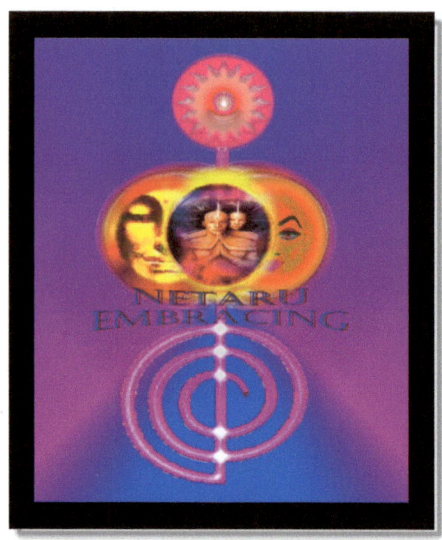

NETARU
"Embracing"

NETARU indicates the time in our relationships where both partners feel open and trusting in the power of the love shared is at a place where both are fully engaged in the relationship and desire to move through and heal points of tension or wounding that naturally arise. It is where both are interested in generating and cultivating the energy that allows them to grow in themselves and in the relationship. This is the phase which also allows them to move into a more of tantric sexual connection. Netaru symbolizes what tantric sex means within Reiki. Tantra is a meditative practice by which the ritualistic or deep sharing of spiritual essence between two people in purposely performed in order to experience higher spiritual state of oneness consciously or to intensify the energy of love to manifest certain intention. Before Tantra can be enduring and meaningful, it needs the foundation that Tohnomen and Tehgah represent.

In a healthy relationship where the desire to give and receive love is mutually respected and honored, sexual communion is not the first priority of either partner, it is the desire to know and experience more of what the other is about and to express ones feelings for the other in a way that words cannot express fully. It's after this part of the relationship has been developed that the natural progression into Netaru or tantric sexual bonding takes place. This is a special, sacred sexual expression between two people that Reiki enhances. It is also a matter of choice at every step, and can die out easily if not cared for within a mutually sustained loving commitment.

The top circle represents the transcendental wisdom of the masculine solar energy and the lower spiral represents the uncoiling of the feminine earth energy. The two circles, within the symbol represent masculine and feminine essences, partly merged and partly separate implying that the energies rise in loving union to the degree of intimacy (into me see) established between them. The middle circle is where the heart chakras commune and allow the energy to ascend. The energy rises up to the crown to the degree that masculine and feminine merge in loving synergy with each other.

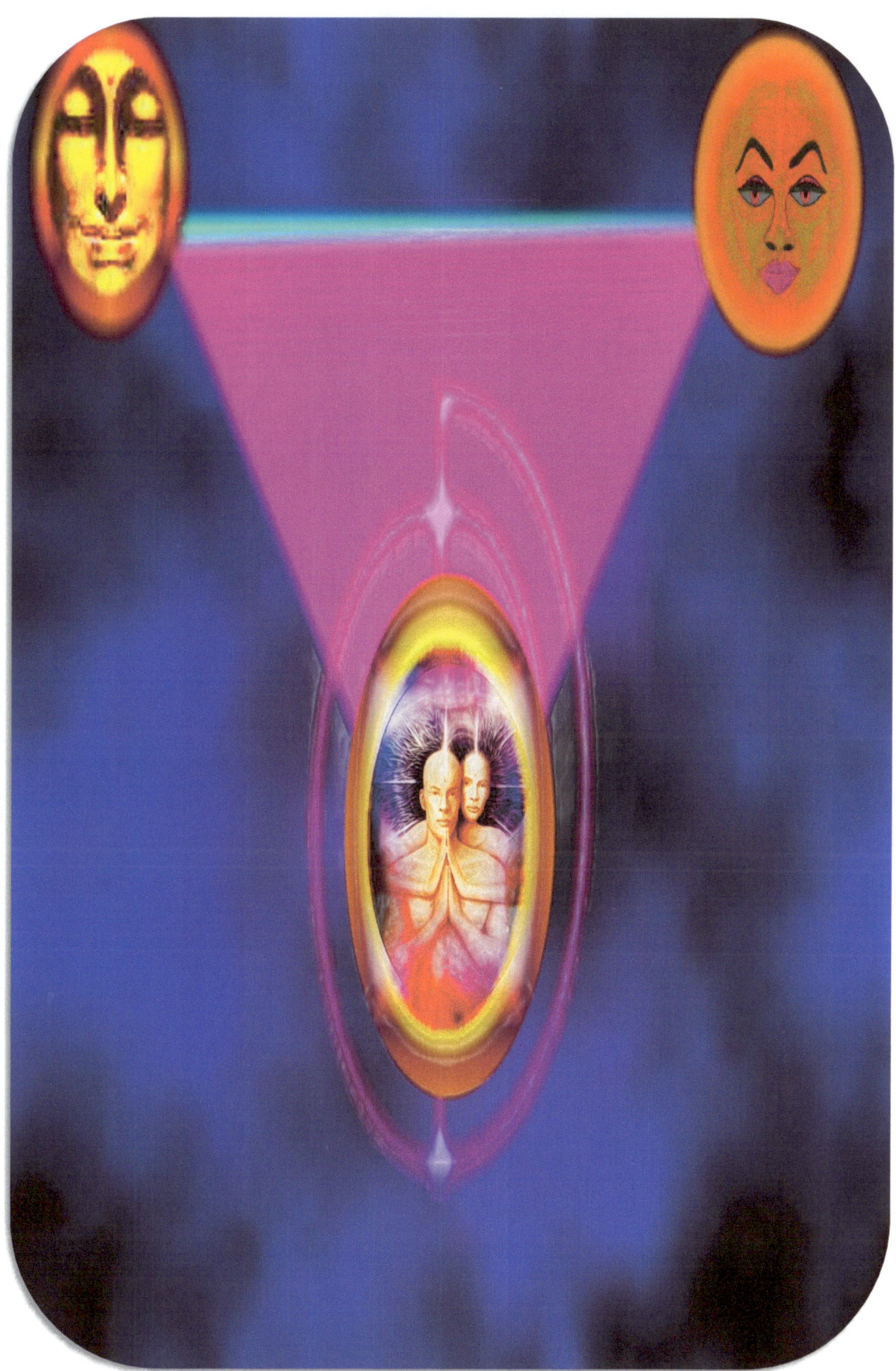

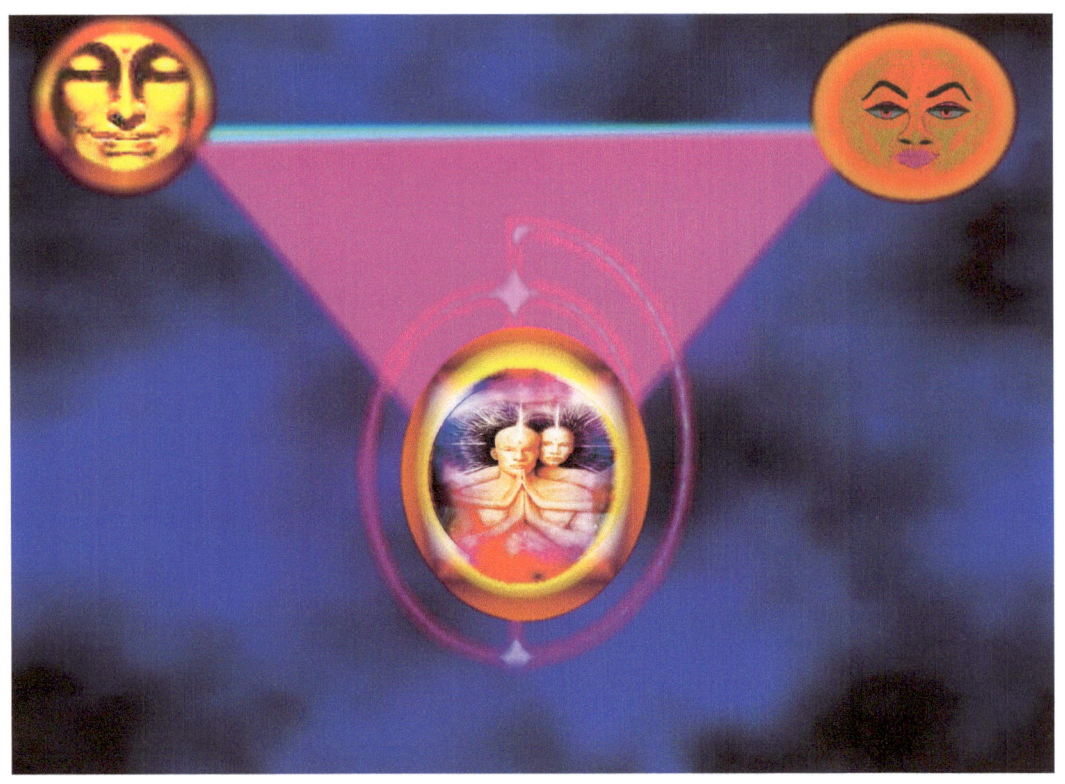

TEPHANU
"Resolving"

In all relationships there are differences in upbringing and traditions, differences of opinions and levels of spirit/soul evolution, and differences in roles and the ways in which each person operates and lives life. Tephanu assist us in innerstanding the balance and support that both bring to each other and the wisdom to create harmony in love by releasing negative connotations learned about the opposite genders and by opening the 1st eye to innerstand, accept, and cultivate the androgynous aspects of cosmic and elemental life force energies that exist within the universe and within us and to drawing upon this.

TEPHANU provides us with the inspiration to become whole and complete both individually and collectively and can be used for resolving issues and differences within oneself, with loved ones, and those within the world that derive from programmed beliefs about masculine and feminine energies and their role within society.

Tephanu helps us to identify and embrace the masculine and feminine aspects that we ourselves embody and to embrace them with the innerstanding that we have chosen them in order to better fulfill our purpose of raising the consciousness our Oneness and to transcend gender labeling. It helps to awaken our appreciation for versus our judgment of each other based on our unique and individual contributions towards humanities evolution in love without placing societal expectation on another. It helps one to comprehend, innerstand, accept and appreciate each person's unique expression and our divine right to love whomever we feel drawn to love without negative repercussions.

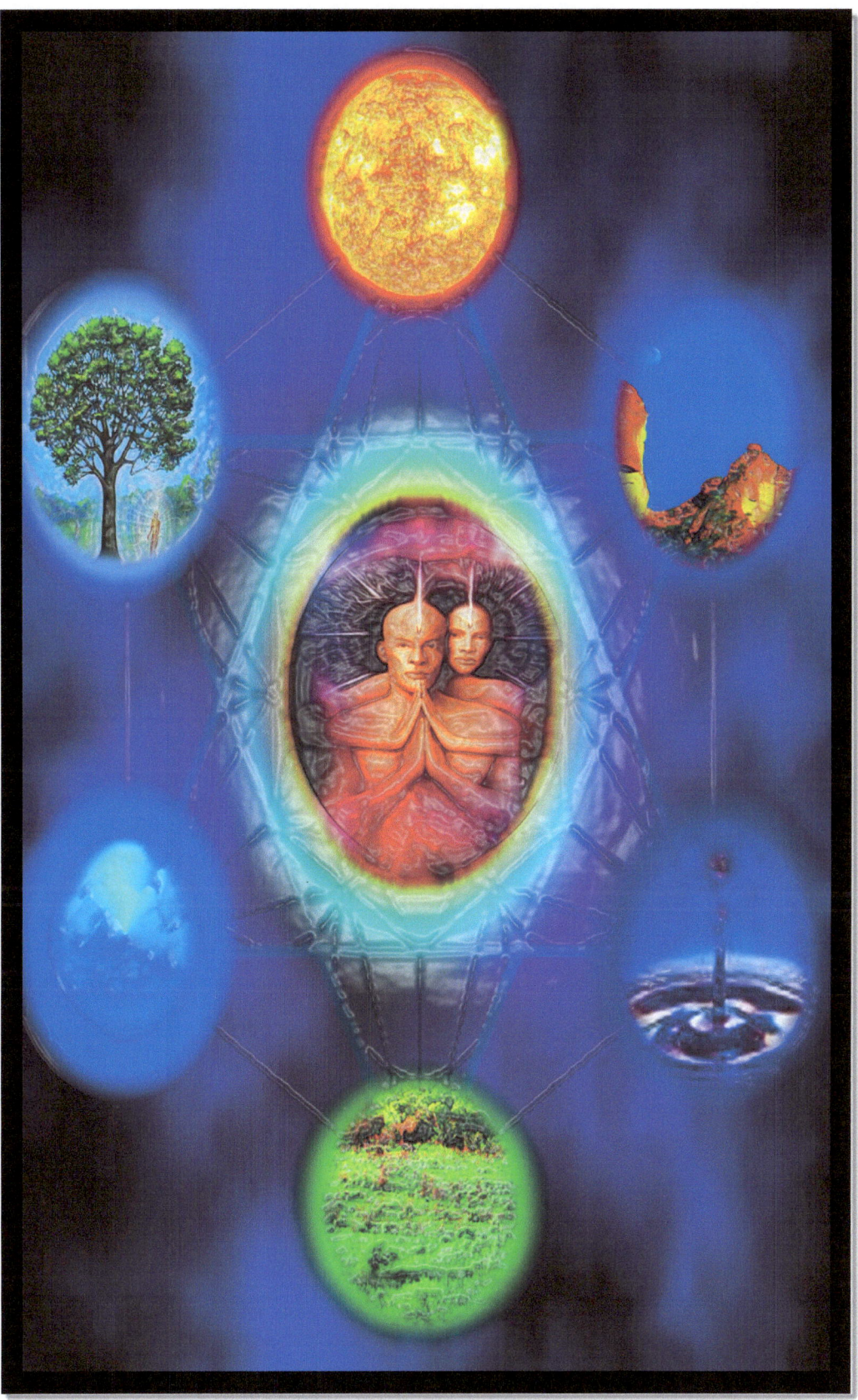

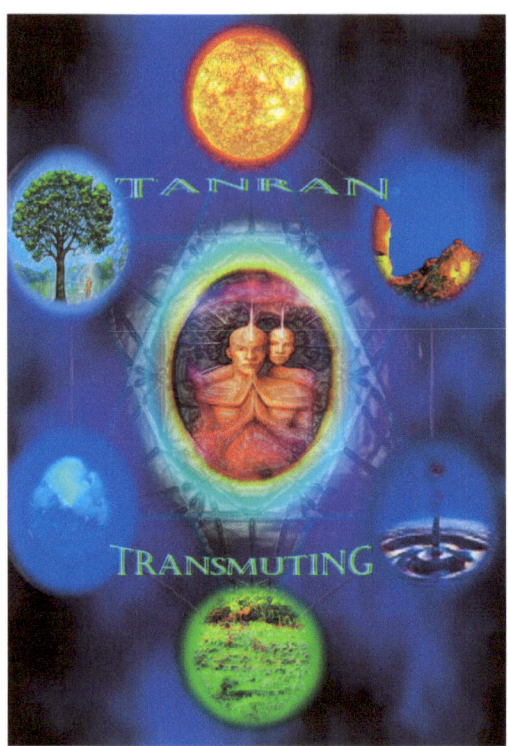

TANRAN
"Transmuting"

As a part of the relationship set, Tanran represents the way in which harmony can exist between differing life force elements and can be achieved through meditative breathing. Deep rhythmic breathing induces a meditative state which allows the calming and balancing qualities of Nature's life force to affect us in the moment which can reverse our resistance against negativity. It helps us to identify the root of our fear-based reactions and transcend them, rather than close down and/or defend against another's negative projection. By recognizing the way in which the elements serve to teach us that in reality turmoil does not have to be perceived as having a malicious intent, it can be viewed as a means to create clarity, deeper harmony, greater honesty and trust. Like the caterpillar and the butterfly, dying to the old mindsets and beliefs open the gate to moving into a Higher perspective of self and life with the capability to harmonize in the midst of uncertainty or turmoil. Tanran symbol can be used as a ritual for opening the heart to face every fear (Falsified Evidence Affecting Reality), with love allowing it to pass without reaction. Know that in most cases, hostility, anger, and negative behavior are an underlying call for love and innerstanding and acceptance without judgments or rebuke. By mastering this we come to discover how love & peace of hearts are larger than the negativity faced.

In conjunction with The Compassion and empathic connection invoked by Tanran, this symbol helps one to not fear but hold space for the pains of others by actively listening without any motive to fix. This allows one to embrace their partner in a committed way without judgment, fear, shame, or triggering any type of negativity from past experience. It generates the feeling of what it's like to truly be heard and loved without conditions. This symbol opens the soul's innerstanding of the growth potential that our past experiences were meant to teach us and inspires us to integrate these transformative changes into our current relationship interactions as a means of creating more authentic, loving, and supportive experiences.

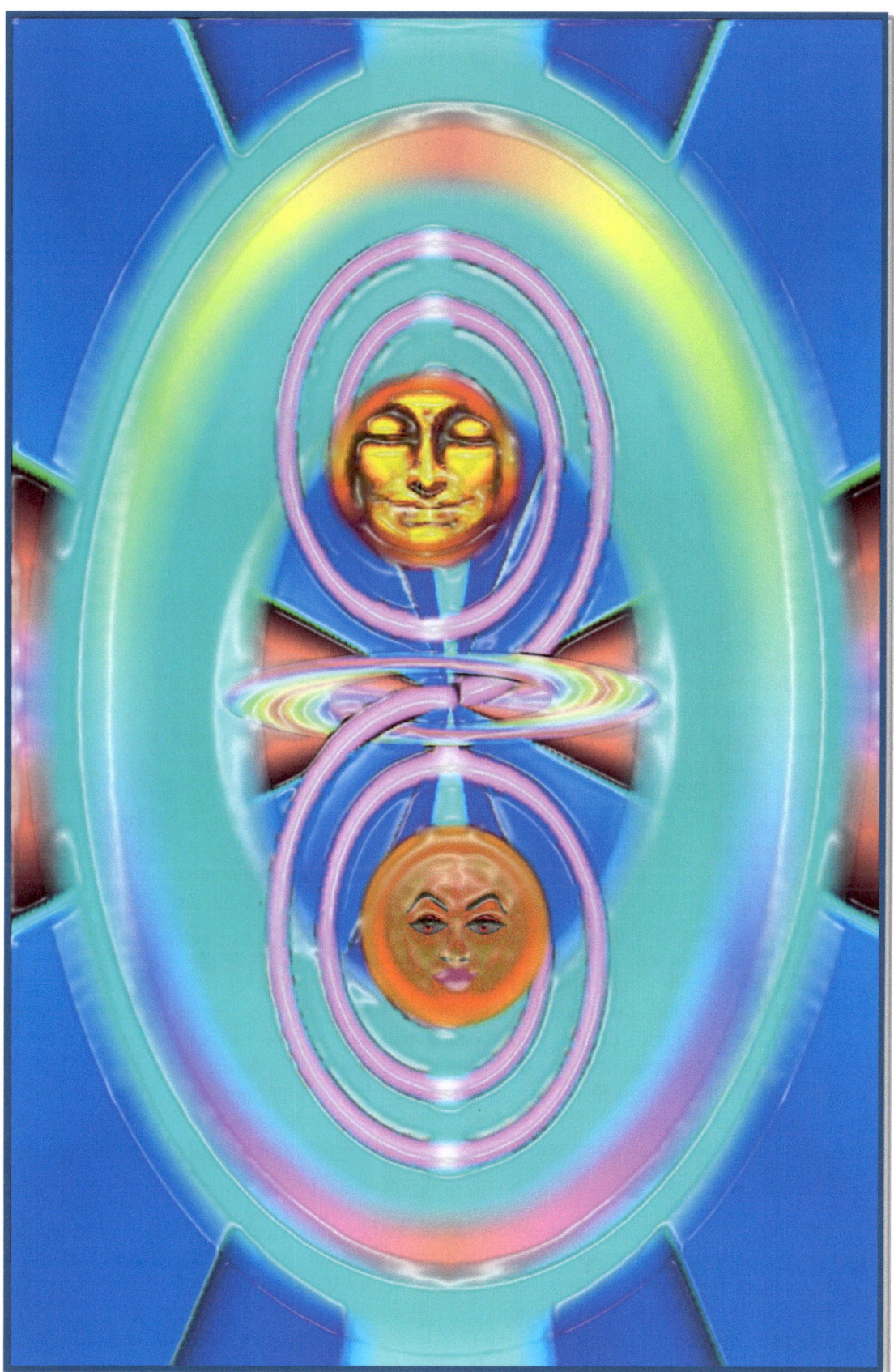

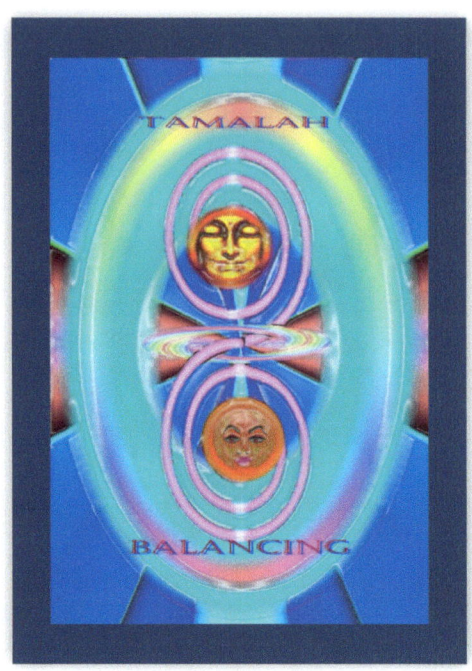

TAMALAH
"Balancing Oneness"

TAMALAH represents the time when a couple has moved from exploring the possibilities of union into having chosen to commit to functioning more and more as one organism. Just as our cells provide equal yet differing attributes in order for our bodies to function as a whole so it necessary for harmony to exist within relationships. The key in this phase of bonding is being able to remain detached from preconceived role expectations yet open to discover how each best connects and how each can best serve the relationship as a whole by what each shares of themselves within it. By this both partners are better able to feel that what they contribute is valued and that both partners are doing their part in maintaining this union harmoniously.

The spirals of this symbol represent opposites as each spiral moves in the opposite direction. The radiant outer circle is the consecrated space that surrounds the male and female in their union. Within this consecrated space, both male and female breathe operating as one which is symbolized by the small oval between the spirals. Unlike the infinity symbol there is no longer any alternations or give and take, it has become the shared space that has grown out of the union where the couple become one body, one heart, one mind. There is something dynamic about the recognition of this phase where complementariness and mutual support of strengths are acknowledged and shared. The uncoiling and recoiling of the spirals reflects the pulse and rhythm that this level of union creates. Energy flows in when the lovers are alone and merges when they are together.

Tamalah allows the opposites to meet in a sacred container of oneness so that they can let go and float in the middle in a peaceful trust of the love, respect, and commitment to union that they've developed between them. The strong feelings of individualism, justice, and the protection of the masculine nature, as well as that of the connectedness and caring of the feminine nature, are what creates the balance of opposites. Both are paradoxically necessary in order to discover deeper levels of harmony and wholeness.

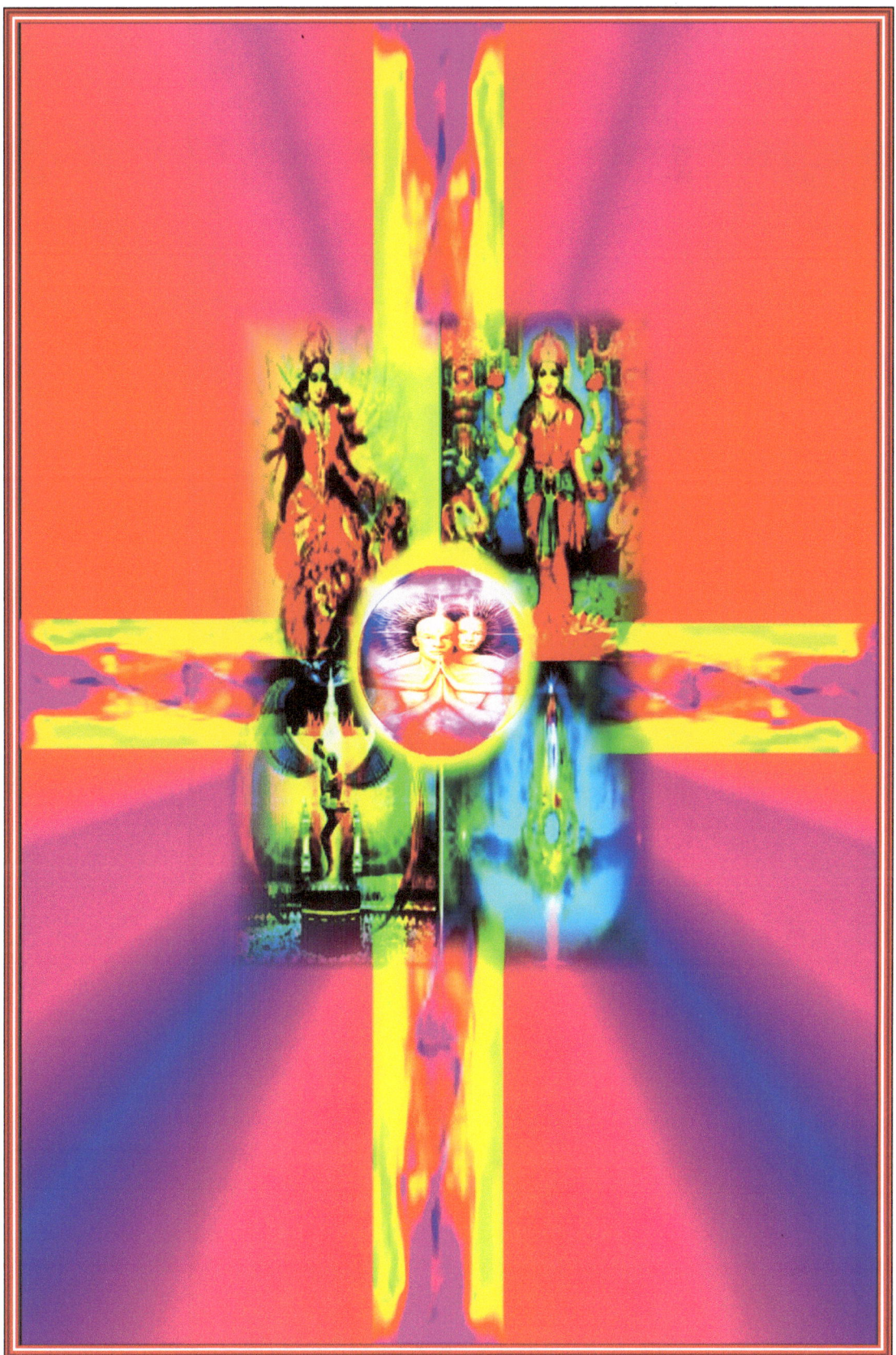

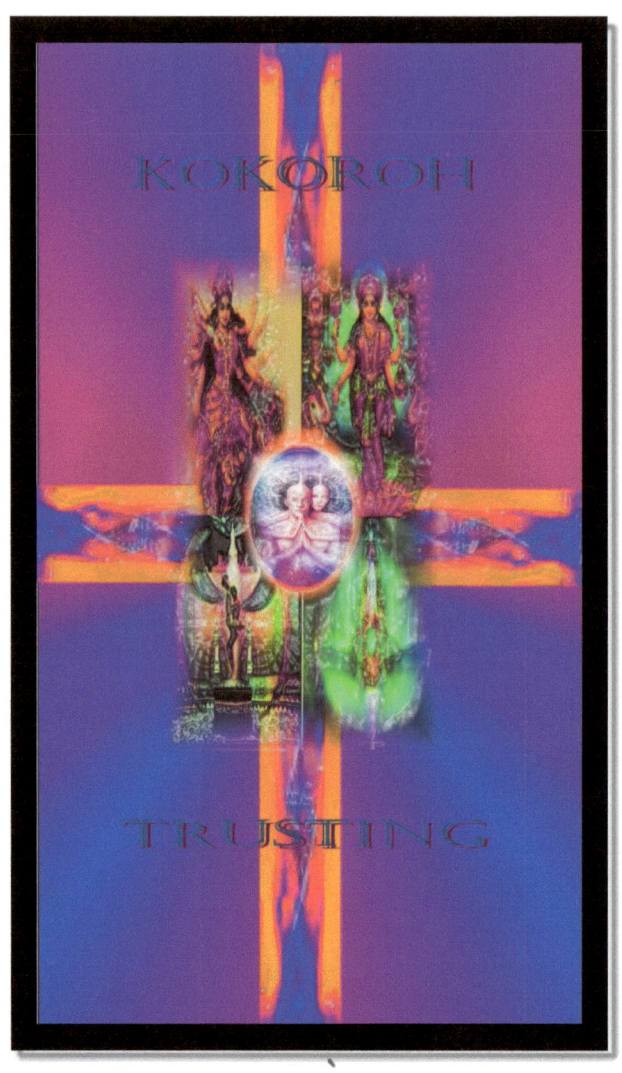

KOHKOROH
"Supportive Honoring"

KOKOROH-is about organizing our relationships in terms of whom and what is truly supportive of us and whom and what we are supportive of. It helps create synergistic energy exchanges that naturally grow around us that are honored and cultivated. It's about interdependence innerstanding the ways to live in independent oneness with everything that surrounds us harmoniously. When we inner-stand this, we learn to serve and be served within this interdependence. It breaks the illusion of isolated individuality and the belief in separation that sometimes offers false security for people. When we feel disconnected or ostracized from others, then we become manipulative, dominant and possessive as a means of controlling those who fill the sense of love and self-worth that they provide us. Or, we try to fearfully run away and live without risking relationship with others and growing from the natural challenges that relating present. We also try to manipulatively give to others, conforming to what they want, in order to strategically get our own needs met in return. When we rest in interdependence, than we are able to trust life and relax into giving and receiving freely out of the desire to give for giving's sake without self-serving or ulterior motive.

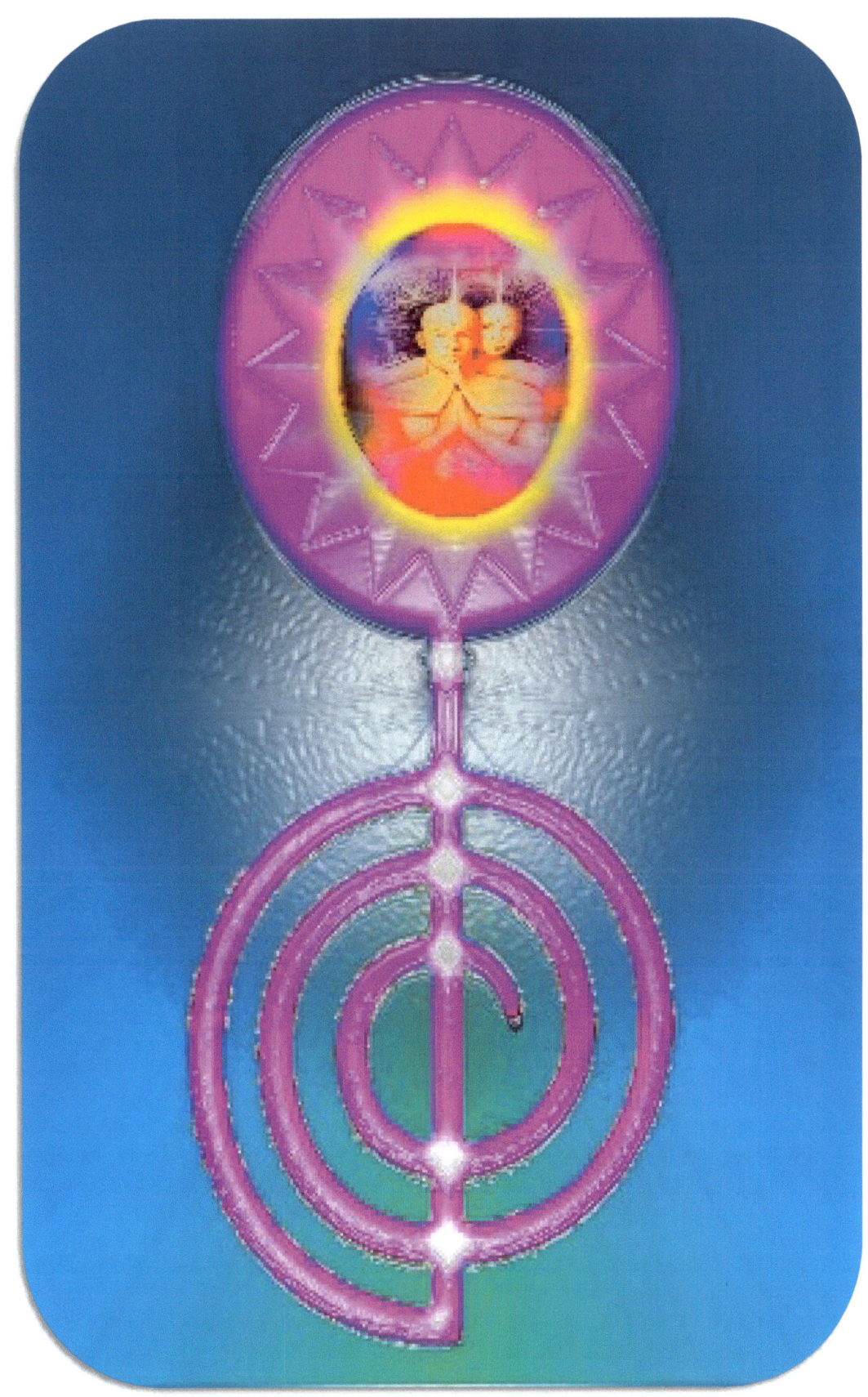

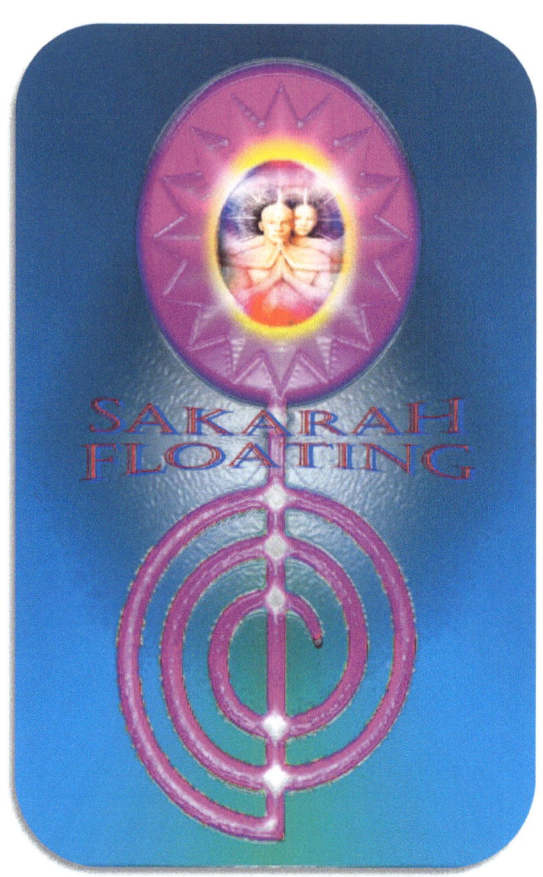

SAKARAH
"Life Wave Floating"

SAKARAH is an Itanamic (ee-tan-ah-mic) word for the level of enlightenment reached within oneself where wholeness of truth is not only illuminated inside of them enabling them to accept themselves and all others as they are, but moves into the conscious awareness of all opposites meeting, balancing, and seeing the innate harmony and necessity for each other. It works to integrate the two as differing aspects of the same spectrum versus viewing them as polar opposites. This symbol represents the point of heart awakening when one for the first-time experiences and innerstand the power of non-judgment, and is able to drop past opinions which have kept one's heart closed and limited in its experiences of giving and receiving love. When this happens we're able to embrace everything without condemnation and to see ourselves reflected within another. The energy spirals out de-activating the need to be in control one's actions that are outside of social conformity as well as the actions of others. One is able to let go of their need to be right that lies within power center of the solar plexus. The energy of Sakarah assists one to embody the desire to truly live and let live without attachment and concern of what others may think.

SAKARAH radiates the sense of knowing that life is always supporting you and creating a peaceful floating quality to living life where the universe fulfills your needs and desires effortlessly showing up at the times when you are truly wanting or needing it to without necessarily being consciously aware of what one is truly needing.

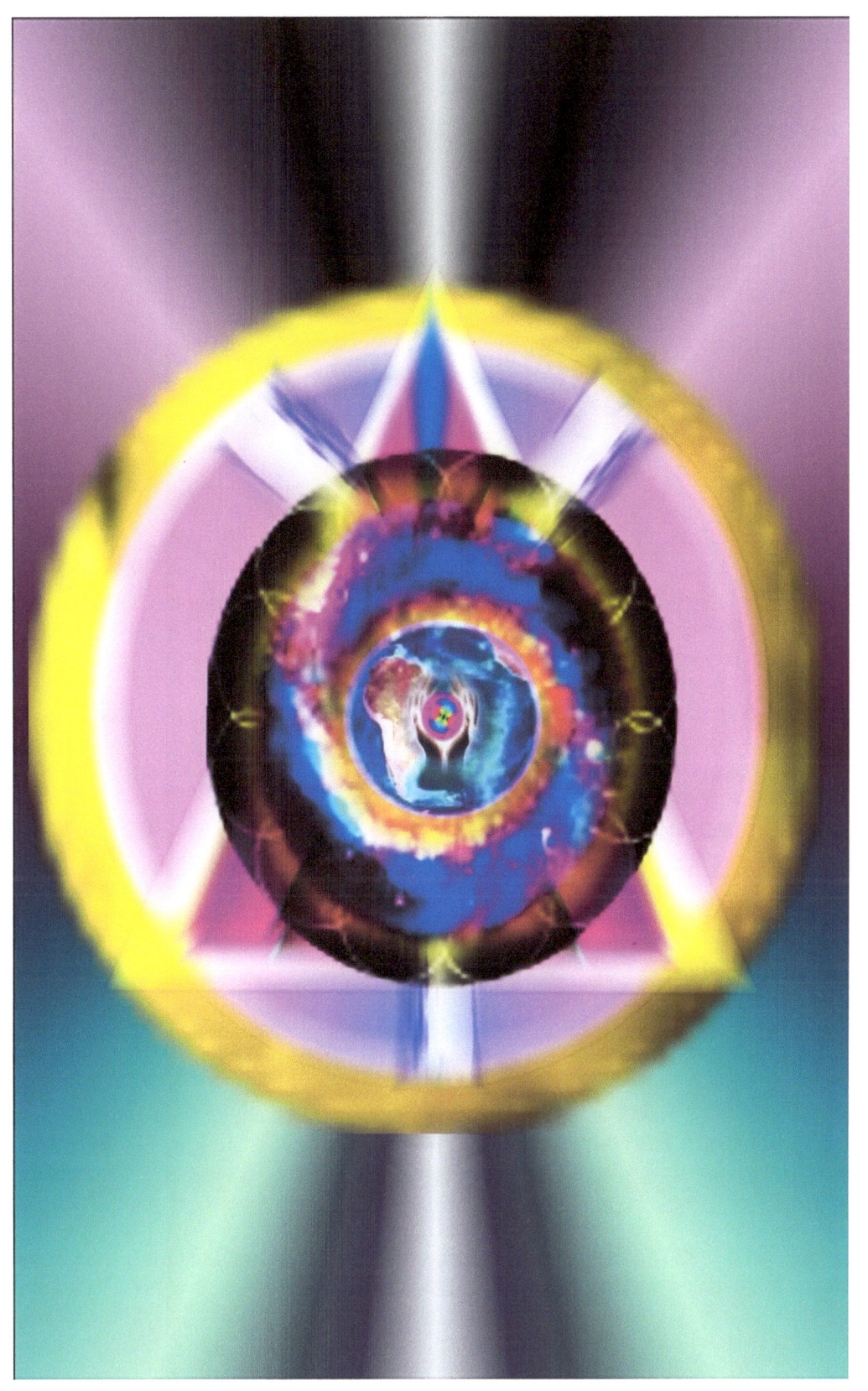

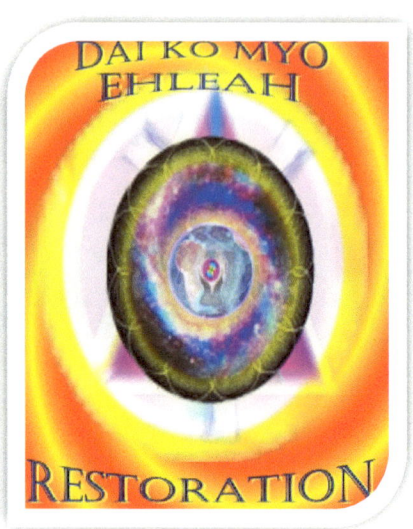

DAIKOMYOLEAH
"Planetary Restoration"

Within this planetary symbol **DAI KO MYO** and **EHLEAH** combine for the healing and restoration of Mother Earth. It opens the portal to human awareness of her consciousness linking it to our own so that we may once again innerstand her true sentient state and our reciprocal responsibility towards her care as offspring. We are being reminded of her original state, the purity of her essence as it existed prior to man's destructive misuse of the richness of her sustenance and her natural beauty. Not just visually but the beauty of her sentient nurturing essence that has and continues to sustain all life that dwells here on Earth.

The sentient soul retrieval aspects of Ehleah and the holistic healing power of Dai Ko Myo when sent by intention out into the universe, shifts our conscious awareness and re-awakens our innerstanding and desire to create the ways and means to adapt our modernized way of life to one that is more aligned with the natural flow in respect to the elements and their life force. It inspires in us a desire to live in harmony with all of creation and inspires us with ideas such as solar heating, wind and solar energy and the use of biodegradable forms of fuel, all being alternatives to continuing to strip her of her inner resources. It also has inspired changes in the way in which we deal with waste products by implementing measures that are less harmful to the environment and all of life forms that exist here.

The influences of the information age have had the effect of a double edged sword. Though it has played a major part in restoring our conscious awareness of connection to the elements of life here, (the plant life, insects, animal kingdom, sea life, mineral kingdom, the air, water, sun, moon, and stars), it at the same time often consumes our attention away from participating actively with her. With the re-discoveries that modern science has made of the sentience and interconnectedness of all matter and the access to this new information through the internet there is no longer a blinder over our consciousness which forces us to become more accountable for our choices. because of this technological medium there is limitless knowledge that we are able to access and share thus inspire to bring about the new paradigm shift to a more synchronized existence with Mother Earth and all of creation.